It's Vintage, Darling!

how to be a clothes connoisseur

D1103181

CHRISTA WEIL

It's Vintage, Darling!

how to be a clothes connoisseur

HODDER &
STOUGHTON

A CIP catalogue record for this title is
available from the British Library

ISBN 978 0 340 92276 7

Typeset in Adobe Caslon by Palimpsest Book Production Limited,
Grangemouth, Stirlingshire

Printed and bound by
Mackays of Chatham Ltd, Chatham, Kent

Hodder Headline's policy is to use papers that are natural, renewable and
recyclable products and made from wood grown in sustainable forests.
The logging and manufacturing processes are expected to conform to the
environmental regulations of the country of origin.

Hodder and Stoughton Ltd
A division of Hodder Headline
338 Euston Road
London NW1 3BH

To Heather

Contents

Foreword

We're always searching for something fresh, something that sparks us up. Take the wedgie shoes we all wore in the 1970s – those platforms with a cork sole – I had pairs in metallic pink and natural leather. We *loved* those shoes, wore them until they came apart and them mended them and wore them some more. Well, Browns have just redone them and they're flying out of the store. Somehow that style looks right again.

It's all about cycles, isn't it, in fashion and in life. After working for twenty years designing fabrics for the home, I felt like I wanted to start working with the human form again – dressing a body in motion, material in three dimensions that will move and catch the breeze, which offers such a different set of challenges from, say, fabric for a curtain or a sofa. Inacio Ribeiro asked me to collaborate with Cacharel, which I did for two seasons, and then Topshop became interested. I couldn't imagine a better time to be working with them – there's such energy, such a buzz. We all sat down and had a good look over my sketchbooks from the 1960s and 1970s. Many of those designs had been worked into fabrics that my husband, Ossie Clark, had used in his pieces for the shop Quorum, and later, in our collaboration with the manufacturer Radley. For the new Topshop line, I updated some of the vintage prints, like Mystic Daisy, which I think is one of my best. Others, like Posh Dot, are completely new but have that vintage-y air.

My mother was a seamstress, so I was aware of how clothes are put together. Great fit and immaculate construction were things my sisters and

I were fortunate enough to take for granted. I remember going to Kendal's in Manchester and seeing a dress that was absolutely fabulous, in black silk with pleats around the bottom. I asked my mother to try to copy it. We were all quite demanding of her, but she was a terribly nice mother so she did. In the very early days Ossie would come over and ask her advice on setting a sleeve or a particular cut.

Of course with time he developed an architectural understanding of women's bodies, how to cut his patterns in very complicated ways and make them work. His joy was in creating intricate shapes. He was most happy when he'd come home and say 'I've just worked out a new way of cutting this dress'. The handicraft, the attention to detail – I think that's why, at the V&A retrospective of his work, so many women were able to put on their old Ossies and look marvellous.

Of course, many of his shapes were inspired by pieces in the V&A, or by ruined old clothes with a wonderful detail I'd bring him from Portobello market. Nothing's new really. Markets have always been a fantastic source of ideas. When I was younger I'd frequently go to Portobello at weekends. There was a wonderful doctor lady who sold boxes of Victorian lace, she always had interesting things. There was also a man there who sold old cashmere and tweeds. He was just an ordinary bloke who lived down the road and he'd have these wonderful suits that must have been worn by somebody who stuck pheasants in all the pockets. I loved decking out my friends in all these extraordinary things. Clothes like that don't go away. They're like great old paintings. They just *move around*, don't they?

Marc Jacobs typifies the idea of the past echoing in the present. I'm certain he haunted the vintage emporiums in SoHo. There you'd see masses of those wonderful winceyette nightclothes, the ones with the big buttons, so evocative of the fifties, and now of course big buttons have become one of his hallmarks. He captures something in his lines that I value immensely: a sense of innocence – sprightly and uncontrived. You see it so clearly in silent movies, in the kinds of costumes Clara Bow would wear. Or a school-girl in uniform. I think girls have an instinctive sense of style, taking something very basic like that and addressing it in just their own way. What could be prettier?

I saw Coco Chanel once many years ago when I was in Paris with Ossie. She was sitting on the staircase in her shop on the rue Cambon, reflected in the mirrors, wearing a little hat. She took that idea of a uniform and made it into the height of elegance. Simplicity with a flourish, a touch of idiosyncratic style. A bit of old lace, or marvellous tweed, a pattern that catches the eye but doesn't blind it – it's all in the touches.

I think it's just so nice to see someone dressed properly. Walk down the High Street and you inevitably see a few girls who look astonishing. They have put themselves together in a way that's not simply about following trends. They don't care what everybody else thinks. They're a law unto themselves – and that is the essence of stylishness.

Celia Birtwell

London, May 2006

Introduction

Wouldn't it be wonderful to slip into the role of Hitchcock heroine in a nipped-waist, sharp-shouldered suit; a siren in a basque; a free-spirited bohemian in an amazing beaded kaftan; a poetic pre-Raphaelite muse in a cameo-perfect lacy blouse?

Dressing up is all about imagining yourself in other lives. The joy of vintage is that, with well-informed shopping, you can make your dreams come true. Clothes provide a key to unlocking a side of yourself worthy of exploration, empowerment, adornment. They allow you to be the leading lady in dramas of your own creating. Even without a red carpet you can look every inch a star.

Let's face it – anyone can walk down the High Street, spend some money and get a fairly fashionable look. But why not try for something more – an outfit that suggests hidden depths, imagination, allure. Whether it's Topshop customised with a fabulous chiffon scarf or an original Ossie Clark, *It's Vintage, Darling!* shows you how to find those special pieces that not only look great on the hanger, they also look great on you.

You don't have to be a striking model to possess striking style – it's all in the presentation. Think about the Hollywood stars of the 1940s and 1950s. They always looked the part, not because they weighed eight stone, but because their clothes fit beautifully and flattered the best elements of their figures. Sadly, none of us has arch-costumer Edith Head at our disposal, but we can learn from her tricks – things like how garments should fall across the shoulders; which hemline best suits our legs; the silhouettes that will always be classics; and how to alter an outfit so it looks like it was sewn on. Clothes may not make the man, or even the woman, but they do provide an entrée into a realm beyond the ordinary. This is a companion guide through that realm, describing how to find clothing that surpasses in every way: beautifully made, utterly flattering, and worthy of the admiration – the lingering gaze – of others.

The most brilliant contemporary designers continually plunder history's attic, seeking out the arresting lines, fabrics, construction, accessorising, and attitudes of decades and even centuries ago. They pick and choose from the old to re-invent the looks of the world's most fashionable women. You can do exactly the same thing for yourself, whether you're a vintage queen, a charity shop princess, or a dress agency diva, or a combination of all three. You can renew yourself with breathtaking garments that others were naive enough to let go. A great piece of clothing, be it a beautifully preserved relic or a nearly-new piece so stylishly crafted it is destined to endure, is not only a means of self-exploration. It is also a delicate piece of armour against the slings and arrows that are an inevitable aspect of life. A totem, a charm, a source of power. On even the most trying of days, when you are carrying a bag spangled in sequins, or are swathed in cashmere so soft you could purr, or are wearing a fedora tilted just so, you can look in the mirror and know that one thing, at least, is absolutely right.

You may be a fixture at the local Oxfam. The stall holders at the best markets may know you by name. But if you still come home with purchases that felt like incredible bargains (£30 for an Azzedine Alaïa, what a steal! are you kidding?) that are quickly banished to the land of wardrobe mistakes (sure it was £30, but it was also two sizes too small) then it's time to upgrade your know-how. Women who can spot the two kinds of value – based on a garment's general excellence and on how precisely it meets their individual needs – have made themselves something very special, and very rare: *connoisseurs* in the art of dressing with high style.

As if to make up for the great originality, enduring style and reasonable prices there for the taking, second-hand shopping makes significant demands on your time. Even in vintage stores and dress agencies, where the quality is pre-screened, it can take hours to find just one suitable piece, or – *sob* – nothing at all. Connoisseurship helps streamline the process. It comes to your aid no matter what your preferred habitat: church jumble sale or Hampstead dress agency. With your expertise refined and assessment skills ramped up, you can move down a rail *at speed*. Your fingertips are sensitised to top-quality fabrics. Your eyes latch onto the properly set-in shoulder, the expensive button, the extraordinary tweed. In this way, you go directly to the very best pieces, leaving the also-rans behind for less selective shoppers.

It takes commitment and discipline to do anything well, and that includes becoming a second-hand connoisseur. I began shopping this way many years ago, while working in publishing in New York City. This 'glamour' job paid a very unglamorous salary, one that barely covered food and shelter, never mind fashion sprees. Still, I loved *the idea* of beautiful clothes and didn't want to settle for cheaply made stuff. Then, as now, Manhattan's Upper East side abounded with charity shops and dress agencies, places where the Park Avenue Princesses and the Ladies Who Lunch retired their clothing after an outing or two. One of my very first buys was a chocolate silk blouse by Isaac Mizrahi, the brilliant American designer. The silk was heavy, radiant, and so sensual against the skin that it seemed almost illicit to be wearing it by day, in a cubicle, no less. Every time I put it on, I *knew* there was a world of possibilities beyond that workstation. Flash forward to London, where at Steinberg & Tolkein on the King's Road, I come across a Givenchy jacket of unknown vintage, black, quilted and appliquéd with bright yellow felt flowers. It alludes to Mao jackets, smoking jackets, and nursery school all at the same time, and, improbably, looks fantastic on. It's also timeless, and I'll be wearing it for the rest of my life. Then there's the 1980s Chanel jacket I just found on eBay, which will look great over a satin camisole . . .

These pieces and the others in my wardrobe have taught me invaluable lessons about what quality is. They are why I no longer settle for anything that falls short of fabulous. In the chapters that follow, I share what I've learned over many years spent in the company of amazing old clothes. Say it loud, say it proud: '*It's Vintage, Darling!*' tells the world that while we still adore playing dress-up, we've become unerringly sophisticated in our choices.

The Second-hand Fashion Fundamentals

All about the
second-hand market

While a freshly minted Best Actress gliding to the podium in a vintage ball gown (Reese Witherspoon, we're talking about you) is a relatively recent phenomenon, the second-hand clothing trade is not. It's a good bet that the very first used-clothing transaction took place in a cave. Since then, the business has had a long, successful and extremely colourful history. Take a peek at a Victorian market through the eyes of a nineteenth-century reporter: 'Petticoat Lane is essentially the old clothes district. Embracing the streets and alleys adjacent to Petticoat Lane and including the rows of old boots and shoes on the ground, there is perhaps two or three miles of old clothes . . . gowns of every shade and pattern are hanging up. Dress coats, frock coats, great coats, livery and game keepers' coats, paletots, tunics, trousers, knee breeches, waistcoats, capes, pilot coats, working jackets, plaids, hats, dressing gowns, skirts, Guernsey frocks, are all displayed.' Frock coats! Waistcoats! Paletots! (Whatever those are!) But the experience wasn't exactly serene. The reporter goes on to explain that 'clothes first come through the Old Clothes Exchange. The Exchange had been so noisy that the East

India Company, who had warehouses nearby, complained; sometimes it took 200 constables to keep order.' Just imagine what it was like during sales.

If Petticoat Lane represented the hurly-burly of the used-clothing biz, the royal courts of France, where exacting rituals of dress and decorum reigned, saw a far more genteel version, steeped in feminine frivolity. *The Culture of Clothes*, a sociological history of clothing in that country, notes that the most esteemed eighteenth-century Parisian resellers were the *revendeuses à la toilette* (who called during noblewomen's lengthy, gossipy preparations for an appearance in court). *Revendeuses* bought and sold old fabrics, lace, jewels and other items from the rich and resold them to equally upper-class customers. The women are depicted in engravings of the period acting as 'both confidantes and merchants at the morning toilets of the ladies'.

The second-hand clothing business is still stratified according to the type of garment a shop typically sells and the starriness of the names on the labels. Unlike times past, however, shoppers today do not strictly segregate themselves within a particular sphere. Trustafarians who could buy out a Prada boutique with nary a blip in resting pulse rate instead find their hearts racing in charity shops. Impoverished students tarry in the poshest of dress agencies. Even traditional boundaries between High Street retailers and second-hand stores have blurred, with the London Topshop giving over valuable floorspace to a vintage collection.

First things first: a few definitions

— *Vintage*

Fashionistas tend to be a bit obsessed (i.e. completely insane) when it comes to current *tendences*, deeming a garment vintage if it's more than one season old. For the rest of us, ten years is roughly sufficient for a given era to recycle back into wearability, though many of us will be forever (and rightly) loath to wear any style we favoured in puberty. Depending on the shop or stallholder, vintage possibilities range from polyester disco shirts with lapels wide enough to land a small plane through nineteenth-century side-saddle riding habits to post-war New Look ball gowns. Vintage sellers often specialise in particular eras – 'retro', for example, which roughly refers to garments of the 1970s, 1980s and 1990s – or types of clothes, like the wonderfully loud Hawaiian shirts adopted by buoyant American GIs coming home from Pacific tours of duty.

While they're extremely cagey about divulging sources, shop owners and stallholders obtain their stock from wholesalers, car-boot sales, charity shops (though this source is drying up fast), and from individuals who have recently undertaken a major loft clear-out.

Beyond bricks-and-mortar shops, and vintage expos that draw multiple sellers under one roof, the internet is a vast electronic vintage mall, with UK and international sellers operating marvellous sites filled with free information and links a couple of mouse-clicks away from the scans of the clothes. And then there's eBay, which has become a behemoth player catering to those who love the buzz of bidding for old clothes at auction. How to take advantage of these particular buying opportunities is described in greater detail in the chapters that follow.

While we all agree that vintage clothing is fabulous, the shopping experience is a special one that has its own particular upsides and downsides. You probably know most of them already, but it's worth reviewing them generally here before we get more specific later in the book.

ADVANTAGES OF SHOPPING AT VINTAGE OUTLETS:

Distinctiveness – most of the items are truly one-of-a-kind.

Volume – if you love Chantilly lace, you'll find it in quantity if you discover the right shop.

Craftsmanship – the better clothing of the past has construction to die for.

Research opportunities – vintage shops are like style museums; you can learn even if you don't care to buy.

DISADVANTAGES OF SHOPPING AT VINTAGE OUTLETS:

Possible high £££ – reflecting rarity and quality of the garments.

Fragility – many of the clothes are too delicate for everyday wear.

Condition – not always impeccable.

Sizes – can be very tricky to get right.

— Dress Agencies

Dress agencies typically sell new or lightly worn designer clothing that is under five years old. The very best of these pieces will be iconic twenty years from now. I've always found it puzzling that dress agencies don't enjoy the same cachet in the UK that they do in the States, where once upon a time they outfitted my entire working wardrobe. Even if you're not inclined to shop in them habitually, they are always worth a look-in, for the fine lines and beautiful workmanship of the stand-out pieces can be an invaluable mainstay of the stylish girl's wardrobe. In a sense, shopping at a dress agency allows you to get a jump on the vintage finds of the future.

Why do the owners of these wonderful pieces ever let them go in the first place? Some women are so rich, bless them, they can afford to completely refurbish their wardrobes twice a year. Other women travel in circles so fashionably correct, so hell-bent on the new, that they daren't wear the Balenciaga frock that was the darling of the trendsetters last year. Still others are in the throes of yet another personal crisis that demands that they raise cash quick – and their husbands will never notice that twenty pairs of shoes have mysteriously gone missing.

In the shucking of the old to make room for the new, the shop acts as middleman for sellers (also known as consignors). Lady Raffia, for example, recently lost two stone on her spa retreat in Bhutan and can no longer wear her Etro paisley silk skirt, purchased at the Harvey Nick's sale a year ago for £399. When she brings it in to her neighbourhood dress agency, the manager takes a good look, making sure it is clean (a must), free of damage and obvious signs of wear, is of a recent season and is suitable for the shop's clientele. If the skirt is accepted, the shop might price it anywhere from £5 to £500, but most likely in the region of £200. If the garment sells, Lady R. might expect to receive 40–60% of the selling price. A dress agency typically displays a piece for 60–90 days. If it doesn't sell at the original price after a set period, it may be marked down. If it still hasn't sold within an agreed-upon period (often another 6–8 weeks), Lady Raffia is expected to reclaim it. If it does sell, she collects a cheque.

In this way, clothing is sourced from the wealthy, the famous, the fashion insiders – some of the best-dressed ladies in town. As for their names, the shop will keep mum. The owner of Encore on New York's Madison Avenue, said to be the oldest dress agency in the United States, only confirmed that Jackie Onassis was a frequent consignor long after the story was repeatedly published. This is business as usual among the top dress-agency owners – they would rather wear sackcloth than divulge their consignors' secrets. That spangly Miu Miu tunic you've just brought home from the dress agency in South Kensington might have spent a day on the back of a football wife, a pop tart, an Oscar hopeful. You never know – but what you can get is part of the fun.

ADVANTAGES OF SHOPPING AT DRESS AGENCIES:

Time saving – the items have been pre-screened by the management.

Rational display – usually the clothing is sized, and sometimes arranged by colour. Sale goods are often on a special rack.

Consistency of goods – the owner pre-screens so you don't have to wade through piles of nothing.

Condition of clothing – most shops accept only dry-cleaned clothes with little sign of wear.

Real dressing rooms – privacy, good lighting.

Mark-down policy – pricing can range anywhere from 25%

(for brand-new, current items) to 75% of the original retail cost. Bargains to be found if shop holds clearance sales.

Service – frequent customers get top-notch treatment.

DISADVANTAGES OF SHOPPING AT DRESS AGENCIES:

High £££ – reflecting original cost of garments.

Inadequate service – if you're an unfamiliar face, you may be left to your own devices.

Attitude – while the vast majority of shopkeepers are lovely and helpful, a few can be snobbish.

— Charity Shops

While vintage clothing brings zest and individuality to a world otherwise ruled by fashion clones, a woman does not live by petticoats alone. Or cork platforms. Or plaid plus-fours (if that's what she's into). There is a valid and pressing need for wardrobe basics against which to display the stars of a personal vintage trove. Super-stylish jeans. The perfect scoop-necked white T-shirt. Really cute flat shoes. There is no better place to find simple pieces like these for mere pennies than in charity shops, where as often as not they're brand new. Charity shops are also superb sources for the kind of trendy, indifferently-made-but-who-cares guilty pleasures (ponchos, anyone? Boho belts?) we can't resist from time to time, but still don't want to waste a fortune on. Other charity-shop holdings that routinely draw models and stylists are: highly distressed jackets, oddball hats, clothes that are *slightly wrong*, thrown on to skew an ensemble away from perfection. This is not something we all can carry off, but when worn with confidence and a razor-sharp sense of where to stop, thrift-store grunge can look fierce.

All this, and charity shops also regularly reward us with extraordinarily fine, inexplicably ignored skirts, trousers, tops and coats. No wonder the places are so habit-forming. UK charity shops, true to their name, are run by not-for-profit organisations (in the US, the thrift-store equivalents are occasionally run by individuals for profit). Conveniently, they tend to cluster two or three to a block, as they do in Golders Green Road in north London, affording an entire morning or afternoon of bouncing from door to door and rifling through the rails. The merchandise is generally sourced from individual donations, but sometimes the shops have special arrangements with High Street stores and/or manufacturers, resulting in the special guest appearance of new, unworn, recent-season goods selling for a pittance.

In recent years, shops have instituted set-aside 'designer rails', where the brand names are a bit starrier and prices are more assertive. But in my experience the so-called designer merchandise is not much better or worse than the shop's unheralded offerings. The most reliable gauge of the quality in a given store is the price of properties in the surrounding neighbourhood.

ADVANTAGES OF SHOPPING AT CHARITY SHOPS:

Basics – the best everyday pieces are found here for less.

Street style – this is where wardrobes get their edge.

Variety – new merchandise constantly coming in.

New clothes available – thanks to manufacturers and others donating unsold goods.

Comprehensive – most charity shops sell everything from overcoats to earrings, making it possible to pull together an outfit in one place.

'Designer racks' – may help hone search.

Charitable – you're supporting a worthy cause by buying there.

DISADVANTAGES OF SHOPPING AT CHARITY SHOPS:

Atmosphere – possibly lacking in lustre.

Time drain – lots needed for focused shopping.

Condition of clothes – there is no guarantee that clothes are clean, much less in good condition.

Vertigo – clothes may be unsized, or haphazardly arranged.

Fitting rooms – possibly communal, possibly absent.

— *Other important stuff*

WHAT SORT OF PEOPLE AM I GOING TO RUN INTO?

The cliché is eccentrics, e.g. dotty grande dames, goths, people who believe life is one big fancy-dress party. On any given day, there will probably be a few of these types enlivening the shop floor. They are part of the ambiance, and frankly are a lot more entertaining than the crowd at Bluewater.

And then there's everybody else, including the freelance stylist for a top fashion magazine, hunting down a pair of 1980s stilettos to counterbalance the luxe of a couture ball gown. And that big guy with the little helper running ahead, tossing back garments for inspection? He designed the gown, and is looking for inspiration for next season's line.

WHERE DO I FIND THE SHOPS?

The resources section at the back of this book provides an excellent starting point for finding vintage sellers, charity shops, dress agencies and related organisations in the UK. Also, have a look in the Yellow Pages (see *Charitable Organisations, Dress Agencies, Second-hand, Charity Shops, Vintage, Retro*). If you have internet access, look up the keywords above together with your target city or town. City guides frequently list second-hand shopping opportunities. Be bold and start up a conversation with your fellow second-hand shoppers. Like all good hobbyists, they're apt to happily share information and lore.

ISN'T THERE SOMETHING TAWDRY ABOUT SECOND-HAND CLOTHING?

Sure, occasionally the clothes can be grubby. But garments aren't always pristine in first-run stores either, especially towards the end of the season, by which time hundreds of people may have tried a blouse on, smeared it with Juicy Tube, stained it with still-damp fake tan, stepped on it, borrowed it for a night out, etc. If you're in the habit of going to the gym, you'll encounter more fresh germs on a Pilates mat than in a charity shop.

I can think of nothing more depressing than entering a High Street shop late on Saturday afternoon to find a bedlam of garments tossed here and there, items mis-sized, dressing rooms heaped with other people's discards, and salespeople nursing the career option of mass murderer. All this and I'm still paying a fortune? *Merci, non.* I'd rather forsake glitzy fittings and too-cool-for-school sales help by patronising a vintage or charity store. This will leave me more to spend on atmosphere that counts – a great club or restaurant, and the black cab to get there. (Which means I can wear really unsensible shoes.)

I'VE BEEN SECOND-HAND SHOPPING AND THE PRICES
WEREN'T MUCH BETTER THAN RETAIL.
Odds are, the place was a high-calibre dress agency or vintage-clothing shop, which can and will sell garments priced well beyond High Street retail. A beautiful Christian Lacroix embroidered jacket that cost £800 new is still a bargain at £275, if it is in immaculate condition. A John Galliano suit rightly commands serious money in a dress agency, for it is likely to become a piece of fashion history.

IT TAKES TOO MUCH TIME TO FIND ANYTHING.
No arguing with this, it is the unavoidable downside of shopping for second-hand clothing. One can hunt for hours and still come up empty-handed. Which is why the core curriculum of this book is how to streamline the process: how to find marvellous pieces with the systematic use of sight and touch, and then make realistic judgments about whether or not it is a good buy. Using these techniques, it's possible to become a faster, more efficient and more effective shopper. And hey, you can spend a day on the High Street and come home empty-handed too.

WEARING SOMEBODY ELSE'S OLD CLOTHES GIVES ME THE CREEPS.
Many pieces that land up with second-hand merchants haven't been worn at all. There are some crazy shoppers out there, people who regularly furnish second-hand stockrooms with brand-new goods. You probably know one.

Maybe you *are* one. I'm talking about women who love shopping so much, they buy simply because they were born to. Once a woman like this has brought her adorable Anya Hindmarch shoes home from Harrods, they instantly become less interesting than the Ginas in the Bond Street shop window, which, once acquired, will pale before the glory of the Jimmy Choo slingbacks *on sale*, and so on. It's too late to return anything, the shoe cubbies in her wardrobe runneth over, so off the purchases go to a dress agency, eBay or – happy day – a charity shop. Compulsive shopping is not a modern phenomenon: the equivalent can occur with vintage clothing, when someone decides to clear out a shopaholic nan's old trunks. Buyers like these make my world go round. Other contributors to the new-merchandise flow include:

- ◉ Women who have recently lost or gained weight, or who buy clothing as a futile incentive to do so.
- ◉ Love-rat boyfriends or ex-husbands, whose gifts of clothing will never – *ever* – be worn.
- ◉ Fashion industry insiders who are a wellspring of sample merchandise.
- ◉ People like us who make mistakes, especially when it comes to shoes.

So much for the negative aspects of second-hand shopping. What about the positives?

YOU CAN ASSEMBLE A VAST WARDROBE.
Though I advise against this again and again, many die-hard shoppers will merrily ignore it.

THIS MODE OF SHOPPING CAN HELP DETERMINE
YOUR BEST STYLE OPTIONS.
Charity shops, vintage stores and dress agencies can stock a wider variety of styles, colours and labels than a standard shop could ever possibly afford. You can try on countless different styles – not to buy, necessarily, but to

learn what flatters. This is especially true when conventional High Street and department stores are all beaming down the same three seasonal gimmicks, i.e., ankle-length skirts, crocheted tops and acid green.

EXPERIENCED SECOND-HAND CLOTHES SHOPPERS
CAN ASSEMBLE A COMPLETE OUTFIT IN ONE GO.
If you know your stuff, you can work wonders in a second-hand shop, because most stock not only clothing, but shoes, scarves, bags and jewellery, all within paces of each other.

PERSONALIZED SERVICE IS AVAILABLE.
If you are a steady customer at a cracking dress agency, you can expect a level of service akin to that lavished on bold-faced names in high-end boutiques. The shop owner will call you when pieces arrive in your size and style, and act as a partner in helping build your wardrobe. Even if you are a first-time customer, a good dress agency should offer the kind of warmth and attention that is hard to come by at identikit retailers.

YOU'LL GET HONEST OPINIONS FROM SALES
STAFF AND OTHER CUSTOMERS.
It does a shop owner no good to tell a customer something looks great when it doesn't. They have a stake in making clients look good. Especially in vintage and charity shops, you can get honest opinion from fellow shoppers, some of whom live to give opinions. Which brings me to another point about shopping in second-hand stores.

IT'S A CHANCE TO USE YOUR WITS.
In a retail environment, it takes no brains at all to assemble an outfit the magazines say is hot, plop it down at the till, and go. But at a second-hand store, you must be on your toes. At a very basic level, it's calling hunt-and-gather instincts into play. But it holds the possibility of another ancient skill as well: negotiation. (How, when and where to haggle is discussed in Chapters 13, 14 and 15.)

YOU CAN GET BETTER LONG-TERM VALUE FOR
YOUR MONEY AT SECOND-HAND STORES.

Given the quality of the fabric, workmanship and trimmings, a previously owned jacket made to superior standards will look better and wear longer than new garments made to inferior standards. This is why an Yves Saint Laurent couture piece ends its life in a fashion museum, while a lesser imitator ends up in a landfill.

SPEAKING OF WHICH: SECOND-HAND IS GOOD
FOR THE ENVIRONMENT.

We've all heard about the waste stream, the over-consumption of resources, the ecological and even psychological damage that accompanies the apparel manufacturing process, most notably in the lesser-developed nations. Where our grandparents would have mended, altered and handed down garments until they fell apart, we have become accustomed to the idea of disposable goods. In addition to clogging the landfills, we need to account for the environmental cost of making the textiles in the first place. Huge volumes of waste water are generated in their manufacture, water which may contain heavy metals from the dyeing process, as well as run-off dyes themselves. Growing cotton efficiently requires pesticides and fertiliser, and oil is consumed in the manufacture of synthetic fibres. By making the decision to purchase second-hand clothing, you are helping to prolong the useful life of a garment, reducing waste and amortising the cost of its manufacture upon the environment.

BY SHOPPING AT CHARITY SHOPS, YOU ARE SUPPORTING
THE EFFORTS OF VITAL ORGANISATIONS.

Non-profit charity shops help pay for programmes that are increasingly necessary as government funding diminishes.

SHOPPING SECOND-HAND HELPS LOCAL BUSINESS.

Mega-retailing is a fact of modern life, with every High Street in every city featuring the usual round of cookie-cutter stores. The rise of shopping-centre culture has taken a toll on small-business owners because these operations are not able to compete when it comes to buying power and price-cutting policies. Yet one kind of business has flourished in the face of monster retailing – second-hand shops. The people running these places are your neighbours, part of your community in a way that the higher-ups at Gap will never be. Shopping second-hand doesn't just keep good clothing going, it keeps good people going too. See? You can be a fabulous dresser and a nice person. Who said fashionable people are shallow?

The wonders that we weave: fabrics and how they got that way

Any fashion insider will tell you that appreciating fabric is the foundation of appreciating fine clothing. Understanding fibres and their particular characteristics is the first step in becoming a clothes connoisseur. As this book aims to teach you *everything* there is to know about buying stand-out pieces, this chapter offers a look at how fabrics are made, followed by an overview of the most popular natural and artificial fibres. OK. I admit it. These first chapters are more anorak than adorable cropped trench coat, but stick with me here. They set the stage for Chapter 3, devoted to training your eyes and hands to detect brilliance amid dross. You will be amazed at how a little extra knowledge will help you shop smarter, faster, better. After reading this chapter and the one that follows, you'll find it much easier to find the fabrics you love best, whether it's Egyptian cotton or duppioni silk. With your new savoir-faire, you'll set higher personal standards about what is welcome against your skin and what is not. Finally, once you've found wonderful pieces, you'll know whether their qualities work with your lifestyle.

— *Nice threads!*

At the end of the day, clothes *are* threads, woven or knitted, or even pounded together to make fabric. Let's take a closer look at how this happens. Imagine a simple cotton-polyester T-shirt. Unravel the knit, and you get threads. Untwist the threads, and you're down to the absolute basic element, the fibres. **Fibre** is a catch-all term used to describe the wisps of cotton and strands of polyester that are blended together in this particular T-shirt. But experts often make a further distinction. They'll say yes, cotton is a fibre, but, technically speaking, polyester is a **filament**. The main difference between the two is their length. Fibres are on the short side. Filaments go on and on and on. Silk is the only natural filament – unspool a silk cocoon and you get a single strand that averages a mile long. All the other kinds of filament are synthetically made, and theoretically could unreel forever.

Since they're so short, fibres must be **spun** in order to make yarn or thread. In basic terms, spinning is similar to what happens when you pull some fluff off the end of a cotton bud and roll it between your fingers, forming a long, tight mass. Whether the fibres originate from cotton plants or camels, the choicest ones are usually the longest, because when spun they form the tightest, hardest, smoothest threads – resulting in the most finely textured, elegant fabric. Shorter fibres make a fuzzier thread or yarn (all those stubby ends sticking out) – resulting in a bulkier, more rough-hewn look and feel. Filaments are also usually spun because their diameter (thickness) is so small you can barely see them, much less weave or knit them, until a bunch are twisted together.

As we'll see, the **length** and **diameter** of the fibres play a key role in determining how a fabric looks and feels. Other qualities are important too, such as the **crimp** (kinkiness), **absorbency, smoothness, stretchiness** and **resilience** (ability to bounce back).

— What textile mills do

Once the thread or yarn is spun, it must be configured into fabric. Two methods have been used since time immemorial: **weaving** and **knitting**.

Woven fabric is produced on a loom. On this machine, long rows of up-and-down, or **warp**, threads are stretched tight like piano wires – creating a framework for a **filling thread** to pass over and under. The simplest and most common type of weave is the **plain weave**, where the filling thread goes over * under * over * under. Another popular weave is **twill**, where the filling thread goes something like over * under * under * over * under * under, and then, when it moves up a row, keeps the same rhythm but shifts one thread over. This makes a diagonal pattern – one you may be able to spot in a pair of jeans that are older than five years or so, which were typically made with a twill weave (now jeans manufacturers are diversifying like crazy, with left-hand weave, triple-somersault-with-a-flip weave, but that's another story). The last important type of woven fabric is the **satin weave**. It's a common misconception that satin is a type of fibre, like silk. It's not. Satin can be made with cotton, wool, silk or polyester, as long as the weave goes something like over * over * over * under * over * over * over * under * over * over – you get the idea. Here, the filling threads 'float' for long stretches across the top of the weave. Their unbroken length helps give satin its distinctive gleam.

Knitted fabrics are different. Some are easy to spot, like fuzzy mohair mufflers. Others are trickier – possibly because they're not made of wool (knits don't need to be), possibly because the interlock is so teeny the fabric looks woven until you get really really close. (Diane von Furstenberg's silk jersey wrap dresses are a good example.) Whether they're made with a pair of needles or a turbocharged knitting machine, all knits have one thing in common: they're made up of **interlocking loops** rather than crisscrossed threads or yarn. In a performance comparison, wovens tend to be stronger than knits, and knits tend to be stretchier than wovens.

The stretchiness of a given garment is also determined by the manufacturing process. Finished fabric has distinct **grains** – running horizontally and up and down. The cross grain usually has a bit of stretch. For its part, the vertical grain doesn't have comparable give (kind of like your lips, which can stretch way wide for a smile or a kiss, but don't yield nearly as much up and down). Clothing manufacturers consciously use these qualities when assembling a garment to ensure that it fits and hangs well.

The main determinant of the stretchiness of a fabric is the material that it's made of. Which brings us to the fibres themselves. You thought your closet was jammed with clothes? Brace yourself. Thanks to 10,000 years of fabric history, it's also loaded with ancient rites, swashbuckling exploration and scientific genius.

Can I borrow your coat?
A round-up of natural fibres

— Wool

Once upon a time in Spain, the Merino sheep was so highly prized that anyone caught smuggling one out of the country was sentenced to death. Harsh, but hardly surprising – the woolly wonders earned their masters so much money that the taxes alone financed Columbus's trip to America. Today, the Merino is still the king of the wool-producing breeds. Its fibres are white (easy to dye) and very fine (about the same diameter as a human hair, which makes for a delightfully soft yarn or thread).

Wool is obtained by shearing, usually in the spring, once it's warm enough for the sheep to go without a heavy coat. After a long winter, the fleece is festooned with mud, twigs and everything else the animal happens to bumble into. So after shearing, it's a hot bath and a good scrub (for the wool, not the sheep) to remove the dirt, debris and most of the natural oils. Then the wool is 'carded' to get all the fibres running in roughly the same direction. Next it's combed, which winnows out all fibres of two inches or less. These shorter hairs will be used to make **woollen** or fuzzy fabrics, such as bulky knits and tweeds. The longer fibres will be used to make fine sweaters and suiting fabric, known in the fashion business as **worsteds**.

Wool has many appealing characteristics. First, its natural crimp helps it trap pockets of air, which keep the sheep (and you) toasty no matter how bleak the weather. Also, wool sheds water droplets (ask any Aran fisherman), but absorbs water vapour, meaning it can pull perspiration right off the body (ask any Aran fisherman after an entire winter wearing that now-reeking jumper). Finally, wool springs back when crushed or stretched – even up to a third of its length – meaning it packs without wrinkles (ask any Palm Beach fisherman).

A label specifying 'Virgin Wool' does not refer to the animal's behind-the-barn activities, or lack thereof. It simply means the fibre is new, rather than recycled from old fabric. 'Lambswool' on a label indicates that the source animal was under seven months old, so the fleece is correspondingly finer, lighter and softer.

Despite all these fine qualities, wool has its disadvantages. If a wool garment is accidentally tossed into the wash, the knock-out combination of heat, moisture and pressure causes the tiny scales running along the fibres' surface to intersnag and coil. The resulting itty-bitty jumper would be comical, if it weren't so tragic. This is why woollen items are best hand-washed or dry-cleaned.

SPECIALITY ANIMAL FIBRES

Wool doesn't necessarily come from sheep. Camels, alpaca, even rabbits, also supply the goods. With modern garments, the contents label may specify the source animal, with older pieces the label may be unforthcoming, or missing altogether. If in the course of shopping your hand feels something softer, finer and more appealing than other garments, pull it out and see if the label offers enlightenment. It could be you've found something very special.

Alpaca: A South American cousin of the goat, the alpaca lives high in the Andes mountains. It evolved a lightweight, lustrous soft wool with lots of crimp to keep warm in chilly temperatures. In former days alpaca was used with some frequency in better clothing (you may find it in a fine vintage coat or jacket) but is now used only in deluxe pieces.

Angora fur: Not to be confused with the Angora goat, which yields mohair (see below). Angora fur comes from a special breed of domesticated rabbit, whose coat is clipped or combed every 3–4 months. Angora is the ultimate sweater-girl material: with its soft, longish fibres, it's extraordinarily touchable.

Camel hair: It gets mighty chilly in Outer Mongolia. That's why the two-humped Bactrian camel develops a fuzzy under-layer of hair as insulation. Very warm, yet extremely lightweight: some claim a 22 oz camel-hair fabric is as warm as a 32 oz garment made of wool. Of a lovely toffee-brown colour, the hair is usually left undyed. Camel's hair coats, which had their heyday in the 1950s, may be made of camel hair, sheep's wool, or a combination of the two.

Cashmere: Semi-wild goats living in the mountainous Kashmir region of India provided the world with its first cashmere. Now China has taken over, along with Australia, New Zealand and, of course, Scotland. Why is this fibre so prized? Once you feel it or, better, wear it, you'll never ask again. With its tiny diameter and buoyant crimp, cashmere makes for a super-soft, snugly warm, yet light-as-air raiment. True **pashmina**, made of the finest possible cashmere thread, is said to be so delicate that a large shawl may be drawn through a wedding band. But cashmere comes at a cost. The goat's delightful undercoat is intermingled with less delightful thick guard hairs. The strands must be separated by hand, making for a labour-intensive process.

Mohair: Made from the fleece of Angora goats, which originated in the Himalayas and have since been widely imported elsewhere. Mohair is praised for its resilience and lustrous sheen. When woven, mohair is indistinguishable from fine sheep's wool. In knit form, it is the hairiest of the speciality fibres, making for jumpers with a distinctive snow-bunny or earth-mother vibe (exactly which is down to the hue and hearth).

— Cotton

In 1350, the English explorer Sir John Mandeville came back from India hopping with news: 'There is a wonderful tree which bore tiny lambs on the ends of its branches.' These days, we'd gently draw him aside and tell him he found a cotton plant. Thanks to the world's love of jeans, cotton is the most-used fibre of all, holding a 65% share of the total apparel market. It all starts 4–6 weeks after planting, when cotton flowers fall off to reveal the tiny boll, or seedpod. This spends a few weeks ripening. When it can't get any fatter, it splits, revealing the white, fluffy interior fibre that protects the seeds. After the fibre is picked it is deseeded and sent to a mill where it is drawn, combed and spun into yarn or thread. As with wool, the length and diameter of the fibres determine their end use. The longest, choicest fibres, traditionally from the **Sea Island** and **Egyptian** species (and the Egyptian subspecies **Pima**), are used to make the fine, tight threads that go into the best cotton shirting fabric – the kind you see in Jermyn Street windows. Most everyday cotton clothing is made from average-length fibres.

COMFORT FACTOR

Clothing manufacturers – especially in the sporting-goods market – love to talk about the comfort factor of their fabrics, but what does all the jargon mean? At the most basic level, if a fabric is loosely knitted or woven (like cheese cloth), air passes easily from one side to the other, making for high **breathability**. Another factor is a fabric's **conductivity**: how well the fibres transfer heat from inside to out. Low-conductivity fabrics like Orlon and silk help keep heat close to the body. High-conductivity fabrics like cotton and linen allow heat to pass through. Still another aspect is **absorbency**. If perspiration sits on the skin unabsorbed, it makes us feel clammy (if it's cold), or sweaty (if it's warm). All natural fibres absorb sweat. Synthetic fibres don't, which in the past lent them a poor reputation. But today, manufacturers are able to engineer these fibres with tiny grooves running along their surfaces. This encourages **wickability**, allowing moisture to pass off the skin onto the garment, where it quickly dries.

As you might expect from a fibre that flourishes in semi-tropical sun and pelting rains, cotton easily withstands the rigors of the washing machine – even at boiling-hot temperatures. It is also highly absorbent, making it comfortable to wear in humid conditions. Cotton's downside is that it wrinkles easily, which is why it's often blended with polyester, which doesn't wrinkle at all.

— Silk

Legend has it that silk was discovered by a Chinese princess, Hsi Ling-Chi, in 2640 BC, when she accidentally dropped a silkworm cocoon into hot water and saw big potential when it began to unravel. For thousands of years, the Chinese jealously guarded the manufacturing process, and the trading route into that country, known as the Silk Road, was well-trodden by merchants who made a fortune selling the material to the courts of Europe. Now, after 4,500 years of intense cultivation, silk moths have become so domesticated they can't fly. Once the moths have laid their eggs, they are collected, and the hatched silkworm (actually a caterpillar) spends the next 4–5 weeks feasting on mulberry leaves, which are replenished every 2–3 hours. When it can't take another bite, the caterpillar latches onto a twig and starts to spin its cocoon. The cocoon material is silk. The animal manoeuvres the filament over and around itself for 2–3 days. The finished cocoons are gathered and baked to kill the animals inside (ethical vegetarians take note). They're then placed in tanks of warm water to loosen the silk's gummy coating and reveal the end of the filaments, which are carefully unspooled. Any broken fibres are used to make **spun silk**, which is of lesser quality. **Raw silk** is spun silk that has been brushed to give it a cottony effect. **Wild silk** is from worms eating a less exquisite diet, usually oak leaves, which is reflected in the rougher quality of the finished fabric. **Shantung** (also called **duppioni**) **silk** is high-quality fabric distinguished by its slubs, or irregularly nubby threads. In the silk business, professionals measure the fabric in units called momme: lesser-quality, washable and other types of silk range from 6–12 momme; heavier, better-quality silk such as crepe de chine average from 14–18 or even higher momme, and silks used in suiting fabric are the heaviest at up to 22 momme.

> 'Whereas in silks my Julia goes
> Then (methinks) how sweetly flows
> That liquefaction of her clothes.'
> **Robert Herrick, English poet, 1591–1674**

In the Roman Empire, silk sold for its weight in gold, which is hardly surprising given its characteristics. The filament is extremely fine – the finest of all natural fibres – very smooth, and shaped like a prism. These qualities give it a lustre that can only be matched by artificial fabrics. Another quality of silk is tremendous strength despite extremely light weight – nature made it this way to protect the developing animal from the elements and to keep the cocoon firmly attached to its twig, no matter how hard the wind would blow. Also, because the cocooned worm must develop at a consistently warm temperature, silk does not readily let heat escape. This low conductivity makes it somewhat like the insulation that wraps a house, and is why the fabric is warm to wear despite its light weight. But because silk is so labour-intensive, it is an expensive fibre.

—Linen and Ramie

Said to be the oldest fibre, linen was also the world's most important until cotton took over at the end of the eighteenth century. Linen is made from the inner bark of the long stems of the flax plant, which is cultivated in temperate and subtropical regions around the world. To this day, flax fibres are prepared for spinning using an efficient age-old process: the stems are cut near the roots and are thrown into a pond or tank for a few days, where the natural rotting action of bacteria eats away at the unusable inner core. The fibres are then cleaned, straightened and spun. The natural waxes present in flax are what gives linen its lustre.

Any material that keeps a four-foot-tall plant standing upright has to be extremely strong. This strength carries over to the finished fabric. Linen is also incredibly long-wearing – this is the fibre ancient Egyptians used to wrap mummies for their voyage to the afterworld.

I once saw a piece of mummy fabric up close in the textile department of the Cooper-Hewitt Museum in New York. Apart from some mysterious stains, it looked exactly like one of my grandmother's old table runners. (Come to think of it, the runner had stains too, but I'm pretty sure that was tea.) Anyway, linen's strength is why so many antique bedclothes turn up at jumble and car-boot sales; with proper care, it lasts and lasts. But there's also a downside. Flax fibres are designed by nature to point in a single direction: up towards the sun. If linen gets bent out of shape, it tends to stay that way, wrinkling easily in fabric form. If creased sharply enough in the same place over a long period, linen fibres may even snap and fray, which is why the fabric should never be too crisply ironed, and why heirloom garments should be refolded every so often. Back on the plus side, linen is an excellent conductor of heat, explaining its popularity as a cool summer fabric.

Ramie is a natural fibre resembling linen, but originating from the stem of the ramie shrub, which grows in the United States and the Far East. The difficulty in processing ramie has limited its use, but it is an extremely strong fibre, and occasionally turns up in summer garments.

Pulp it up: the roster of artificial fibres

Without getting too technical about it, there are two kinds of artificial fibres: **man-made** and **synthetic**. Rayon, acetate and triacetate – the man-made ones – in fact originate with plant material, which has been tweaked in the textile lab to create filaments with unique appearance and wear characteristics. To put it in very simple terms, man-made fibres are the Pringles potato snack of the fabric world.

—Rayon and Lyocell (Viscose, Cupro, Tencel)

Rayon was the very first man-made fibre. It was patented in 1855 by the Swiss George Audemars, who figured if a lowly caterpillar could produce a beautiful, hard-wearing filament, so could he. Through much of the nineteenth and early twentieth centuries, rayon was extremely popular as a hosiery fibre – it lent the look of silk stockings at an affordable price. The material came by its name because, like silk, it brightly reflects rays of light.

The basic recipe for rayon has gone largely unchanged since Audemars made the first batch. Wood pulp, usually from pine trees, is purified and chemically treated so that it forms a thick, gluey sludge. This is forced through a device known as a **spinneret**, which looks something like a showerhead. The emerging identical strands harden upon contact with an acid bath. Further chemical treatment makes them even tougher, then they're spun into thread. **Viscose** and **cupro** are two specific kinds of rayon.

Because it originates in the plant kingdom, rayon behaves a lot like its cousin cotton – it is absorbent, drapes well, and feels lovely against the skin. Formerly, it had the unfortunate tendency to spot in the rain and go to pieces if accidentally machine-washed. Today, it is usually coated to prevent spotting, and is made in a machine-washable form (called **lyocell**, which you may see marketed under the trade name Tencel). Since certain kinds of rayon remain dry-clean only, it's very important to check (and pay attention to!) the care label. If the piece is vintage and you suspect it might be rayon (it's always wise to ask *before* you buy), take pains to hand-wash or dry-clean it.

—Acetate and Triacetate

Also made from wood, or possibly cotton fibres that are too short to spin, acetate is manufactured in a process similar to rayon. Chemically, acetate is akin to Uhu glue: in the manufacturing process it hardens upon contact with air. This chemical connection makes acetate a bit high-strung as fibres go – it melts upon contact with heat and is liable to dissolve under the influence of alcohol, or, for that matter, acetone-based nail-polish remover. But its shimmering beauty makes all forgivable. You probably know acetate best as a lining for coats and jackets; it's a favourite here because it won't bobble even under the constant abrasion of sliding sleeves. But, lately, the fibre has come out of its shell, and is being worn as an outer fabric in its own right. While acetate is dry-clean only, **triacetate** is a washable variant.

Parlez-vous polyester?
The wonderful world of synthetics

Acrylic, polyester, nylon, spandex – let's give the chemists a round of applause. Somehow they figured out how to make coal tar, water, petroleum and air – ordinarily poor mixers – hook up into one long conga-line of a molecule. This was the first step towards making plastic, and the plastic fibres we call synthetics.

—Acrylic (Orlon)

This fibre hopes to pull the wool over your eyes. Even though it starts out as coal, water, petroleum and limestone, acrylic's ultimate warmth, fluffiness and softness does an excellent imitation of sheep's wool. This has as much to do with the *way* it's made as with the chemicals involved. As a

MICROFIBRES

These are artificial fibres finer than any found in nature. Microfibres may be of polyester, nylon, acrylic or rayon, or a blend. Microfibres' tiny diameter means they have a silky feel and can be woven very tight, making them resistant to rain, cold and wind. For this reason, they're often used to make rainwear.

first step, prefabricated acrylic chips are melted, then forced through a spinneret to make fine filaments. These are then crimped (to mimic the kinkiness of wool), chopped (to mimic the short fibres of wool) and spun, creating an end-product that looks and acts like wool yarn. But, unlike the latter, acrylic is machine-washable and moths hate the taste. Also, acrylic is relatively inexpensive to process, which is why it often turns up in lower-priced jumpers. One problem with acrylic – indeed with most knitted fibres but especially knitted synthetics – it tends to bobble. You know these, the irksome balls of fluff that accumulate where the material gets wear and tear. There's little you can do to prevent bobbling, but the balls can be razored or carefully snipped off for a (temporary) freshening-up of the garment.

—Polyester (Crimplene, Terylene, Dacron)

Introduced in 1953 by DuPont, polyester is a widely used synthetic fibre. Not long ago its image was poor, due to its propensity to trap heat and sweat, as well as its extensive use in budget-priced finery. But today it's a different story, thanks to smart PR on the part of manufacturers, the rise of microfibres, and the renaissance of 1970s boogie-down gear.

Despite all the changes, polyester retains its most impressive quality – ease of care. Poly easily holds its own against the washing machine and dryer, doesn't shrink and is the most wrinkle-resistant fibre known. This is why it's often blended with cotton and other fabrics that tend to loose their shape, or helps support other synthetics that could suffer a breakdown if forced to go it alone in the washing machine. On the negative side, polyester doesn't always let oily stains go. Vintage shoppers should keep this in mind if they come across a fabulous polyester blouse with a conspicuous splotch.

— Nylon (Polyamide)

If you're looking for strength, look no further than nylon – it's the strongest fibre known to man. Nylon carried parachuting soldiers through the skies in World War II. Nylon is used to make rip-stop luggage. Nylon is used to make bullet-proof vests. Nylon is used to make tights –

go figure. In an extremely complicated series of chemical steps, nylon is made from air, water and coal, then is extruded into filaments, of which fishing line is a relatively thick example. Why a fibre able to haul in a 200 lb fighting marlin can't withstand the pressure of my pinkie toe is mysterious to say the least, and I would love an explanation from the tights manufacturers. In the meantime, let's take it on faith that nylon is used on its own and in countless blends to give strength and durability to weaker materials. Because it is light, the fibre doesn't add bulk, which is particularly helpful in sportswear. Chemically speaking, nylon is a member of the **polyamide** family, and you'll often see it labelled as such in European content labels.

— Spandex (Elastane, Lycra®)

During World War II, scientists worked feverishly to create a chemical substance that could act as a substitute for rubber. While critical to the war effort, rubber was difficult to procure, since it came from tropical trees within striking range of Japan's air force. Science persevered, and spandex was the spectacular result. A stretchy fibre, it can be drawn out to 500% of its original length and snap back the same as before. Moreover, spandex can do this again and again and again, which is why it easily keeps pace in Boxercise class long after you yourself are near collapse.

Spandex is never used on its own. It's invariably a small percentage of the total fibre content of a fabric. Moreover, it's expensive, so budget-minded manufacturers strive to keep it to a minimum. The more spandex present (especially over 10%), the more stubbornly the garment will hold its shape. But even as little as 2% goes a long way in preventing baggy knees and saggy bottoms (on the clothes – Boxercise being the way forward on you).

I can't believe it's not leather: a few more synthetics

— Ultra suede

Made of polyester and polyurethane, ultra suede is made in Japan in a top-secret, hush-hush process. The fabric looks and feels like suede, but is washable. Not surprisingly, given its care characteristics, many ultra suede garments still look brand new twenty years on.

— Polyvinylchloride (PVC)

Typically used in jackets and trousers, PVC looks like leather but in fact is plastic. It does not breathe so can get uncomfortably warm to wear (not that a goth would let on). Playing to this audience (and the rest of us trying on a cheap 'n' surly look), this material wipes clean, repels rain and takes a lot of abuse.

Closet safari

Back at the beginning of the chapter, I mentioned that many of the fibres profiled here are hanging out in your own wardrobe. Why not see what you've got? Pull the pieces out and have a look at the contents label, which will be found, if present, on the collar, waistband or an inner side seam (a fibre-content label has been mandatory on UK garments since 1976). As you work your way through, glance back at the fibre profiles to remind yourself of their individual characteristics. If fibres haven't appeared on your radar before, you might be surprised by what you find. You may discover that cashmere or high-percentage spandex is running rampant through your closet. Or that your favourite suit contains nylon. Close your eyes and spend some time **feeling** the differences between the fibres and blends – how slippery acetate lining is, how spongy polyester. If you love the feel of a particular piece of clothing, try to commit those sensations to memory.

Next, look very carefully at how cleaning has affected the garments, and which fibres show the most signs of wear. If you have two pieces with identical fibre content, notice how manufacturers can make the same material look and feel slightly different, depending on the weight and manufacturing technique. Really get to know your fabrics in the privacy of your home. Next, we'll be hitting the shops.

Getting the handle
of fine fabrics

Are you getting enough fibre? Your GP and I are concerned. She's thinking about your diet. I'm thinking about what you know about clothes. We're devoting a lot of attention to fibres and fabrics early on in this book, but the in-depth immersion will prove worthwhile. This is why:

Connoisseur's Tip:
The quality of the fabric used in a garment is the best indicator of its quality overall. Or, to put it more bluntly: shoddy fabric equals shoddy merchandise.

Finding the finest examples of wool, silk, cotton and other materials on a long rail of mixed-quality clothing is tantamount to finding the Jean Patou tweed jacket, the 1950s rayon dress, the overlooked Missoni jumper. A manufacturer will not splash out on a superior textile only to undercut it with cheap trimmings and indifferent assembly. Top fabric equals a top piece. Don't worry if your ability to detect it isn't cracking at this point. None of us were born with the skill. It has to be nurtured through focused effort, and will come to life as soon as you start thinking about what you're doing. In fact, the learning process is very natural, especially if you love to browse. It all comes down to developing your senses – sight, sound and, most especially, touch.

— Please do touch the merchandise

If you're like most people, when you're browsing in a second-hand shop you rely on your eyes, zeroing in on colours and cuts. This is certainly the best way to shop in a department store, where the styles are arranged logically and there's a bounty of sizes to choose from. But in the second-hand environment, using only your eyes is inefficient. Does this sound familiar? Relying only on sight, you work your way down a rail, picking out the colours and prints that catch your fancy. Unfortunately, upon closer look, none of the pieces hold up. This jacket's massive shoulder pads would better suit an American football linebacker. That blouse's seams are a few wears away from structural collapse. Frustrated, you go *back* down the same rack, painstakingly examining every piece. No wonder second-hand shopping takes forever!

But, if you put faith in your sense of touch and get your hands working the first time around, you'll also pull out clothing that *feels* marvellous. This means more potential fabulous finds, less time wasted on no-hopers. Expertise in your fingertips reinforces your ability to detect fashion greatness. It's also invaluable in the murky corners of underlit vintage and charity shops. Second-hand shopping is a lot more efficient once you've got the touch.

—*I've never felt this way before*

Strange, isn't it, how society caters to all of our senses but touch. We have art museums to delight the eyes. MP3 players to captivate the ears. Gelato sample spoons for taste, perfume counters for smell. But touch is given short shrift. Certainly we can pay to *be* touched, legally or otherwise, but the flip side – arrays of sensations to delight the fingertips – seem to be missing from the pleasure sector. I think we all fill the gap in a semi-conscious way, every time we hit the shops. Why else browse when there's no money to spend? Simply touching a Ballantyne triple-ply cashmere cardie is marvellous, and it makes us feel better to do it.

In a famous study some years ago, premature babies that were wrapped in fleecy blankets gained weight faster than those that were not – the babies thrived because they were being bombarded by pleasing tactile sensations. Maybe that's why so many of us unwind at lunchtime or after a bad day with a quick run through a shop – to touch, hold, examine. They don't call it 'retail therapy' for nothing. Somehow the simple act of exercising the senses sweeps all the tension away.

We're born to touch, to grasp, to hold. What are the first words most children learn? 'Don't touch!' But we do. We can't help it. Cats have whiskers, dogs have a keen sense of smell, we have fingers and a highly mobile thumb to help us find our way through the world. Nature made touching such an easy thing to do. Our fingertips are ridged – not to help Scotland Yard track us down, but to snag items more easily, like the dots on the fingertips of rubber gloves. They also help us detect minute changes in texture.

But it's not the ridges themselves that do the feeling – that happens one skin layer down. Here, little bulbs called **Meissner's corpuscles** sit at the end of sensory nerves. Where they're the densest, for instance in our fingertips, there can be as many as 9,000 per square inch. Each bulb has a bunch of bedspring-like sensors within. If one of them detects gentle pressure, it shoots a nerve impulse up the arm to the spinal cord, then on to the cerebral cortex in the brain, which figures out what's being felt.

The attention span of sense receptors is famously short. Just as you can't smell your tea after your nose has been over the cup for more than a few seconds, your touch receptors will stop firing after a very brief period of time. This is why we stroke fabric instead of simply putting down a fingertip. We not only get more information, we get more *different* information – tiny variations in surface texture – which gives us a fuller picture of the touched object. How sensitive are our hands to different surface qualities? Have you ever felt the symphony of textures offered by an antique boned corset? Silk lining, frilly trim, stiff whalebone, cotton laces, metal hooks . . .

—*I wanna hold your hand*

When a fashion designer considers a textile for use in a clothing line, a key element of the appraisal is how that fabric feels. In fact, the pros use a specific word to describe that feeling – the fabric's **hand**. *Fairchild's Dictionary of Textiles* defines hand this way:

> *A quality or characteristic of fabrics perceived by the sense of touch, e.g. softness, firmness, drapeability, fineness, resilience – in other words, its tactile quality.*

Weaving, knitting and chemical treatment play an important role in how a fibre feels – even like fibres can feel unrelated depending on their manufacturing origins. By the same token, entirely different fibres can be made to feel remarkably similar. This is frequently the case if a given texture – slick, scrunchy, ultra-soft – is one of the important trends in a given fashion season.

Evaluating fabrics like an expert is not terribly difficult. With a little practise, we're all capable of distinguishing great from the not-so-good. It comes down to feeling – really feeling – the sensations provided by fabrics at all points along the quality scale. In this way, we create so-called 'sense memories' that can be called upon again and again. Sense memories of deluxe fabrics are invaluable, for these reasons:

1) They help us detect the top-notch pieces.
2) They help us shop faster (especially under less-than-ideal conditions).
3) They give us a one-up on less-skilled shoppers (who still rely mostly on their eyes).

'The quality that most distinguishes the work of the best designers is their immediate and total response to the feel of the fabric.'
Frances Kennett, *Secrets of the Couturiers*

— *Experience at your fingertips*

Is your sense memory underdeveloped? Not to worry. It's so easy, even fun, to sharpen this expertise. All you need to do is:

1) Introduce your hands to as many fine fabrics as possible.
2) Spend time feeling, examining and comparing them.
3) With any given fabric, decide which qualities stand out (heaviness, smooth drape, fuzzy surface, scratchiness – or, if you're poetic, liquidity, oomph, candlewick bedspread, etc.).
4) Write your impressions down.

The note-taking may sound suspiciously like work, but a bit of effort will more than repay your shopping excursions later on. Memory alone has its limitations. Writing a quick description of, say, three-ply cashmere, concentrates the mind, lodging the sense memory. For some reason, the small effort of writing helps fleeting impressions endure.

Since you're not a textile production manager or fashion journalist, you don't need to use expert terminology as you go. People experience sensations in their own unique way, so its only natural that everybody's impressions – and descriptions – will differ. Where your sister might describe heavy silk as having a slightly suede-y, dry-feeling, non-slip surface, you might say it feels like the pad you use to apply foundation. Either way is fine, as long as it sticks in your mind.

— Where to find a range of fabrics?

There are two ways to go about building your sense memories. One is easy, and works as follows. Have a pen and small notepad at the ready in your handbag. Over a period of months, whenever you have occasion to shop or browse, check the fabric content of a variety of pieces (by looking at the contents label). Make a quick note of what the fabric or blend is, and your tactile impressions of it. If you haven't written descriptively since school, don't worry; the notes are for you alone. You'll find it much easier to refer to earlier insights if they're all gathered in one place. Try to pay special attention to the finer fabrics, the ones you'd like to add to your wardrobe. Eventually, you'll become more and more familiar with the assorted tactile values, to the point where you can guess what a fibre is without even a glance at the contents label.

The other way to build sense memories is the crash programme. This takes a couple of weeks and is very intense, but the effort will swiftly enhance your shopping skills. Again, it involves doing field work, but this time in a focused way. You will be examining specific fabrics ranging from the mediocre to tip-top, within square footage that can be covered without raising blisters. Your destination: a department store. If you don't have a such a store within striking distance, make do with High Street shops until a serious excursion is a possibility.

You can learn more about clothes in a redoubtable, old-school emporium than just about anywhere else. If it helps, consider it a temple of learning, like a library, and be sure to leave the cash cards at home. Also be aware that for the purpose of this exercise, we're largely staying clear of the women's departments, the better to avoid unnecessary distractions.

Once on site, you'll be spending time in various departments (or, if you're on the High Street, in various shops) in order to familiarise yourself with specific fabrics (the exact locations are described in the **Fabric Finder** section coming up). Once you've decided which fabric you'll focus on, the basic procedure is as follows:

Step 1: To build sense memories of, say, fine cotton, consult the Fabric Finder, which in this case will direct you to the Men's Dress Shirts area. Once there, take a quick look around, establishing the whereabouts of the least-expensive brands, all the way up to the priciest. (For these purposes, price is a fairly reliable indicator of overall quality.)

Step 2: Pick out about 3 or 4 sample shirts in a range of prices. Check the contents labels or tags to ensure you have 100% cotton (or whatever) in hand.

Step 3: If you're having trouble finding a representative range, consider enlisting the help of the sales staff. Service-oriented salespeople should be delighted to point you to good examples.

Step 4: Once you have identified your samples, give them all your attention, noting the tactile qualities (with eyes closed), then examining up close to assess the fineness of the fibres and tightness of weave. Rub the fabric between your fingertips and listen to the sound. Heft the shirts to feel any difference in weight. In other words, get to know the best stuff so intimately you'd be able to detect it label-less and wrinkled at a charity shop around the corner. Likewise, spend some time examining the less distinguished garments, the better to know what to avoid. After you've communed with the fabric, take some notes.

You might feel tempted to dash from point to point, cramming the knowledge all in one go. Bad idea. If you don't pass out, you'll burn out, and feel negative about the whole undertaking. Instead, space the sessions over a number of trips, and in the meantime use every opportunity to informally feel different fabrics.

In-store fabric finder

— Wools

The **men's suit department** (or a shop like **Reiss**) is the No.1 location for fine worsted wools – the kind that the top designers also use in their upmarket women's lines. This is the place to see how beautifully wool drapes, and how it springs back into place when it's crunched. Be sure to check the hangtags – worsteds labelled 'superfine' or 'super100s' are the best examples going, and worth getting to know very well. Another place to find fine woven wools is in the **men's scarf** department, where challis, cashmere and other examples will be on hand in the winter months.

Deluxe woven wools feel lighter and more refined than lesser-quality counterparts, like you could wear them in summertime without sweltering. Also, when you hold this finer fabric up close, you don't see as much superficial fuzz.

For excellence in wool knits, your next stop is **men's jumpers** (or a shop like **Benetton**). Seek out the lambswool, merino and cashmere (obviously, there will be more on hand during the cooler months). Compare these woollens with each other, and against the lowest-priced pure wool knit on offer. Feel the differences in softness and weight, and have a good look at the curly fibres themselves.

Cashmere fibres are so small you can barely make them out – one of the reasons this fibre feels so soft. Also, compared with other knitted sweaters of the same approximate dimensions, the cashmere is likely to weigh less.

— Silks

The **women's scarf department** (or **a sari supplier**, if there's one anywhere near) is a good place to compare different kinds of silks. Hermès, one of the most expensive brands on the planet, is famous for the heavyweight silk they use in their squares. Ferragamo, Gucci and other top labels will offer similarly luxurious silk weights. Scarves of this quality are usually kept under the counter. Be sure to bring over a bargain-priced silk scarf to compare with the deluxe goods. If the store has a **bridal department**, or if there's a **bridal shop** in your area, continue your silk research there – the most expensive dresses will be made of shantung (the nubbly silk made when twin cocoons are unspooled together, also called duppioni) or heavy silk satin. One more place to get a good sense of the heaviness and intense, vibrant colour possible with fine silk is in **designer ties**.

To me, the finer silks feel remarkably like skin, while the cheaper examples are closer to tissue paper. Lighter-weight fabrics crinkle easily, heavier ones don't. The surface of lesser-quality spun silk often looks chalky. A notable quality of raw silk: it has a highly distinctive sweetish smell.

— Cottons

If you want to learn about cotton knits, your destination is **men's underwear**, tops and bottoms. (Another locale with reams of cotton in various grades is **Gap**). One easy way to gauge the thickness of white cotton knits is to look at your fingertips through the fabric – if you see a lot of flesh colour, the knit is skimpy. Better-quality knit cotton is a lot heavier than the cheap stuff.

The best woven cottons will be found in the **men's dress shirt department** (or in a **T.M. Lewin**). Try to hunt down an example of Sea Island or Egyptian cotton, and use this as the model all the others must live up to. While you're there, find a cotton-poly blend and carefully examine the difference between this and the pure fibre. Another place to see fine cottons is in the **bedding section** (**The White Company** is another possibility) – especially if the shop stocks high-end sheets. Here, too, you can get a better sense of the differences between pure cottons and blends.

Notice how pure cotton holds a crease mark you make with your finger, while polyester blends pop creases right out. Also notice how poly-cotton blends feel less silky than pure cotton.

— Linen

While you're in **bedding**, see if the store stocks linen sheets. Otherwise, head to **tablewear**, and take a look at the tablecloths and napkins. Note how pure linen holds a wrinkle, and how a linen-poly blend does not.

One of linen's stand-out qualities is the irregularity of the individual fibres (it *looks* natural). Notice, too, the coolness, and the slight scratchy sound it makes when rubbed. Also, when you put a crease in, it stays.

— Rayon

Your best bet for high-volume rayon is the **girls' dress department** – start out there, then make a quick dash into **women's dresses** to get a sense of the top-quality material (**Monsoon** and **Accessorize** usually have rayon goods on offer). Rayon is a chameleon fibre par excellence. Note how many guises it can appear in – from gauzy Indian import-style fabric to viscose that looks like the finest silk. Viscose and cupro, a kind of rayon, may look like silk, but feel slightly warmer to the touch.

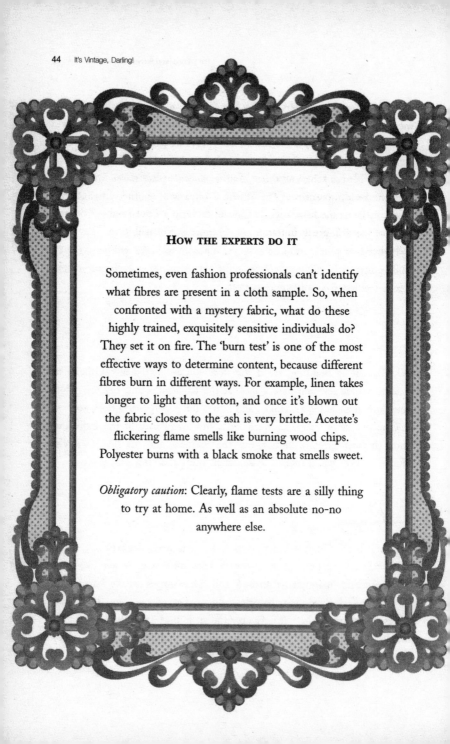

HOW THE EXPERTS DO IT

Sometimes, even fashion professionals can't identify what fibres are present in a cloth sample. So, when confronted with a mystery fabric, what do these highly trained, exquisitely sensitive individuals do? They set it on fire. The 'burn test' is one of the most effective ways to determine content, because different fibres burn in different ways. For example, linen takes longer to light than cotton, and once it's blown out the fabric closest to the ash is very brittle. Acetate's flickering flame smells like burning wood chips. Polyester burns with a black smoke that smells sweet.

Obligatory caution: Clearly, flame tests are a silly thing to try at home. As well as an absolute no-no anywhere else.

— *Synthetics and microfibres*

As a true connoisseur, you'll want to know an inexpensive synthetic the instant you feel it. In a very good department store these may be harder to find, but **children's active wear** (or **Woolies'**) usually does not disappoint. Finding excellent examples of microfibres is easy – simply head to the **rain-wear department** (or have a look at the clothing in a **Foot Locker**).

Acrylic does a great imitation of cashmere, but will often have a telltale sheen.

The telltale indicators of top-quality clothes

Here's a riddle:

Faithful visits to your favourite vintage shop have finally paid off in the form of two 1950s-era nipped-waist suits that Bette Davis and Joan Crawford might have worn at duelling sides of the MGM studio cafeteria. Both suits fit you and both of them flatter. Each one is priced at a reasonable £50. The bad news is, that's exactly the amount you're able to spend, and you're torn over which one to take home. What do you do?

What do you do? *What do you do?*

If the suits were contemporary, you might say, 'Check the labels and go for the most fashionable name.' This response would be sad and wrong. Whether a garment is brand new or decades old, the label should not be significant in your decision-making process. The innate quality of the piece is the best measure of its true value.

Labels don't point the way to fabulous buys. Connoisseurship does: the ability to distinguish the great from the merely so-so by using your powers of observation. By now, you should be growing adept at detecting fine fabric. Now we'll take a look at the other elements that make up great clothes.

You're probably aware of some of them already, and consciously or not take them into account as part of your decision to purchase. What this chapter is going to teach you is how to assess these indicators consistently, rationally and systematically, every time a piece catches your eye.

Doing so will help minimise buying mistakes and save precious time. Women who are wise to the telltale indicators can spot a fabulous button at twenty paces, and know it's attached to a prize piece. The quickest flash of a splendid lining has the same effect. On the flip side, connoisseurs know that irregular seams are a sign that the garment was made in a slapdash fashion, and it will probably have other flaws as well. By putting construction details before labels, you become an independent decision-maker in a world largely brainwashed by the all-pervasive force of fashion marketing.

Connoisseur's Tip:
A garment's true value lies not in its label, but in its workmanship.

— Clothing stripped bare

Strip away the sex-soaked ads, the bombastic catwalk shows, the glittering designer showcases that are the Oscars, Baftas and MTV Music Awards, and what's left to fashion are a few fundamentals.

First is a garment's design – the position of the waistband, the shape of the lapel, the drape of the fabric. Taken as a whole, these reflect the aesthetic vision of the creator and the important tendencies of the season, both of which are reported in the fashion press – and, if that reporter is Suzie Menkes or Sarah Mower, among other greats, described with a laser-precise eye for detail.

Beyond the aesthetics are two more fundamentals that the fashion media, for its own mysterious reasons, rarely discusses in more than a superficial way. They are:

1)   The quality of materials (the fabric and trimmings).
2)   The quality of assembly (the workmanship used to put it together).

Materials and assembly are the primary reasons that a haute-couture skirt costs £2,500 while its cut-rate counterpart is £35. The couture piece is made from the finest materials available and is hand-sewn to ensure perfect fit. Meanwhile, the bargain-buy skirt is put together with low-cost fabric and lightning-fast assembly, so that it can be sold at the lowest possible price point. It's as though these garments exist in alternative universes of materials and workmanship. In the couture universe, a big black hole sucks down the pounds in the name of perfection. In the bargain universe, the production budget's so tight even an asteroid belt is out of the question.

The economic mechanisms of the fashion business can be as complex as a Commes des Garcons cut-and-fold dress. But as long as you understand that materials and assembly are the two main benchmarks of quality, you know enough to cut through the malarkey and get to the true value of clothes.

It really couldn't be simpler. *The better the materials and more painstaking the assembly, the higher the inherent value of the piece.* When you see these aspects for what they are, unswayed by ad hype and fashion's other smoke-and-mirror tricks, you will be a true connoisseur. One more thing: it doesn't matter whether your fashion fever spikes with the clothes of the 1920s, the 1980s or late last week – quality is quality, the principle is timeless.

The telltale indicators

Telltale indicators of quality are where it all begins. Some of these may already be familiar, perhaps because you go pedal-to-the-metal on a Singer sewing machine, perhaps because you're naturally curious about how things are put together, or perhaps because you were blessed with a mother, grandmother or some other wise soul who bored you rigid with this stuff when you were younger. (Every so often you'll see somebody like this lecturing some cringing teenager in the Young Miss department, turning merchandise inside out, sticking their hands inside pockets, and going on at length about seams.) If you never had such a mentor, or if your teenage psyche blocked it due to sheer public embarrassment, guess what? Here's another chance. This information is all quite interesting, especially if you really love clothes, but if the technical nature starts making your eyes glaze over, for goodness sake shut the book and read a trashy magazine with photos of stars looking dreadful. Then, once you're fresh, come back and have another go.

Let's return to those two suits from a couple of pages back, re-examining them for the quality indicators. A true connoisseur would take about a minute to decide that one is superior in all aspects of materials and workmanship. The manufacturer's aspirations are evident throughout. If second-hand pricing were rational, this suit would cost twice as much as the other. But, as we know, second-hand prices and rationality do not always join hands.

—Fabric

The quality of the fabric used in a garment is the best indicator of its quality overall.

Remember this one? Here's where we put it to the test. Both suits are made of wool. But the fabric of the first is lighter in weight and finer to the touch. It's also softer, where the rival suit feels slightly coarse and scratchy. Why is there such a big difference when both are made of the same stuff? Probably because the former was woven with high-quality worsted wool, whose longer, tighter-spun fibres make a finer thread, resulting in a better grade of cloth.

If we examine the fabric minutely, more evidence comes to light. There's more fuzz visible atop the second suit's fabric, reinforcing the notion that it was made with shorter, less desirable fibres. We can't be sure of the wool's background, of course, but it really doesn't matter. The important point is this: which fabric would you prefer to have against bare skin? The first one wins the touch test hands down.

> 'Fine cloth is never out of fashion.'
> **Thomas Fuller, 1654–1734**

—Pattern matching

Making our evaluation easier is the fact that both suits are fashionably pinstriped. On the first, the stripes link up cleanly across most seams, darts and breaks. On the second, the stripes weave and wobble so badly the fashion police ought to give it a breath test.

In superb clothing, stripes, checks, plaids and other bold motifs are carefully aligned across breaks in the fabric, creating an illusion of seamlessness. A splendid example from the past is one of Yves Saint Laurent's 1985 haute-couture ensembles, a Chinese-inspired silk evening trouser suit. Here, sinuous black peonies climb uninterrupted across a pink field, *not only* across the armhole seams, *not only* across the front fastening of the tunic jacket, *but across the spatial divide from jacket to trousers* – not a stem or delicate petal broken. The outfit is breathtaking, and so, no surprise, was its original price.

On a less sublime level, manufacturers have production costs to consider, and perfect pattern matching is an expensive proposition. For one thing, a significant amount of fabric will be wasted in lining up the assorted motifs. For another, the sewing-machine operator requires more time to meticulously align the pieces. For these reasons, the manufacturer may be inclined to forgo perfect match-ups.

It's unreasonable to expect premium pattern matching in budget-priced clothing. Even mid-priced pieces are, alas, not always perfectly matched. Still, when you check a garment over, you should see evidence of *honest effort* to get the motifs coming together as cleanly as possible. If the job is truly sloppy, you can be sure that the rest of the construction will be of the same standard, and the garment is worth no more of your time.

In order of importance, here's where pattern matches come to the test:

1) Patterns (especially plaids and other horizontal motifs) should connect cleanly across any front fastening.
2) Vertical motifs (such as stripes and plaids) should appear to connect from collar to back.
3) Motifs on lapels and pockets should appear to be symmetrical on the two sides (in other words, mirror each other).
4) Vertical motifs should drop evenly alongside side seams (without a lot of wavering in and out).

5)   The main lines of patterns should continue straight through any pockets.
6)   Motifs should link gracefully across darts.

MORE PATTERN NOTES:

◎   Due to complicated technicalities involving curves and fabric grain, the pattern will rarely match perfectly over the shoulder when the sleeves are 'set-in' (the normal kind of sleeve, with a seam at the armhole).

◎   In certain high-quality pieces, buttons or other fastenings are hidden, to emphasise the smooth flow of the pattern.

◎   Pattern matching offers a *near-instant indicator of superb quality*. If you spot a garment with a bold pattern, run your eyes quickly over its seams. If the matches are dead on, this is a superior piece.

— *Interior finish*

Constructing a garment is a lot like joinery. It's all about measuring, cutting, connecting and sealing so the finished product looks great and won't fall apart. As we all know, there are good joiners and there are cowboys. The good ones show up on time, work efficiently and don't leave a mess. Most importantly, they leave you with cabinets that look as nice on the inside as they do on the outside.

Then there are the cowboys. The blokes who show up late, tramp in mud, take constant tea breaks, and leave you with cabinets that look fine on the outside but the inside reveals a wreckage of pencil marks, splintered wood, sloppy painting and last Friday's *Sun*. The cowboy may be a lot cheaper, he may be the spitting image of Ewan McGregor, but every time you open that cabinet you want to stick his hammer right up the toolkit, where it belongs.

Joinery is a lot like clothing manufacture, with one exception. With a garment, we can give the interior a good checking over before we lay down a penny. Oddly enough, many of us don't. From now on, think about the joiners and clothes manufacturers laughing all the way to the bank and turn that piece of clothing inside out.

What you're looking for is tidy workmanship, especially at the seams. Whenever a seam is sewn, two raw fabric edges remain. If left unfinished, they will fray, which looks shoddy, and even the meanest garment maker wouldn't dare leave them in this state. Instead, the industry has a number of different techniques to control raw edges. The most traditional technique is tucking the edges under and sewing them in place. This can be done with a simple tuck or with more complex folds and overlapping – the choice depends on the weight and/or type of fabric, the location of the seam and the finished look desired for the piece. The following are some of the most widely used seam finishes – the ones every connoisseur should recognise. If you're interested in learning about other kinds of seam finishes, you'll find in-depth descriptions in a good sewing guide.

Clean-finished: One of the simplest of finishes. Here, the raw edges of fabric are pressed flat, like a butterfly's wings, down along either side of the seam on the interior of the garment, with the edges turned under and stitched closed.

Bound: Like the clean-finished seam, the raw edges are pressed flat, butterfly-style, but in this case the edges are then bound, or wrapped (also possibly called 'taped') with thin strips of matching fabric. Finishing a seam this way requires more labour, so *bound seams are found on high-quality pieces*, especially so-called 'unconstructed' clothing without a lining.

Flat-fell: Here the seam is sewn so that the raw edges appear on the exterior of the garment. They are then tucked under and stitched flat from the top (topstitching), creating the kind of seam you see running down the legs of blue jeans. What with all the folding, tucking and double-stitching, this seam is incredibly strong. It is widely used in sports, casual and active wear.

French: With this seam, all you see is a crease on the exterior and a narrow flap of fabric on the interior. *A highly refined finish*, this is often used to assemble fine blouses and other clothes made of delicate, sheer or very light-weight woven fabric.

These seams are all made with the traditional sewing machine. But the manufacturer has another technique for finishing raw edges. He can **overlock** them with a special machine called a serger. Never heard of it? No surprise there. This unglamorous workhorse of garment assembly is never going to get a centrefold in *Vogue* magazine. But it's a good bet that many of your contemporary clothes feature the telltale overlock finish, in which tightly spaced loops of thread – reminiscent of a spiral notepad binder – encase and bind the raw seam.

Of all the seam-finishing options, overlocking is the fastest and most efficient. The serger machine can trim the fabric, sew the seam and bind the raw edges all in a single operation. In manufacturing, fastest tends to be cheapest, and the 5-thread overlock is the method of choice in lower-to-mid-priced clothes.

While overlocking is cost-effective, you shouldn't disdain it, for with certain fabrics it's the only way to go. Due to the tendency of the raw edges to curl, *knits are almost always overlocked with a 3–4-thread method*, whether they're from Chanel or Bargain Barn. (The difference is, Chanel will use the same yarn to overlock as was used to knit the garment, while Bargain Barn may employ a cheaper substitute.) Very flimsy, hard-to-sew fabrics like chiffon are also often finished on the overlock machine, because this formidable beast, with its multiple thrashing knives and needles, can grip the fabric much better than can the standard sewing machine. Linens and brocades may be overlocked as a means to cut down on fraying. And, finally, an overlocked seam may, for various reasons, be an aesthetic choice rather than one based on budget. What is naughty – very naughty – on the part of a manufacturer are thread chains (the tail ends of the overlock threads) still evident in the interior. This is sloppy, and an indicator that the rest of the garment will be poorly assembled as well.

It is a plus when a more time-consuming and refined seam-finishing technique (like those mentioned earlier) is used with woven fabrics. The manufacturer willing to bind raw edges or use French seams is likely to strive for exquisite quality all around.

Once you've inspected the seams in a garment's interior, have a look at the exterior seamlines as well. Unsightly bumps, bulges and ripples here are sometimes intentionally sewn in for a rough-hewn effect. Most of the time, though, they're flaws.

— Button, Button

There's something undeniably magical about buttons. In my favourite vintage shop a while back, the owner spilled her sackful of repair buttons onto the counter, preparing to do some mending. At the sound of the clatter all shopping stopped and everybody came over to have a look, even though the buttons weren't for sale.

Why do we love buttons? Probably something basic about human nature: we find it hard to resist anything small, bright and shiny. A great button is a joy unto itself, but, for a smart shopper, it's much more. It's also a prime marker of a marvellous piece of clothing. If you spy, barely visible in the racks, a button gleaming brighter than the rest, zoom in for a closer look. Odds are, the garment it adorns is also a treasure.

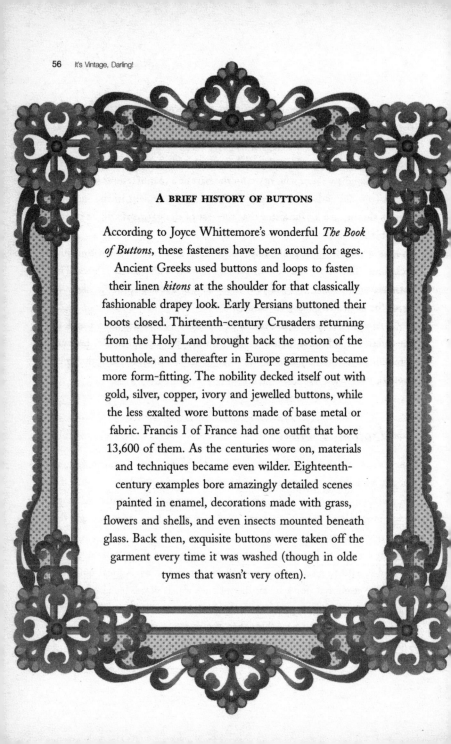

A BRIEF HISTORY OF BUTTONS

According to Joyce Whittemore's wonderful *The Book of Buttons*, these fasteners have been around for ages. Ancient Greeks used buttons and loops to fasten their linen *kitons* at the shoulder for that classically fashionable drapey look. Early Persians buttoned their boots closed. Thirteenth-century Crusaders returning from the Holy Land brought back the notion of the buttonhole, and thereafter in Europe garments became more form-fitting. The nobility decked itself out with gold, silver, copper, ivory and jewelled buttons, while the less exalted wore buttons made of base metal or fabric. Francis I of France had one outfit that bore 13,600 of them. As the centuries wore on, materials and techniques became even wilder. Eighteenth-century examples bore amazingly detailed scenes painted in enamel, decorations made with grass, flowers and shells, and even insects mounted beneath glass. Back then, exquisite buttons were taken off the garment every time it was washed (though in olde tymes that wasn't very often).

Even though they have the entire button world at their beck and call, high-end designers often use rigorously plain (and quite inexpensive) nylon or polyester buttons in order to maintain a clean-lined look. So, *a boring button does not indicate inferior quality*. But the flip side can be stated with assurance:

An extraordinary button points to an extraordinary garment.

Here's the sort of thing to look for:

Real brass: Since synthetics are cheaper to mould and stamp, they are frequently used as substitutes for real metal. If you spy a metallic-looking button and aren't sure if it's authentic, weigh it in your hand. Impostor buttons feel oddly light. They're also oddly warm, and if you flick them with a fingertip they click, whereas you might get a little tone off metal. Pseudo-metal may also carry telltale scratches. Synthetics are generally made of an acetate core coated with copper, followed by a gold or silver metal-look finish. If the coating is damaged, you sometimes see the greenish colour of the copper or the white of the core showing through, which wouldn't be the case with real brass.

Pearl: Pearl buttons aren't made from real pearls; they're drilled from the inner lining (mother-of-pearl) of harvested shells. Back in the days of seafaring trade, the shells usually came from Australia, India, China and Japan, loaded in the hulls to act as ballast for the trip home. Real pearl buttons tend to be cool to the touch, irregular or rough on the back, and fleetingly iridescent (pinpoints of shine, as in silk). Moulded synthetic imitations are warm, entirely smooth, and any iridescence will have fake-looking uniformity, like frosted nail polish.

Horn: These are cut from the horns and hooves of cattle. They were the original 'plastic' buttons, as this material softens when heated and can be pressed into various shapes. Horn buttons may appear as rough-edged chips (favoured especially on Alpine-style loden coats), finely polished dress buttons (seen on all kinds of elegant garments) or horn tips (sporty duffel coats and pea jackets). While the beautiful, irregular grain of horn is difficult to capture in synthetics, it's still often impossible to distinguish the fake from the real thing.

Speaking of animal by-products, bet you didn't know that one William Niles of Jersey City, New Jersey, gained a patent in 1879 for the 'manufacture of ornamental buttons made from blood and other materials'.

Couturier buttons: Also known as *passementerie* buttons, these handmade beauties are often used in haute couture. They are made from a silken cord wrapped again and again around a button form in an attractive and intricate decorative pattern, then tied off with a central knot.

'House' buttons: Many design houses use distinctive buttons, bearing either a special motif (such as Chanel's crossed Cs and lion heads – Coco was a Leo, or Versace's medusas) or the house's name (even some mid-level makers now do this).

Eccentric buttons: Buttons don't have to be 'jewelly' to be wonderful. In 1938, the Parisian couturier Elsa Schiaparelli made a jacket with buttons in the form of moulded plastic locusts – insects otherwise known for their starring role in Biblical plagues. All of Paris swooned at the wit. Needless to say, these didn't come out of stock – they had to be custom designed. This is important to remember when you see a button that has a peculiar shape, an unusual size or some outlandish detail. Odds are it was specially commissioned for the garment, and as such is a great tip-off to high quality.

A button has a silent partner that is equally important in the fastening role:

the hole. If you've never given buttonholes a second thought, you'd be surprised at the kinds of stories they tell:

Machine-worked: This is the most common type of buttonhole, and will be found on 99% of the garments in your closet. It feels rough inside and out, and usually sports a couple of dangly threads, because the stitching is done first, *then* the slit is cut. Some buttonholes are stitched tighter than others – tight is good, because it's neater. Machine-stitched buttonholes may have a slight keyhole shape. This is a detail adopted from the world of men's tailoring – the wider part is meant to accommodate the back loop of a shank button.

Bound: Here the edges of the slit are bound with strips of matching fabric, creating an opening that resembles a letter box on a front door. It looks a lot neater than an ordinary buttonhole, and it takes quite a bit more effort to make up. *If you spot a bound buttonhole, pay extra attention* – somebody's added serious value to the piece.

Hand-stitched: *If you find one of these babies, pounce* – the garment may be haute couture, or at least lovingly hand-made. Here, the slit is cut *before* the stitching takes place, so there are no dangly threads. Also, the stitching around the hole is smooth on the outside, rough on the inside. One more reason why haute couture costs the sun, moon and stars – the time needed to finish just one hand-sewn buttonhole is four hours.

The suits are getting lonely without our attention so let's check back in with them. For once, the second suit comes out a winner – the buttons on the jacket and at the waist of the skirt are of wire filigree, quite a bit spiffier than the utilitarian grey plastic on the first suit. But, as mentioned earlier, a run-of-the-mill button is highly forgivable, as long as other factors shine out.

— Lining notes

Coats, jackets, dresses, skirts and trousers are many-layered things – apart from the visible outermost fabric, there may be up to three more layers between your skin and the outside world.

The garment's hidden **interlinings** are critical to its final appearance. With high-end clothing, different kinds of material are used in different spots, creating varying degrees of stiffness, flex and roll. When a garment 'fits like a second skin', interlinings often deserve the thanks, because they literally help mould the fabric to the shapes of the body. Poor-quality or poorly selected interlinings do just the opposite, causing such flaws as crinkly waistbands, jackets that collapse through the button area, collars that wrinkle and distort, and areas that refuse to iron back into shape.

Equally important, and easier to evaluate, is the **innermost lining**, visible on the inside of the garment. It has four specific roles: covering up raw seams and any intervening layers, maintaining the shape of the outer fabric, making the garment easier to take on and pull off, and making it more comfortable against the skin.

We talk about slipping into and out of pieces of clothing – this would be very tricky indeed if the lining weren't slightly oversized, to allow give, and weren't made of a slippery fabric. In earlier times, cotton or silk did the job. Now lining material is usually acetate, acetate/rayon or rayon. Like every other part of a garment, a lining can be run-of-the-mill or extraordinary. An extraordinary lining heralds a special piece. Some examples of shining linings:

Jacquard lining: Here a name or logo is woven right into the lining fabric to make a subtle pattern, which naturally costs the manufacturer more. Many high-end manufacturers add this nicety, but just as many don't, so it's not a demerit if you don't see it.

Lining of extraordinary colour: An Ozwald Boateng suit stands out for its beautiful tailoring and for the flamboyance of its lining. If the lining of a piece you find deliberately doesn't tone into the outer fabric – say it's apple-green acetate in a black jacket – the maker wants you to look closer. By all means do so; this is probably a winning piece.

Lining of an unusual material: Here's where your hand-development efforts come into play. If the lining doesn't feel like acetate, rayon or a blend of the two, you may have hit the jackpot. Silk linings frequently adorn deluxe contemporary ready-to-wear, vintage pieces and nearly all haute couture.

Intricately constructed lining: All linings start life as pieces of a pattern, but some are more intricately put together than others. Most decent-quality jacket linings have a pleat down the centre of the back, for more give. In more tailored jackets and coats, the linings conform more closely still, possibly with two extra darts in the back panel.

No lining at all, but beautifully finished interior seams: In summer-weight and unconstructed pieces, the lining may be partial or left out altogether. Doing so actually costs the manufacturer more, because it means all the interior seams must be impeccably finished. In this case, a manufacturer is hoping to win your admiration for workmanship that is beautiful inside and out. Likewise, the home sewer of a handmade garment. If you find an unlined vintage piece with beautifully finished interior seams, you are holding a piece tailored with care and pride.

Unfortunately, the maker of our second suit wasn't trying to win anything but a couple more pence per unit – the skirt is unlined altogether. Again, the absence of lining in a jacket, pair of trousers or a skirt is not always an offence. In winter-weight woven wool, however, it's inexcusable. Unless an unlined winter garment is otherwise extraordinary, let it go. It's not worth wasting money on clothes that will cling and make you scratch.

— In the pocket

Pockets are either useful (usually found below the waist) or decorative (usually found above). Either way, they are made from extra pieces of material and require additional sewing time, therefore, they add to the production cost. Some kinds are more expensive to incorporate than others. Here's a pocket summary:

Patch pockets: These are applied to the outside of the garment. While ordinarily square or rectangular, they can take any shape, and may be embellished with flaps, welts or special stitching. *In quality garments, a patch pocket is lined with the same material that lines the interior.*

On less-well-made pieces, such as our suit number two, the seam that attaches the pocket to the outer fabric was left raw and thready inside (the notion being that budget-minded buyers wouldn't check). Meanwhile, suit number one's joins are worthy of a Beverly Hills plastic surgeon – the stitchwork is practically invisible.

A flap positioned just above the pocket adds one more piece of fabric to the total, and is itself worthy of close examination. A fine flap is also lined on the inside, and this lining is invisible when the flap is down. As with pockets, the juncture of flap and the garment should be impeccably clean rather than raw-edged.

Inside pockets: These consist of an opening along a seam line with a fabric sack inside, the sack usually made of the lining material or cotton. Again, the juncture of the main fabric and the sack material should be as clean and unthready as possible.

Slashed pockets: Appearing to float on the front or back of a garment, these are considered the most difficult pocket to construct properly.

As difficulty generally equals expense, their presence indicates that the item is worth your attention. Slashed pockets may have a flap or be welted (the opening has fabric 'lips'). Welting further adds to the complication, especially if it's very narrow, so be on the lookout for this fine point.

GENERAL POCKET NOTES:

◎ Curved or rounded patch pockets are more trouble to sew on perfectly than those with straight edges (and so are more expensive to produce). If you see them, take special note.

◎ When looking at the interior of a high-end unlined garment, any visible pocket sacks should bring to mind origami – absolutely beautiful in their own right. They should also be attached prettily to the interior, so as not to be flapping free.

◎ In haute couture, where one of the aims is to hide figure flaws, designers will actually build in pocket optical illusions to trick the eye, such as making the one on the left breast a shade narrower than the one on the right, to disguise, say, a slightly hunched shoulder. Obviously, with lopsided ready-to-wear pockets, such excuses don't fly.

◎ Along these lines, always inspect pockets carefully to ensure they're hanging at the same level.

◎ Pocket openings are sewn closed in new clothes because the natural urge before a try-on mirror is to strike a pose, namely to jam hands in pockets and look cool. If you come across a jacket where the pockets are still sewn, it's possible that the piece was never worn (though some people never unsnip their pockets, preferring to keep the lines clean).

—Zips, hooks and other fasteners

Buttons don't have a lock on the closure of clothing. Other fasteners include zips, snaps, hooks, frogs (!) and more. On our two suits, the zips themselves are practically identical, but the one sewn on the skirt of the first suit somehow looks neater. Looking more closely, the reason becomes clear: the zip tape (the fabric just around the teeth) perfectly matches the colour of the surrounding wool. The tape used in the other skirt is a less perfect match for its surroundings. Of course this is no reason to drop a garment and run screaming, but it is one more example of how budget manufacture can fall short of perfection.

Though it may be difficult to believe, the zip was originally intended as an enforcer of modesty. Before the 1920s, ladies' garments closed with buttons or hooks. Gaps frequently opened up between these fastenings, especially when the fabric was stressed. The zip, or the 'Slide Fastener' as it was then known, was introduced as a means of preventing this dreaded peekaboo.

Contemporary zips are made of either plastic or metal. There are three basic types: the **open-ended,** which is used to close coats and jackets; the **standard,** which is sealed at the bottom, and seen most often in casual trousers; and the **invisible,** which disappears into a seam and cannot be seen from outside. Whatever type of zip is used:

◎   The raw edge of its tape should be either hidden under a seam or sufficiently neatened so that the eye doesn't come to rest on thready edges.

◎   The teeth should not come in contact with bare skin. A fabric 'zip guard' is provided on all but the cheapest of skirts and trousers. With dresses, the fabric to either side of the zip should be plumped, to hold the teeth away from the skin. Note, though, that even some high-end designers are guilty of over-exposed zips (especially on lightweight slip dresses).

◉   The weight of a zip should correspond to the fabric – zips that are too heavy cause garments to pucker or drape poorly and downgrade the overall look.

If you ever find yourself in Vienna's Kunsthistoriches Museum, consider taking a connoisseur's look at the *Court Jester of Ferrara*, painted by the French artist Jean Fouquet in 1445. For in that painting is the first ever depiction of ye olde **hook and eye**. Some high-end designers are so attuned to aesthetics they will actually wrap this hardware with matching thread.

Self-belts are often of ghastly quality. A plastic belt trying to pass as leather is a dead giveaway of low-end merchandise. But if the belt, and especially the hardware, is neatly covered with matching fabric or silk cord, you can be assured that decent quality was a goal.

Uncommon fastenings – as always, the unusual is a tip-off to the extraordinary. **Snap closures** on a highly tailored suit are audacious, and they must be *great* snaps, impeccably applied, in order to work. In the same vein are the invisible **magnets** that ingeniously close jackets as if by magic. Beautiful silk-cord loop-and-ball **frog closures** have been around for millennia in the Far East, but they still have a delightful visual appeal.

—Label lore

The earlier advice to turn your focus away from the name on the label doesn't mean you should disregard the entire thing, for labels are an important quality indicator. This is because they are *constructed*, just like the garment is. How well a label is put together – the quality and care of its materials and workmanship – is an accurate mirror of the garment as a whole. A budget manufacturer would no sooner put an exquisite (and expensive) jacquard label into a £5.99 T-shirt than a high-end maker would use a cheap printed tag. Let's take a closer look at this usually overlooked element of fashion.

The finest labels are **woven** in a slightly raised pattern on a fabric backing. The more colours used, the costlier the label is, but some very classy designers deliberately go for the simplicity of just two hues. On a fine label, the edges of any lettering and logos will appear smooth and crisp rather than 'stair-stepped', and there will not be a loose-strand 'hairiness' on the reverse side. Indeed, in the best clothing the labels tend to be sewn down on four sides, although this may not be done if the stitching will mar the outside of the item, as in knitwear. Meanwhile, in the cheaper regions of the modern label world, tags are **printed** (which leaves no design evident on the reverse side). What's more, with certain kinds of printing techniques, long strips bearing the name over and over are cut apart with a hot knife, leaving sharp edges that are incredibly irritating once you're wearing the garment.

— The little extras

These are the things that you don't always expect to find inside a garment but, when you do, they give you the warm and fuzzy feeling that the manufacturer has your best interests at heart.

Hidden pockets: These may be found in coats, jackets and smooth-front trousers. While men take hidden pockets for granted, *in women's wear they're practically non-existent, and if you find one, you're holding a stand-out piece of clothing.*

Hanger aides: These are the satiny loops or straps sewn into better garments to keep them hanging steady in the closet. Another variant is the interior neck loop along the collar in jackets and coats – or, even better, a loop of metal chain.

Interior weights: Found only at the highest end of the fashion spectrum, these sewn-in metal slugs or chains help the garment hang more beautifully (a flat gold chain sewn around the lower interior is one of the signatures of a contemporary Chanel jacket).

Spare buttons: Their presence in a sleeve or trouser leg not only indicates a certain level of quality, it hints that the garment is fairly new.

Shoulder pads in jackets, dresses and tops: High-quality shoulder pads are either hidden or detachable, are covered in the same fabric as that used on the exterior (or a reasonably nice equivalent) and are made from padded fabric rather than foam. Bunched-up, wandering and/or unusually large pads are negatives.

What with all the inspecting we find one final flaw in the second of the two suits – a missing button at the cuff. Let's take the first to the till and re-hang the second: it isn't worth any more of our time.

Before closing out the chapter, there is one more important point to be made:

Your quality check must be thorough.

Relying solely on a button or some overlocking to tell the garment's entire story is almost as bad as buying on the basis of a designer name. These factors are simply parts of the whole. Odds are, whenever you assess a garment, some of the indicators will be great and others not – it's the sum that should sway your decisions. And if, after all this, you still take home the occasional gotta-have-it impulse purchase, patterns wildly unmatched, thread chains dangling, buttons cheap as chips, that's fine, as long as you know what you're getting.

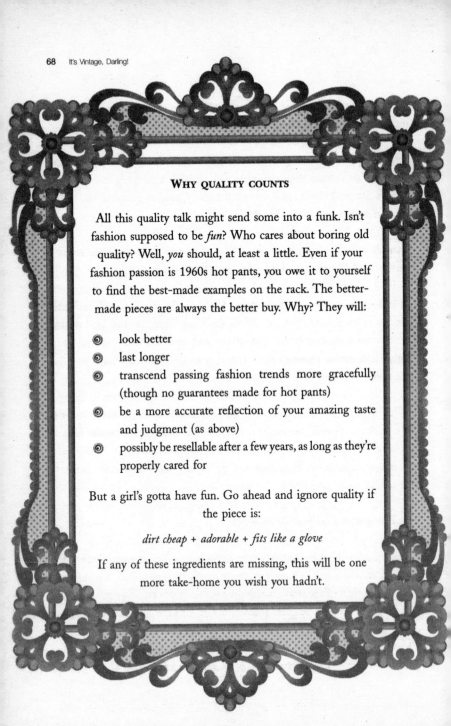

WHY QUALITY COUNTS

All this quality talk might send some into a funk. Isn't fashion supposed to be *fun*? Who cares about boring old quality? Well, *you* should, at least a little. Even if your fashion passion is 1960s hot pants, you owe it to yourself to find the best-made examples on the rack. The better-made pieces are always the better buy. Why? They will:

◎   look better

◎   last longer

◎   transcend passing fashion trends more gracefully (though no guarantees made for hot pants)

◎   be a more accurate reflection of your amazing taste and judgment (as above)

◎   possibly be resellable after a few years, as long as they're properly cared for

But a girl's gotta have fun. Go ahead and ignore quality if the piece is:

dirt cheap + adorable + fits like a glove

If any of these ingredients are missing, this will be one more take-home you wish you hadn't.

5

Garment insider

As we saw in the last chapter, certain characteristics of superior workmanship, like a beautiful bound seam, are found in all sorts of fine clothing. In this chapter, we'll see how specific garments also have their own hallmarks. There are so many ways a manufacturer can build in quality. Given the huge variety of possible cuts, styles and trimmings – even within a category as simple as T-shirts – it's impossible to list every one. The hallmarks provided here are intended as a starting point, meant to get you looking at and thinking about the details that count. It won't take long before you do it subconsciously, rapid-fire. And, once the habit is ingrained, you'll start noticing more and more, expanding your personal tick-list of quality points. The really brilliant thing? All of it applies equally to first-run clothes. With this kind of connoisseurship as second nature, you will have a fashion insider's edge in finding and acquiring exquisite clothes.

> 'Experience isn't interesting until it begins to repeat itself – in
> fact, until it does that, it hardly *is* experience.'
> **Elizabeth Bowen,** *The Death of the Heart*

— Field research

Before we get to the points themselves, a few more words about building that tick-list. The best way is via frequent encounters with gorgeous clothes in fine boutiques, department stores, ultra-select vintage clothing shops, and at vintage clothes auctions (more on these later). Examining and trying on show-stopping pieces doesn't cost a penny, but does give you an expert understanding of materials and workmanship. Naturally, it's frustrating getting so close to garments you can't yet afford, but look on the bright side. If a piece of equal quality and workmanship should appear at your favourite dress agency, charity or vintage shop, you'll instantly recognise it for what it is, getting the jump on less knowledgeable shoppers.

FEAR NOT THE DESIGNER FLOORS

If you're anything like I once was, you may feel intimidated in the posher shops, believing the staff will instantly catch you out as an impostor. Deep down, you believe that unless you can buy, you have no right to try on such beautiful clothes.

This is wrong-headed. Salespeople themselves would be the first to agree. For one thing, who's to know that you won't win the lottery tomorrow? For another, if your body is clean, your make-up smudge-proof and your attitude pleasant, you're already much more welcome than that little Miss Moneybags who flings stuff around, climbs into it with her Choos on and treats the staff like dirt. Finally, if you can discuss workmanship in an interested way, a saleswoman is likely to go out of her way to help, because so few customers actually care. To otherwise ensure good service:

◎ Look smart for visits to high-end boutiques. You'll carry yourself with more authority, which in turn generates more respect. And carry props – a shopping bag or two from a top-flight store. Who's to know that it holds your lunch or a pair of trainers for the journey home?

Salespeople take you more seriously if they think you've been spending loads elsewhere.

◉   After you've had a look inside garments, be sure to hang them like you found them, draping evenly with the pleats aligned. The saleswoman may rush to do it herself, but your effort will be appreciated.

◉   Don't ever bad-mouth the merchandise, even if the price/quality ratio is appalling. These are the saleswoman's livelihood, and she won't appreciate hearing that they are shoddily made.

◉   Serious examination is best done in the dressing room. Take in as many items as allowed in your size, so you can check hang and fit as well as assembly.

◉   If there are other customers around who look like they need help, don't monopolise the salesperson's time.

In your search-and-try-on programme, don't limit your efforts entirely to upmarket stores. Now and again it's a good idea to buzz through the wares of lower-end merchandisers like Hennes or Primark. Why?

1)   The quality might surprise you. Many of these organisations (and their suppliers) are working hard to improve the appeal of their goods. Quality assurance means flawed merchandise is weeded out before it ever reaches the shops. What's more, many – Asda, for example – recognise their customers' hunger for high fashion.

2)   Merchandise of a low-quality level provides a reality check of the kinds of materials and assembly you want to avoid. The clothes will teach you countless lessons about poor workmanship, unappealing fabric and who-cares assembly. By keeping your eyes and hands trained to detect both the top and the bottom of the clothing ranks,

you'll vastly improve your ability to hone in on treasures in the second-hand environment.

—Home study

Shops aren't the only places to check quality. Yet again, you'll be amazed at how much info lurks in your own closet. Get in there and see what you've got, just as you did earlier with fabrics. Enlist tolerant girlfriends and relatives and do the same with their clothes – they'll be fascinated by what you can tell them. If there's a man about the house, look at his clothing, and get ready to weep at its superior tailoring.

A few final words: once you know what you're looking for, quality hallmarks will leap out every time you go over a piece. As with the previous chapter's indicators, it's the overall impression that counts. If a skirt or a top falls short in one area, it may shine in another. Like people, garments are rarely perfect.

—Quality hallmarks

BLOUSES

◎ The tinier the stitches used to assemble the blouse, the better. Sixteen stitches per inch is the sign of a very high standard.

◎ French cuffs (buttonless cuffs held together with cufflinks) are more complicated to construct than regular barrel cuffs. Blouses that feature them are generally very fine overall. If you see French cuffs (and don't mind a bit of extra ironing), pounce. Classic, attractive links can be found at the jewellery counters of many charity shops.

◎ If the buttons are otherwise straightforward, four holes are preferable to two (the buttons are attached more firmly and stay on longer).

◎   A gauntlet button (on the sleeve placket above the wrist) is a nice extra touch. Fashion historians say this button either helped doctors keep their sleeves up during medical procedures, or allowed the wearer to raise hands over the head without the sleeves dropping down.

◎   Buttons at the cuff and collar points should be smaller than those running down the front placket.

◎   Look for pleats at the juncture of sleeve and cuff. If you don't see any, beware: the sleeve may fit awkwardly once on.

◎   Raw edges inside pockets are a huge demerit.

◎   Pockets should hang evenly when the blouse is buttoned.

◎   Long tails (and generous use of fabric overall) is a sign of a generous manufacturer.

◎   The placket upon which the front buttonholes sit should be folded double and/or should be firm enough not to sag under the weight of the buttons.

◎   A manufacturer may tout a 'split' yoke (the piece of fabric that sits on the upper back above the shoulder blades) as a quality indicator, which it is not. The ideal yoke should, however, be *doubled*, that is, made from two layers of fabric.

◎   At the back of the neck, the collar should cover its own seam.

◎   Borrowing from menswear tailoring, ultra-quality blouses may have a bottom hem that is rolled rather than pressed flat.

BUTTON-UP

Button-down collars – today an American
preppie hallmark – were first worn by
British polo players who didn't want them
flapping during matches.

INSTANT QUALITY INDICATOR: A French seam running down the inside
of the arm.

T-SHIRTS

◎   With T-shirts, fabric quality is paramount. Whether it's cotton,
cotton/poly or some other material, make sure the weight is what you
want. Use the fingertip test (how much flesh colour can you see through
the fabric?) as a quick indicator.

◎ Don't let a T-shirt's apparent simplicity fool you into thinking you don't have to try it on. A well-cut tee is less common than you might think. Especially trouble-prone is the area where the arms attach to the main body, where the fabric can bind or sag. Likewise, neck openings can sit bizarrely and fabric can ride up your midriff. *Always* try it on.

◎ Another hard-to-detect problem with tees is fabric cut off the grain, which causes the shirt to twist on the body. This defect will only show up after the first washing, and could be the reason the tee landed in second-hand. *Always* try it on.

◎ Tees cut to contour the body are a sign of value.

◎ 'T'-shaped garments (where sleeves stick straight out) will probably not fit as nicely as those whose sleeves fall closer to the body.

◎ Be sure to check the contents label and washing instructions – some rayon blends must be hand-washed.

◎ Carefully inspect the quality of any embroidery or screen-printing. Note that counterfeiters of designer tees sometimes do a better job than the original makers.

◎ Seams will be overlocked. Be on the lookout for thread chains and loose or sloppy stitching – as with blouses, finer stitching indicates greater quality.

◎ The colour should be crisp and not faded.

◎ A great deal of surface fuzz indicates an older garment.

◎ The neckline and sleeve cuffs should retain elasticity.

◎ Seek out collar and/or shoulder seams that have been reinforced on the interior with tape or fabric strips.

◎ An unusually shaped neck (wide, scoop) is a mark of quality.

◎ A little bit of spandex gives a lot of shape.

◎ The depth of the hems at the sleeves and bottom is part of the design equation – unusually deep hems means that the maker was going for a distinctive look, rather than run-of-the-mill.

◎ A printed label indicates lesser quality. A cheap label bearing a tip-top name points to a counterfeit.

> 'The US Army's 1955 military specification for cotton quarter-sleeve undershirts . . . ran to eight pages of detailed instruction on constructing the perfect t!'
> **John Gordon and Alice Hiller,** *The T-shirt Book*

INSTANT QUALITY INDICATOR: Woven (as opposed to printed) label.

DRESSES

◎ Dresses show their age more starkly than any other garment. If it looks tired on the hanger, it's not likely to look better on your back (unless it's bias-cut fabric, which always looks better on).

◎ Very expensive day dresses of the past fifty years (i.e., those worn by ladies who lunch) have an armour-like quality, due to the substantiality of the fabric and lining (this is true for summer frocks as well – the air is just *frigid* in that restaurant, darling).

◎ With a superior contemporary frock, even if the colour or pattern is relatively muted, the quality of the dyes and printing give it an unmistakable visual 'pop'.

◎ Look carefully at the construction of the lining. If it closely follows that of the dress, the manufacture is of high quality.

◎ The lining should be attached to the dress at the armhole, waist and hips.

◎ The lining should cover the stitching at the hem, but should not drop below the hemline.

◎ Ensure the lining is not distorted from the dress shape by inferior workmanship or improper cleaning.

◎ In cheap dresses, the inner waistband often looks raw and messy.

◎ With a quality dress, the ends of any straps should be trapped between two layers of fabric rather than simply tacked down.

◎ In ultra-quality dresses, beads and sequins are individually sewn on.

◎ If the arms are of sheer fabric, the armhole seam should be neatened as prettily as possible.

◎ Bias-cut dresses look like unfilled sausage skins on the hanger (because the stretchy fabric, cut on an angle, doesn't drape well until it has a body as support). Don't dismiss until you've tried it on. With bias-cut frocks, look inside for hanger loops, which will prevent any distortion from hanging.

◎ With knit dresses, make sure collars and cuffs maintain shape and the backside hasn't bagged (tape reinforcement sewn onto inner seams is a good sign).

◎ Coat-dress styles should have an interior button to hold the inner-most flap securely in place.

◎ The popularity of unlined slip dresses in the nineties saw plenty of raw-edged zips left exposed. This is sloppy – no matter which big-shot designer has perpetrated it.

◎ Make sure longer dresses have a slit or fabric fullness around legs, otherwise you'll find yourself hobbled.

◎ Cheap shoulder pads are covered in sort-of-matching nylon fabric. Better-quality pads are covered in the same material as the dress. They're also removable, or invisible altogether under the lining.

INSTANT QUALITY INDICATOR: A concealed zip running along the side of the torso to the waist. This manufacturer was willing to spend in order to ensure an unbroken expanse front and back.

'You can say what you like about long dresses, but they cover a multitude of shins.'
Mae West, *Peel Me a Grape*

SKIRTS

◎ If the skirt is made of wool or other fabric that might cling, it ought to be lined.

◎ With a basic straight skirt, look for a generous hem. Hems will be less deep on full/flared/circular skirts.

◎ Check the interior lower edge of waistband. Is it concealed in the lining (best), bound with satin (good), or overlocked (OK)?

◎ A zip flap ought to be positioned between its teeth and your skin, or the lining around the zip should be slightly raised, to prevent chafing.

◎ The lining may be either attached to the outer fabric or loose. If it hangs loose, a short thread chain holding it in place at the hem is a nice touch.

◎ Carefully check the top of slit openings for splits or tears. An arrow-head-shaped sewn reinforcement on a kick pleat is an elegant means of strengthening the fabric at this weak spot.

◎ If there is a slit, mitred corners sharpen the look of the adjacent fabric.

◎ A dual button fastening above the zip is generally more secure and comfortable than a hook and eye.

INSTANT QUALITY HALLMARK: Front 'tulip' closure or other curvy hemline (note – these styles are difficult to alter).

TROUSERS

◎ All wool and/or potentially clingy trousers should be lined.

◎   Linings attach to the trousers at the knee, crotch and ankle.

◎   Check the interior lower edge of waistband. Is it concealed in the lining (best), bound with satin (good), or overlocked (OK)?

◎   Check pockets for raw seam edges.

◎   Check the point at which belt loops attach to the waistband. In deluxe trousers, this will be hemmed clean. In lesser-quality trousers, a bit of rough edge may appear. In no-quality trousers, fraying will abound.

◎   Belt loops should be generous – in cheaper trousers, they tend to be skimpy.

◎   If waistband is elasticised, gathers should be uniform.

◎   The edges of the fly's zip tape should be concealed behind the lining.

◎   Check any rivets for signs of rust.

◎   Any big tag on rear waistband of jeans should be real leather, not plastic or cardboard.

◎   Extra-plush corduroy is unusual and generally a sign of good quality.

◎   Corduroy shouldn't show signs of wear at the seat or knees.

INSTANT QUALITY INDICATOR: Floating welt pockets at the hip (see Chapter 4).

> 'When a man says he likes a woman in a skirt,
> I tell him to try one.'
> **Katherine Hepburn**

JACKETS

◎ The key quality hallmarks of sports/active wear and casual jackets are even stitching, a distinctive silhouette, contemporary fabric and effective hardware.

◎ Look carefully at the colour of white active-wear jackets – sometimes these have been treated with special brighteners that can be stripped out by improper dry-cleaning, leaving the colour dingy.

◎ The more tailored the jacket, the more important the inner structure (interlinings, padding), since these help the piece conform to the body.

◎ With tailored jackets, the meeting point of the sleeve and shoulder should be as sleek as the lines of a Porsche, with no bumps, ridges or wavering seams. Generally speaking, the closer set-in sleeves hang to the body, the better the construction. Watch out especially for the outline of shoulder pads – you shouldn't be able to see them from the exterior. A hollow under the end of the shoulder is especially bad.

◎ Some couturiers (notably Yves Saint Laurent and John Galliano) have favoured padded sleeve caps (the point at which the sleeve meets the shoulder), so that they are slightly peaked. Work of this kind should show no dimples or breaks.

◎ The attachment points of epaulets and other embellishments should be hemmed clean.

◎ An eye-catching tweed (multi-textured, possibly incorporating unexpected materials) points to a stand-out garment.

◎ In exquisitely well-made jackets, two-holed buttons will be sewn on to match the orientation of the buttonhole slits (vertical or horizontal).

◎ In superior tailored jackets, buttons will be attached to fabric with twisted shanks of thread, allowing some play of movement.

◎ The lining of the finest jackets may be quilted (stitched down in a square or diamond pattern, often seen in Chanel).

◎ Look for a pleat down the centre of the back panel of the lining. In very well-made tailored jackets, darts are often placed to either side of midline.

◎ In finer tailored jackets, the collar may be hand-sewn onto the jacket body.

◎ A felt lining underneath a collar is a tailoring detail that indicates ambition on the part of the manufacturer. It must be invisible when the collar is in normal position, and any visible stitching should be attractively done.

◎ The interlinings should be neither visible (ripples) nor audible (crackles) when you handle the fabric.

◉   Lapels should have enough substance so they don't fold or droop. In the best jackets, they are constructed to gently roll towards the chest.

◉   Collars in a contrasting fabric (such as velvet) are costlier to incorporate and so are a good tip-off to a better-made piece.

◉   Real suede patches or leather patches at the collar or elbows are another excellent quality indicator (beware, though, that such pieces can be the devil to clean).

INSTANT QUALITY INDICATOR: Unusual cuffs (for example, scalloped, curved or turned-back).

JUMPERS
◉   The component pieces of fully fashioned jumpers are pre-shaped on the knitting machine to conform to the finished outlines of the garment (rather than being cut and sewn after knitting is completed), and there is inconspicuous ribbing wherever the width of the jumper changes, for example at the shoulder seams. Such jumpers tend to be more tailored and have less bulky seams than cut-and-sewn.

◉   With wool and cashmere, the finer the knit, the more refined the quality. Sometimes, though, a bulkier, toasty Shetland may be the better buy, depending on wardrobe needs.

◉   Cotton knit jumpers tend to look like hell once they've been through the dryer. Check such garments carefully for signs of fading.

◉   If you must wear them, check the inside of colourful motif jumpers for long stretches of floating yarn. In a well-finished jumper, these will be anchored (technically speaking, 'stranded' or 'woven') after every five loops or so. This is to prevent the strands from snagging.

◎ Intricately patterned ribs, cables and stitches are part of the knitter's art, and should be sought out.

◎ A true 'fisherman's knit' cable allows a careful pinkie finger underneath a braid that appears to be attached flat to the garment.

◎ Make sure the top edge of a polo neck isn't rippling.

◎ Buttons and buttonholes on better cardigans will have reinforcement in the form of a fabric or grosgrain ribbon placket to prevent sagging.

◎ Thread used to overlock the seams of jumpers is ideally identical to that used to knit the garment. Otherwise, it should be as close a match as possible.

INSTANT QUALITY INDICATOR: Extra-fine cables or weave.

COATS

◎ Unless it's for a special occasion, a coat should be cut generously enough to allow for a suit jacket or jumper underneath.

◎ Linings should also be generous – look out for signs of wear around underarms (though linings can be replaced fairly easily).

◎ Extreme softness in a wool coat indicates the presence of cashmere.

◎ Capes of woven wool tend to be of fine quality. Consider them for between-season wear.

◎   A detachable wool lining in raincoats is a sign of good quality.

◎   On casual coats, look for heavy-duty hardware.

◎   Many lesser-quality trench coats have cheaply made and attached epaulets, patch pockets, fold-over lapels, etc. Check the attachment points and seams very carefully to distinguish the great from the pretenders.

◎   With suede and leather, the stiffer it is (check especially around the collar), the dirtier – or the poorer the quality.

◎   Due to fur's fall in popularity, it now abounds at vintage and charity shops. Especially with older furs, be on the alert for gaping seams, moth-eaten patches, stiffness in the pelts and general lack of gloss. Unless you enjoy terrorising small children, don't buy martins with heads and paws still attached.

◎   Look for a heavy fabric loop inside the coat collar for hanging, but do opt for a hanger whenever possible.

INSTANT QUALITY INDICATOR: Metal-chain hanging loop just inside neck.

'The trick of wearing mink is to look as though you are wearing a cloth coat. The trick of wearing a cloth coat is to look as though you are wearing mink.'
Pierre Balmain, couturier, 1955

Bringing the Past to Life with Period Clothes
by Jenny Beavan, Oscar-winning Costume Designer

Ordinarily when we create the costumes for a film, the
aim is to be incredibly honest – the clothing should be
as true to the period and place as possible. We often
use actual vintage pieces. For *The Black Dahlia*, which
is set in 1947 Los Angeles, 90% of the costumes –
there were 750 complete outfits in all – were vintage.
Much of it was rented from costume stock houses but
we also did a lot of buying from flea markets – at the
Santa Monica Airport and at the Rose Bowl, for
example. Los Angeles is heaving with forties pieces,
rack upon rack – it was effectively untouched by the
war for much of the decade and the clothes were at
the height of fashion, while over here it was make
do and mend . . .

The film I most enjoyed working on was *Gosford Park*,
because of the overall-ness and the simplicity of it. One
frock in that film was key – an emerald silk gown that
Claudie Blakley's character wore every evening to dinner
– she couldn't afford any others, and was made to pay

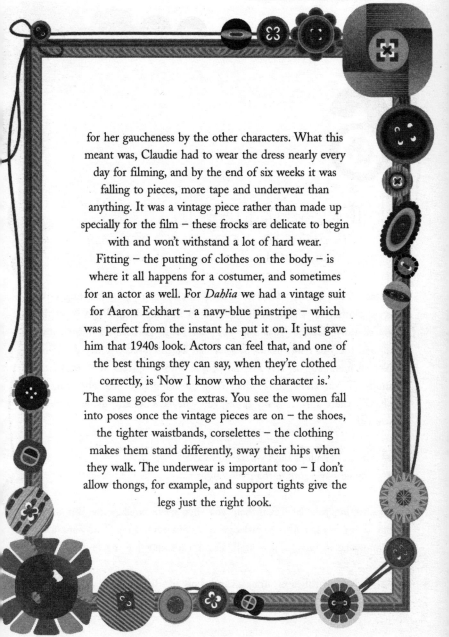

for her gaucheness by the other characters. What this
meant was, Claudie had to wear the dress nearly every
day for filming, and by the end of six weeks it was
falling to pieces, more tape and underwear than
anything. It was a vintage piece rather than made up
specially for the film – these frocks are delicate to begin
with and won't withstand a lot of hard wear.

Fitting – the putting of clothes on the body – is
where it all happens for a costumer, and sometimes
for an actor as well. For *Dahlia* we had a vintage suit
for Aaron Eckhart – a navy-blue pinstripe – which
was perfect from the instant he put it on. It just gave
him that 1940s look. Actors can feel that, and one of
the best things they can say, when they're clothed
correctly, is 'Now I know who the character is.'
The same goes for the extras. You see the women fall
into poses once the vintage pieces are on – the shoes,
the tighter waistbands, corselettes – the clothing
makes them stand differently, sway their hips when
they walk. The underwear is important too – I don't
allow thongs, for example, and support tights give the
legs just the right look.

Tag, you're it

After all the earlier advice to ignore labels when you're hunting down great clothes, this chapter is devoted to nothing but. Why? Now that you're fully fledged, meaning you can judge garments on their own merits, the full truth of the matter can be disclosed. Names do count. Not so much for us, but for the people who set prices at second-hand shops. If you know better than they do about how the label game is played, where a name really ranks, you will have the advantage. It means you can:

◎ target fabulous buys where they exist
◎ avoid paying more than you ought to

So knowing your labels can help you shop more intelligently. But, as the old saying goes, a *little* knowledge is a dangerous thing. You want to be connoisseur in this realm as well. This means knowing things like:

◎ what a diffusion line is and how it differs from a designer's collection pieces

◉ instances when respected names may produce less-than-stellar goods
◉ how to spot counterfeits

— When the name doesn't ring a bell

Here's an example of how a superficial knowledge about labels can be more hindrance than help: label-struck shoppers may ignore killer pieces *simply because they don't recognise the name on the tag*. How silly is that? Given the thousands upon thousands of brands out there, it's easy to understand the desire to streamline the process. But it's also easy to narrow down too far. Some women are so eager to find superstar names they bypass a brilliant up-and-comer, or a lesser-known designer of the past whose cult status is known to only a select few, or a piece that is truly outstanding whose label is missing in action.

Connoisseur's Tip:
Never ignore a garment because the label is unfamiliar, or is missing, or is odd. Acclaimed designer Martin Margiela's label is blank, embellished only with quadrangle stitches.

— The time-honoured tradition of designer hype

You often hear that designer mania is a new phenomenon, arising in the 1980s as part of that decade's obsession with money and power. In fact, couturiers have been astral bodies unto themselves for centuries. Rose Bertin, dressmaker to Queen Marie-Antoinette in the late 1700s, was, as one historian puts it, 'famous enough in her day to be regarded as something of a minister of fashion'. France set the style for European fashion, and Bertin's fame quickly spread. Soon she dressed royalty as far away as Madrid and St Petersburg – until history's wheel turned. With the French Revolution, the frivolity of worrying about fashionable necklines became bitterly clear to Bertin's clientele. She herself escaped and went on to write scandalous memoirs.

A hundred years later, the dressmaker Charles Worth had a similarly starry career, minus the mob's rude interruptions. He adopted a god-like *hauteur* that has been widely imitated in the fashion scene ever since:

> So keen was he to raise the study of dress to a new level that he adopted a completely unprecedented attitude towards his customers. A lady did not go to Maison Worth as she would to an ordinary dressmaker and say that she wanted a dress in green silk by Friday. First she made an appointment (for Worth was an extremely busy man), which was most unusual, and when admitted to his presence she would find that her own ideas counted for nothing. Worth would study her, note her colouring, her hair, her jewels, her style and then he would design a gown which he thought suited her. Anyone going to Worth had to submit to his taste, while his overseas customers had to rely on his taste completely, it did not matter if they were the Empress Marie Feodorovna in St Petersburg or Mrs J. Pierpont Morgan in New York, they were sent what Worth judged would suit them best.
>
> (Diana de Marly, *The History of Haute Couture, 1850–1950*)

Fashion historian Colin McDowell has a sharper opinion of Worth's contribution to design history:

> High fashion required a dictator who would show how much he scorned his clients for their lack of fashion culture. By treating them

abominably and over-charging them disgracefully, Worth ensured the lasting success of the breed he had brought into existence.

(Colin McDowell, *Dressed to Kill*)

— *The haute couture*

Once upon a time, the activities of Worth and his followers concerned only a razor-thin slice of society – women with the money and leisure to have frocks made to measure in Paris. So it remained until recent decades, when haute couture became a circus for the masses. Along with the widespread media coverage came a blurring of the term's meaning. Now, merchandisers happily slap the 'haute couture' label onto everything from hosiery to pet collars. Yet it really only means one thing: garments made by hand, over the course of several fittings, by a limited number of design houses in Paris – sold directly to buyers rather than through shops.

The list is strictly controlled by the Paris-based Chambre Syndicale de la Couture et des Créateurs de la Mode, which acts like a union for this crème de la crème industry. Until a few years ago, the membership requirements were very strict. Haute-couture houses were obligated to have a significant presence in Paris (employing a specified number of *mains* or sewing hands). Moreover, fashion shows had to be presented twice a year, featuring a set number of garments. But now the rules are loosening, in an effort to bring in fresh talent and interest.

The Chambre is fighting for the life of this old-line industry because the number of steady haute-couture customers in the entire world ranges from the hundreds to the low thousands, depending on who's doing the counting. Though these ladies are willing to spend up to £50,000 for a single ball gown, even they cannot keep the business afloat. Haute couture is always a money-losing operation. How could it be otherwise, when ten people are employed to hand-sew seed pearls all over a mermaid-inspired dress? Or produced marvels like a jacket with no visible point of entry?

The very thought of such clothing makes all of us giddy, but reality must enter in: *haute-couture pieces rarely materialise in second-hand shops*. They do appear with some frequency at vintage auctions, but there the expertly assessed estimated prices reflect their deluxe pedigree. The scarcity of couture down your local Oxfam is in part due to the fact that it costs too much to simply cast away (a young relative or household staffer is a likely beneficiary), in part because the couture houses' free alteration service means nobody has to grow out of them, in part because they wear beautifully for decades, and in part because they often get donated to museums instead. Still, *rarely* isn't the same as *never*. It pays to be on the alert, for you just never know. A Nina Ricci couture jacket recently showed up at my local charity shop for £50 – a few decimal points to the west of where it was originally priced. Tragically, it didn't fit.

— The haute-couture labels

The following names represent the ultimate in the art of high fashion – the grand French couture houses, as well as little-known couturiers who have been dressing some of the most stylish women in the world under the radar, and also some great names from the past. The best way to keep abreast of who's who and what's what is to regularly read magazines such as *Vogue, Tatler, Harper's Bazaar, In Style* and the *International Herald Tribune* newspaper's fashion coverage. Do bear in mind that if a former couture line is no longer produced (Versace's, for example), pieces may still be circulating in the second-hand world, and are still of intrisically great value.

(Certain nationalities – *et vous connaissez bien qui vous êtes* – are notorious for being sticklers about pronunciation. To remove all doubts are the parenthetical guides . . .)

Adeline André (Ah-de-leen
  AHN-dray)

Balmain (Ball-meh)

Chanel (Shah-nel)

Christian Lacroix (CHREES-tee-
  ah La-CWAH)

Dior (Dee-aw)

Dominique Sirop (Doe-mee-neek
  SEE-row)

Elie Saab (El-EE Sab)

Emanuel Ungaro (Ay-ma-new-
  ELLE OONG-ah-ro)

Franck Sorbier (SOR-beeay)

Givenchy (GEE-vahn-SHEE)

Hanae Mori (Ha-nay MOR-ee)

Jean-Louis Scherrer (Shawn
  Loo-EE SHER-ay)

Jean Paul Gaultier (Shawn Poll
  GO-tee-ay)

Josephus Thimister (JO-sephus
  THI-mister)

Lecoanet Hemant (Le-co-ah-nay
  AY-mahn)

Louis Féraud (Fay-row)

Nina Ricci (Nee-nah Ree-chee)

Olcimar Versolato (OHL-chee-mar
  Ver-so-LAH-toe)

Paco Rabanne (Rah-BAHN)

Pascal Humbert (PAH-scahl
  OOM-ber)

Per Spook (Per SPOOK)

Rochas (ROW-chah)

Ted Lapidus (LAH-pee-duss)

Thierry Mugler (Tyeh-REE
  MOOG-lay)

Valentino (Vah-len-TEE-no)

Versace (VER-sah-chay)

Yves Saint Laurent (EEV Sahn
  Low-RAHN)

— The international set

Besides the one-of-a-kind pieces they make for the wealthiest women in
the world, the haute-couture houses also produce ready-to-wear (*pret-à-
porter*) lines every season, distributed through boutiques and department
stores. The prices for individual garments usually top out in the low thousands, attracting a steady stream of wealthy customers and offsetting some
of the losses in couture. The cachet of an ultra-hot designer is greatly
dependent on the models, starlets and It Girls (or, in many cases, the stylists

employed by these women) who take a fancy to a given piece. A design house will strategically gift to oft-photographed celebrities, and restrict supply to bona-fide buyers, in order to attain cult status for a particular garment or accessory. All of this adds up to big-time exclusivity. The consequent waiting lists only add to the house's allure.

Paris has no lock on this fashion level: the couturiers share the stage with *pret-à-porter* designers from the world's other major fashion centres. London, New York, Milan, Paris – they are the major launch pads of the ready-to-wear collections. 'Collection' is another fashion term that is flung around with abandon, but in the strict sense it means the most deluxe pieces a designer sells in shops – in other words, the line that is the top-of-the-line.

The following elite group of *pret-à-porter* design houses (including a few now defunct) has achieved such success that they are instantly recognised all over the world. Today they fill the best dress agencies, tomorrow they will be the go-to garments in vintage shops. And (if you're very, very lucky) they may appear in the occasional charity shop in between.

Alaïa (Ah-lee-a)

Alber Elbaz

Alberta Ferretti (Feh-REH-tee)

Alexander McQueen

Anna Molinari

Balenciaga (Bah-len-chee-AH-ga)

Bill Blass

Calvin Klein

Carolina Herrara (HAY-rah-rah)

Cerruti (Chay-ROO-tee)

Chloé (CLO-ay)

Claude Montana

Diane von Furstenberg

Dolce & Gabbana (DOL-chay ay Gah-BAH-nah)

Donna Karan (CARE-an)

Emilio Pucci (POO-chee)

Escada

Etro (AY-tro)

Fendi

Gianfranco Ferré (Fer-RAY)

Giles by Giles Deacon

Giorgio Armani

Gucci

Guy Laroche (Key La-ROASH)

Helmut Lang (HELL-moot Lahng)

Hermès (Air-MEZZ)

Hervé Léger (Air-VAY LEH-jay)

Isaac Mizrahi (Mizz-RAH-hee)

Issey Miyake (EE-say MEE-yah-kay)

Jil Sander

John Galliano

Karl Lagerfeld (LAH-ger-feld)

Kenzo

Krizia (KREE-zee-ya)

Lanvin (LAW-vah)

Loewe (LO-vay)

Louis Féraud (Loo-EE FAY-row)

Louis Vuitton (Loo-EE
VUEE-tow)

Marc Jacobs

Marni

MaxMara

Michael Kors

Missoni

Miu Miu

Moschino (Mos-KEE-no)

Oscar de la Renta

Prada

Ralph Lauren (LAW-ren)

Rifat Ozbek (REE-faht OZ-beck)

Roberto Cavalli

Roland Mouret (RO-lan MOO-ray)

Romeo Gigli (Ro-MAY-o
GEE-lee)

Salvatore Ferragamo

Sonia Rykiel (REE-kay-ell)

Stella McCartney

Viktor & Rolf

Trussardi

— The Great Brits

There is no better indication of the vibrant creativity of the British fashion pack than the appointment of John Galliano, Alexander McQueen, Phoebe Philo and Julien Macdonald to the helms of fashion dreadnoughts across the channel. At a slightly less exalted level, local stars fill the international fashion pages with the swashbuckling irreverence British Fashion Week is famous for. At the top of their game today, these designers and fashion houses will be among the most coveted creators found in the vintage shops of tomorrow.

Amanda Wakeley

Antoni & Alison

Antonio Berardi

Aquascutum

Basso & Brooke

Bella Freud

Ben De Lisi

Betty Jackson

Boudicca

Boyd

Bruce Oldfield
Burberry
Caroline Charles
Clements Ribeiro
Daks
Duro Olowu
Edina Ronay
Eley Kishimoto
English Eccentrics
Elspeth Gibson
Frost French
Gharani Strok
Ghost
Hussein Chalayan
Jacques Azagury
Jaeger
Jasper Conran
Jenny Packham
Jean Muir
Jonathan Saunders
John Rocha
Joseph

Julien Macdonald
Katherine Hamnett
Luella
Lulu Guinness
Margaret Howell
Maria Grachvogel
Matthew Williamson
Mulberry
Mulligan
N. Peal
Nicole Farhi
Paul Costelloe
Paul Smith
Pierce Fionda
Pringle
Ronit Zilkha
Temperley
Tomasz Starzewski (Star-zee-oo-ski)
Vivienne Westwood
Zandra Rhodes

— *Blasts from the past*

Vintage princesses take note: the names and labels that follow are some of the stand-outs of twentieth-century UK fashion history. This list is by no means comprehensive – you'll find a wealth of further information by speaking with dealers about your finds, making enquiries at a good costume collection (the Victoria & Albert Museum has an expert opinion service, for example), or searching a given brand or name on the internet. Along these lines, *www.vintagefashionguild.org* has a extensive resource section of scanned international vintage labels, along with capsule histories of the designers.

Annacat (1960s)
Apple (1960s)
Barbara Hulanicki (1980s)
Biba (1960s–70s)
Bill Gibb (1960s–70s)
Blanes (1950s–60s)
Body Map (1980s)
Bus Stop (1960s–70s)
Carnegie of London (1960s)
CC41 (1940s–50s)
Clobber (1960s–70s)
Diana Warren (1950s–70s)
Dollyrockers (1960s–70s)
Donald Davies (1970s–80s)
Elsie Whiteley (1930s–70s)
Frank Usher (1940s–present)
Frederick Starke (1920s–60s)
Gerald McCann (1950s–60s)
Gina Fratini (1960s–80s)
Granny Takes a Trip (1960s–70s)
Hardy Amies (1930s–present)
Harella (1940s–70s)
Horrockses (1940s–80s)
Janice Wainwright (1960s–70s)
Jean Allen (1950s–70s)
Jean Varon (1960s–80s)
Jeff Banks (1960s–present)
John Bates (1960s–70s)
John Charles (1950s–80s)
John Stephen (1960s–70s)

Laura Ashley (1950s–present)
Lord Kitcheners (1960s–70s)
Marion Donaldson (1960s–90s)
Marion Foale and Sally Tuffin
   (1960s–70s)
Marshall & Snelgrove
   (1870s–1970s)
Mary Quant (1950s–60s)
Miss London (1950s)
Mr Darren (1970s)
Norman Hartnell (1920s–70s)
Origin (1960s)
Ossie Clark (1960s–70s)
Pam Hogg (1980s)
Quad (1960s)
Quorum (1960s)
Radley (1960s–80s)
Ricci Michaels (1960s)
Robert Dorland (1950s–70s)
Samuel Sherman (1960s–70s)
Sarah Whitworth (1980s)
Shubette (1913–present)
Susan Small (1940s–70s)
Sybil Connolly (1940s–60s)
The White House (1910s–70s)
Twiggy (1960s)
Victor Stiebel (1930s–60s)
Windsmoor (1930s–present)
Workers for Freedom
   (1980s–present)

— The all-Americans

These higher-end contemporary American labels, while well-loved in the United States, don't carry the same buzz at an international level. Not that they are in any way inferior, just not as hugely popular here as they are in New York, Chicago and Los Angeles. Given the ubiquity of Yanks in this country, particularly in London, these names may nonetheless appear in second-hand shops, trailing their owners across the pond.

Adrienne Vittadini
Anna Sui
Antonio Fusco
Badgley Mischka (Badge-lee
   MISH-kah)
Bob Mackie
Fabrice
J. Mendel
Joan & David
Joan Vass
John Bartlett
Lily Pulitzer
Marc Eisen
Mary McFadden
Narciso Rodriguez

Nicole Miller
Norma Kamali
Patrick Robinson
Proenza Schouler
Rebecca Moses
Richard Tyler
Scaasi
Todd Oldham
Tommy Hilfiger
Tse
Vera Wang
Vivienne Tam
Zac Posen
Zang Toi
Zoran

— Foreign finds

While this list isn't comprehensive (there are simply too many designers out there to include one and all), these are among the best-loved names in their home countries.

AUSTRALIA
Alex Perry
Alexandra Nea
Alice McCall
Camilla & Marc
Claude Maus
Collette Dinnigan
Gwendolynne
Kirrily Johnston
Leona Edmiston
Lisa Ho
Mad Cortes
Nicola Finetti
Nobody
Paablo Nevada
Rebecca Davies
Vicious Threads
Wayne Cooper
Zambesi

BELGIUM
Ann Demeulemeester
   (Duh-MULE-uh-MEES-ter)
Dries Van Noten (DREES van
   NOH-ten)
Martin Margiela (Mar-gee-ELL-a)
Veronique Branquinho
   (VAY-ron-eek Brahn-KEE-no)

FRANCE
A.P.C. (Ah Pay Say)
Agnès B. (Ahn-yes BAY)

Atsuro Tayama (AHT-soo-ro Tah-
   YAH-ma)
Cacharel (CAH-shah-rell)
Chantal Thomass (Shawn-TAHL
   TOE-mahs)
Daniel Hechter (DAH-nee-ell
   ECK-tay)
Diapositiv (DEE-a-poe-sa-TEEV)
Dorothée Bis (Do-ro-tay BEE)
Emmanuelle Khanh (AY-mahn-u-
   ell KAHN)
Equipment
Et Vous (Ay Voo)
Galeries Lafayette (GAH-la-ree
   Lahf-eye-ETT)
George Rech (Raysh)
Gerard Darel (JAY-rar Dah-
   RELL)
Ines de la Fressange (EE-ness duh
   lah Fray-SAHN-juh)
Irene van Ryb (EE-ren van
   REEB)
Jacques Fath (Jock Fahth)
Les Copains (Lay Co-PEH)
Lolita Lempicka (LEM-pee-kah)
Lucien Pellat-Finet (LOO-see-ahn
   PAY-lah FEE-nay)
Martine Sitbon (SEET-bow)
Plein Sud (Plan SUE)
Popi Moreni
   (Poe-pee Mow-RAY-nee)
Regina Rubens (Ray-gee-nah

ROO-bens)
Rodier (ROH-dee-ay)
Sisley
Teenflo
Tehen (TAY-hen)
Vertigo (Ver-TEE-go)

GERMANY
Basler
Bogner
Fink
Hugo Boss
Joop!
Joseph Janard
KS/Steilmann
Lancaster
Marc Cain
Olsen
Rena Lange
Searle
Strenesse
Yarell

ITALY
Alessandro Dell' Acqua

Basile (Bah-SEEL)
Byblos (BEE-blows)
Enrico Coveri (Co-VER-ee)
Genny
Giambattista Valli
    (Jam-ba-TEE-sta Va-LEE)
Laura Biagiotti
    (BEE-ah-gee-OH-tee)
Loro Piano (Lo-ro Pee-AH-no)
Malo
Mila Schön (MEE-lah SHINE)
Nino Cerruti (Chay-ROO-tee)
Simonetta (SEE-mo-NAY-tah)

SPAIN
Adolfo Dominguez
    (Do-MING-ez)
Antonio Alverado
    (Al-ver-AH-doh)
Marguerita Nuez (NOO-ez)
Nacho Ruiz (ROO-eez)
Roberto Verinno (Ver-EE-no)
Sybilla (SEE-bee-lah)
Vittorio & Luchino (Vee-TOH-
    ree-oh ay Loo-KEY-no)

— Diffusion confusion

The big-name designers are very much aware of the glitter factor swirling about their names. They are also aware that only a small segment of the public can afford a £1,500 collection suit. That is why, in the 1980s and 1990s, many began to create spin-off lines. The pieces in these secondary lines – sometimes called *diffusion* lines – are made for customers who crave the labels but can't afford the cost of high-end *pret-à-porter*. Lower in price, these garments are also produced in greater volumes, in order to reach as many buyers as possible.

Department stores have jumped into the game, enlisting some of the starriest names in the British fashion universe to create fusion labels. Debenhams, for example, has a cracking line-up including Jasper Conran, Ben de Lisi and Julien Macdonald. In this case, the store and the designer are both present on the label, making an in-store line easy to differentiate from collection pieces (although certain unscrupulous internet resellers may tout the designer but neglect to mention the store).

The diffusion concept has proven such an El Dorado that many designers do not stop with one or two offshoots, but instead offer lines three, four and five price levels removed from the collection pieces. These often have the words 'jeans' or 'sport' somewhere on the label. Usually targeted at younger customers, the items are mass merchandise, typically made with minimal input from the hotshot on the tag. Buyers don't know or don't care. They gladly pay a £30 surcharge for the few grains of stardust a designer logo conveys.

The key question is, how to tell a first-rate *pret-à-porter* piece from a fourth-rate teen-pleaser? In department stores, high-class is separated from teencentric-mass by escalators and a semi-rational pricing system. At dress agencies, vintage shops and charity shops, these pieces could easily end up side by side on the same rack, with similar pricing. Granted, some proprietors are savvy enough to sort it all out, tagging diffusion merchandise according to its quality level. But others are hoodwinked by the label game. That's why discerning the differences between a collection piece and its diffusion third cousin is a critical aspect of connoisseurship. To consistently buy at rational prices, you need to rely on your own judgment. There are three ways to avoid overspending:

1) Know your quality.
2) Remember that a collection label – meaning the label itself – *looks*

different from one on a diffusion piece. The colour is different. Initials are not used – a rough rule of thumb is the more words involved, the tonier the piece. The word 'collection' often features prominently, 'sport' and 'jeans' do not.

3)   Become familiar with the relative merits and demerits of diffusion labels. Quite a few are great, offering serious quality at a reasonable price. A few are so bad it's an insult to fashion and humanity. The best place to educate yourself about the variations among lines and labels is a great department store – as long as you can avoid the temptation to take samples home for in-depth study.

— Counterfeits!

Once spotting quality has become second nature, you may find yourself laughing out loud at a preposterously bad garment bearing a solid-gold label. Easy-to-manufacture pieces like T-shirts, jeans and polo shirts are the usual suspects. All over the world, markets selling nothing but knock-offs cater to shoppers' touching belief that the stuff is real and authentically stolen. Wake up, darlings. It's *never* real.

So how best to defend yourself against the scourge of counterfeits? The label itself is often the giveaway – fake labels are frequently printed rather than woven (remember, printed labels are cheaper to produce). Anyone who believes that Chanel, with its meticulous quality standards, would make a T-shirt with a printed label . . . well, some people are easily fooled.

Labels also point to bogus clothing by their absence – especially the tags indicating country of origin, fabric composition and care instructions. If you don't see them (or signs that they've been cut out) in a brand-new, contemporary item, red alert.

Besides counterfeiters, our other nemeses are consignors up to no good. The owner of an exquisite dress agency in Knightsbridge tells a story about a regular (and *extremely* wealthy) consignor who had an abundance of spare time but not many scruples. In she came to sell a jacket she swore was Chanel. Sure enough, the label confirmed it, and so did the beautiful buttons. Yet our owner remained unimpressed.

'Mrs So-and-so,' he says. 'I'm sorry to have to tell you this is not a Chanel jacket.'

'Are you mad?' she retorts. 'Of course it is. Look at the label, look at the buttons.'

'Madam, with all due respect, this is not Chanel.'

'How can you possibly be so sure?'

'The lining. You forgot to replace it. As far as I know, Chanel has never used one with "Jaeger" all over it.'

Whoops. One more reason to give linings a good look.

Who's That Girl?

Getting great fit

Finding spectacular clothes isn't enough. The real goal is finding spectacular clothes that fit beautifully. Bodies being what they are, this is the ultimate test, and, despite all good intentions, one we routinely cheat. Why? Because going home without something new, especially after shopping for hours, feels like defeat. At moments like these we're especially vulnerable to the voice of the devil on our shoulder, who whispers all the wrong things in our ear:

You: What do you think?
Little devil: Think? Who needs to think? That tweed is perfection with your peach angora jumper! Buy it before somebody else grabs it!

You (straining to fasten the zip): I don't know . . . my bum . . . doesn't it look tight?

Little devil: It's a pencil skirt! It's supposed to look tight! The perfect excuse to lose that half stone . . .

Our accomplice only lurks for so long. The instant money crosses the till, he vanishes. What takes his place? The slow, sickly realisation that, once again, we've failed the fit test, buying something that, once on, makes us feel wrong.

— Combating the little devil

You've been shopping for a few hours and can feel that mania building, a 'buy, buy, buy' fever marked by obsessive trawling through racks and agonised stretches in front of a mirror, visions of carrot sticks dancing in your head. Take a deep breath. Truly great clothes are blissfully, unquestionably, made for you – they shouldn't cause angst of any kind. Soothe the need to take something home with a detour to the jewellery or scarf section. Blow a few quid on a trinket you'll actually wear. This will shut the demon up, and will make you happier in the long run. Another tactic: put the questionable piece on hold and leave the shop altogether. Plan to return in an hour or two, with a cool head. The bother of going back acts like a brisk slap to the subconscious, bringing rationality to the fore. If the item is a must-have, you'll come back; if not, the trouble will hardly seem worth it.

— With liberty and so-so fit for all

If you've ever compromised where fit is concerned, at least you've got plenty of company. Despite the availability of countless makes and styles, despite the media barrage of high-fashion images, poor fit is widespread. We've largely lost a skill that was second nature back when we made up our own clothes, or had them made for us – the ability to assess how fabric sits on the body. The proof can be seen on the street, in corridors at the office, at the pick-n-mix stand at the cinema. Women with carefully styled hair, manicures, nice make-up, undercutting their looks with poor fit. Or, just as bad, undercutting the very point of the clothes that they're wearing. Late 1940s and 1950s jackets are supposed to be *nippy* around the waist – if they puff and slide around, the vintage drama is gone. Corsets are meant to *mould* the figure, not add extra bulges above and below. Even a piece as simple and forgiving as a 1960s babydoll dress needs to fit beautifully at the shoulders – otherwise you'll look less like a doll than a little girl wearing big sister's clothes.

Speaking of which, in certain other countries girls are carefully trained from a very young age about the importance of good fit. If you've read many books on personal style, you'll know this is the point where French and Italian women are trotted out in reproach to British dress sense. Writers don't do this merely to sound sophisticated. In the fashion capitals of Europe, women *do* seem to know things we don't. Not because they're smarter, not because they're richer, but because they're raised with different notions about how to shop and, more important, how to buy. For them, great fit is more important than a great price reduction. Having spent two years in Paris in awe of the native talent, I offer these first-hand observations:

◉ *There, stylishness doesn't mean having a huge wardrobe.* There's more on this in the next chapter, but it boils down to *looking great* every day instead of *looking different* every day – and being much choosier about fit.

◉ *They don't try on clothes during lunch.* In France, lunch hour is for lunch, or for sitting in the park tanning your legs. Before heading back to the office, the girls may indulge in a quick cruise through a boutique, but only to get a notion of what's there. Real shopping is done at the weekends, and the pursuit is savoured rather than rushed.

◎ *They shop to educate themselves as much as to buy.* In a boutique, a French woman and a sales assistant will stand in front of a mirror for a good half-hour, debating the rise of the hemline, pinching at excess fabric, moulding a potential purchase to the figure. The conversation is open and frank, and matters of a quarter inch are debated with great gusto. Then what happens? As often as not, the customer walks out of the ship, *without buying the outfit.* But it's not like she left empty-handed. Now she's even more knowledgeable than she was before about the shapes and colours that suit her. Maybe she'll return in a few days and buy it after all. Or maybe she'll head out to the Réciproque dress agency in the 16th arrondissement and apply that knowledge to her purse's benefit.

◎ *They understand the difference between tight and tailored.* Tight is sleazy. Tailored is flattering. And once you've decided to try tailored your-self, anything less precise (baggy tops, poorly set shoulders, skirts that slide around the body) feels sloppy.

◎ *They emphasise the good, and disguise the bad.* In the fashion capital of the world, women don't give a damn about fashionable hemlines. If it's a face-off between looking beautiful and looking bang-on-trend, beautiful will win out every time. Their skirts always hit the spot that best showcases their legs. And, if their legs aren't so fab, they draw the eye up to more alluring regions, seeing no point in letting one mediocre feature cloud the illusion of perfection.

◎ *They look at their bodies realistically.* The same kind of cool logic that gave the world the philosophical principle 'I think therefore I am' gives French women the ability to say, 'I think I am too broad in the hips to wear shorts, therefore I am going to wear a skirt.'

You wear it well

Even those of us without a drop of Gallic blood can learn to achieve fit *à la Française*. It comes down to applying the same brisk rationality. Truly stylish women manage both the process and the outcome by breaking it into four distinct steps:

'Trifles make perfection, but perfection is no trifle'
Italian proverb

—*Step 1: What's your size?*

Who really knows? We're all haunted by the Ghost of Sizes Past, numbers that were accurate years ago, before weight fluctuations, childbirth, the resolution to swim thirty lengths a week. The human figure changes, for better and for worse, over time. This is why it's so important to get updated numbers every year. If your weight yo-yos, you might want to take measurements more often. Having an accurate idea of your place on the size chart speeds the process of trying clothes on, and also prevents the ego blows that follow on outdated assumptions.

Honing in on your current size means tracking down a tape measure. *A chorus of groans lifts from the crowd.* Women hate tape measures for excellent reasons: memories of hot-faced sessions in the teen bra department, or the vital statistics of brain-dead hotties in lad mags. Never mind. Knowing these numbers is key.

Here's where to take measurements, in inches:

Bust: around the fullest part and across back, try to keep the tape as level as possible.

Waist: hold the tape comfortably – not tight – at the bend of the waist, not necessarily the belly button. If you're not sure where the bend is, take a quick side dip to find the crease.

Hips: around the fullest part – often closer to the upper thighs.

A final important measurement to take – your *inseam*. Knowing this number will help you quickly grab jeans and other casual trousers that are sized by inseam and waist inches on an outer or inner label. The easiest way to take an inseam measurement is to pull out a pair of trousers that hit your ankles right where you want them to. Measure from the ankle hem up to the centre of the crotch, and remember that high heels demand an extra inch or so of inseam.

Size Chart

size	8	10	12	14	16	18	20	22	24	26
bust	31	32	34	36	38	40	42	44	46	48
waist	24	25	27	29	31	33	35	37	39	41
hips	34	35	37	39	41	43	45	47	49	51

Now compare your measurements to this chart. Circle the size or sizes that best conform to your figure. Don't be surprised if you're not a uniform 10 or 16 or whatever – most of us are one measure above the waist and another one below.

Now that you know your approximate size or sizes, jot it down in your notebook, along with the date, and tell yourself it's only a number. In this case, you're more right than you know.

—Step 2: Size matters, but only sort of

Victorian tops made for grown women, while gorgeous, often seem better suited to consumptive sprites. Vintage pieces from the 1940s, 1950s and 1960s notoriously run small – a size 12 from back then might barely be a 10 today. There is no agreed-upon standard for contemporary garment sizes from year to year. This is because the sizes are based on national averages that change over time, due to a number of factors. Nutrition is a big one. So is posture, which has had its own modes and has varied widely throughout the decades.

Location has as much of an effect on garments as time does. From country to country, sizes said to be 'equivalent' to ours ain't necessarily so. In theory, French size 40 trousers should fit a size 12–14 bottom, but, because French hips tend to be narrower, their trousers often run small on our figures.

To make it more complicated, clothing manufacturers size (or, to use the technical term, grade) their lines according to different formulas. Moreover, fit fluctuations may enter in because manufacturers normally allow up to a half-inch leeway between otherwise identical pieces (sewing-machine operators can only be so accurate).

All this explains why size is, at best, a conjecture rather than fact. Every garment has to prove itself: you can't take anything for granted. Even brands or designers that typically fit you like a glove can suddenly go sloppy as an old mitten, for reasons that have nothing to do with your figure.

Connoisseur's Tip:
Always consider clothes one size above and one size below your 'true' one. Given the wide variations possible in cut, the off-size is liable to fit perfectly.

SHAPE SHIFTING THROUGH THE AGES

If your body doesn't fall in with the modernist credo 'less is more', take heart. Retro fashions accommodate all kinds of figures. According to the internet-based expert Vintage Vixen, 'Because vintage clothing encompasses practically any style you can think of, there is always a silhouette to flatter your figure.' Here is her round-up of each era's special characteristics.

1900s: full, rounded bust/very small waist/flat stomach with full backside/legs not visible

1910s A: high, smaller bust/small but emphasised waist/ flattish stomach with full hips/legs not visible

1910s B: solid, but soft bust/medium to large waist/ vague, unoutlined hips/ankles only visible

1920s: no outline of bust, waist or hips/thin breadth/legs visible to knee

1930s: high, small to medium bust/trim waist/little hips/legs visible to calves

1940s: large, broad shoulders/soft, medium to large bust/severe, trim waist/medium hips/legs visible to knee

1950s A: voluptuous, medium to large bust/small, cinched waist/full hips/legs visible to knee

1950s B: small to medium bust/trim waist/rounded hips

1960s: small shoulders and bust/A-line from bust or hip/lots of leg

1970s: no particular shape, but a generally natural silhouette

Reprinted with kind permission of Vintage Vixen Clothing Co. from their website: www.vintagevixen.com

— The rough cut

So it makes sense to grab a range of sizes to try on. But what if a piece *looks* like a great candidate, but . . .

1) the size is snipped out
2) it's a vintage or foreign item labelled in an unfamiliar way
3) the size tag and the piece seem mismatched

Must you go through the bother of schlepping to the dressing room and pulling the thing on, knowing full well it may not fit? Not if you know *how clothes in your size hang atop, rather than on, your body*. This is a technique you can apply right in the aisle, one that can save a lot of dilly-dallying. You probably do it to a degree already. It is, quite simply, the whole-body version of measuring a sleeve against your arm or checking the length of trousers down your leg. Note, though, that the information it yields is rough at best; it is most reliable with straightforwardly cut, non-stretchy pieces.

To get the gist of the technique, your own garments are once again the best teachers. These should include a blouse (with ordinary rather than dropped shoulder seams), trousers, a skirt and dress jacket – all of them non-stretch and a great fit. Once you have them out, and are dressed in a fairly figure-skimming outfit, stand before a full-length mirror. Item by item, you're going to discover exactly where the sample garments hit your figure. Don't be put off by the wordiness of the instructions below – the draping itself is actually quite simple.

BLOUSE

We'll start off with a size-check that's familiar. Place the left armhole seam directly over the crease of your left armpit (if you're left-handed, reverse the sides). Letting the sleeve fall naturally down your straightened left arm, notice where the cuff hits the wrist. This point is the *target zone* for future blouses. If a cuff or hem falls much farther up, the candidate is probably too small. Any farther down, and it's probably too big.

Now make sure all the buttons are done up. Holding the blouse taut by the two armhole seams, lay it across the shoulders as though you had it on. See how these seams fall directly atop your armpit creases – these two points are your *target zones* for shoulder seams on future blouses. If a candidate blouse is too small through the shoulders, the seams will land closer to your neck. On blouses that are too large through the shoulders, the seams will edge down your arms.

Now tuck the collar snugly under your chin. Drape the blouse naturally down your torso and regrasp it by the side seams about an inch below each armpit, so that the fabric rests perfectly smooth across your bust. Your fingertips are now positioned somewhere on your upper ribs – the give-or-take *target zones* for bustline size. If a blouse's side seams bring your fingertips much closer to your breasts, it's probably too small. If your fingers begin heading around your back, the blouse is liable to be too big.

SKIRT

Close all buttons and zips. Hold the skirt taut at its waistband, one hand on either side seam, so the skirt hangs flat and is facing front. Drape it from your waist, as though to check length, but instead note where your thumbs hit your middle. These spots are the *target zones* for future skirts. If, with a skirt under consideration, your thumbs range closer to your belly button, it may be too small. If your thumbs hit farther back, the skirt may be too big.

TROUSERS

Do the same with the waistband for trousers (note that low-rise trousers will have different target zones than higher-waisted ones). Now note where the crotch seam falls relative to your own body (try-on pieces whose crotch falls much higher or lower are going to be very uncomfortable to wear). Finally, to find your *target zones* for length, hold the waistband at proper height and let the legs fall naturally to the ankles. Remember the spots where the hem lands.

JACKET

Button your best-fitting jacket and drape it against your torso. The position of the armhole seams will give you a rough indication of where these should fall on future jackets.

Again, this technique is approximate – a garment put together by a clever designer might break all the rules but still look and feel great. But, if a straightforward piece fails a couple of these tests, move on.

—Step 3: Who says the mirror never lies?

The next stage in the fit process is the try-on, the point at which many of us stumble. And no wonder. Most us depend on the outlines bounced back by the mirror as the sole evidence of what works and what doesn't. On the face of it, this makes perfect sense. The problem is, when our eyes and mind get together in front of a looking glass, all kinds of mischief can happen. Since the late 1960s, there have been a number of scientific studies analysing female self-perception in the mirror. The studies routinely show that in Western cultures, we see ourselves as being fatter than we actually are (while men, bless them, perceive themselves as being more god-like). At its worst, this cognitive warp can fuel anorexia, but to a less dramatic degree it distorts our notion of what fits. Due to the misperception of imaginary flaws, some of us may buy garments that are too baggy.

This isn't the only illusion fostered by mirrors. Another arises when we rely on a single mirror instead of a three-way glass to assess fit. No matter how wide it is, a single mirror imposes a two-dimensional, paper-doll effect on the figure. We compensate, of course, by taking a quick turn to profile – posture-perfect, tummy yanked tight. *Very* realistic. Meanwhile, our backsides remain as obscure as the dark side of the moon. Is it necessary to spell out the consequences? In contrast, a good three-way mirror portrays us in the round, as the world sees us. If your favourite dress agency doesn't have one, gently suggest it to the owner. If your favourite charity shop is doing great to have a mirror at all, remember to bring a small pocket glass to check your hind aspect.

OUR CREASE TO BEAR

As we've just seen, the outlines of a garment in a mirror aren't 100% reliable. So what's the alternative? Something some of us are already expert in – spotting wrinkles. Not the kind on the skin. Not the kind due to poor ironing. I'm talking about *tension wrinkles*, the ones that result when fabric fits poorly. In catalogues and magazines these creases don't exist, but in the real world they're everywhere you look: across the back, under the armpits, over the thighs, around the crotch. Tension wrinkles inevitably point to poor fit. Once you know what you're looking for, they are easy to spot. Whenever you see one, treat it like a symptom – it's telling you where something's wrong. In essence, a taut wrinkle indicates that fabric is straining across a given area – there's too much body for too little fabric. A slack or droopy wrinkle, rather predictably, indicates the opposite problem. Be vigilant! The goal is smooth and elegant, not packed or insufficiently poured-in.

NOT FOR YOUR EYES ONLY

Besides wrinkle cues, there's one other back-up for mirror evidence, and it doesn't require a looking glass at all. When a garment hangs impeccably, it *feels* great, like a second skin. There's that 'ahhh' factor that settles the minute it's on. While our eyes can deceive us, our nerve endings never lie. If you can nail down these sensations so that you recognise them time and again, you'll eventually be able to rely on them routinely. That's why it makes sense to systematically use 'feel' cues as well as visual and wrinkle cues in the quest for getting great fit.

—*Putting it all together*

Here's how the techniques come together: the visual and feel cues plus the wrinkle decoder. Using the three systematically in the fitting room should give you a very accurate idea of when you've got a winner.

BLOUSES

PROPER FIT – VISUAL CUES

◎ Long sleeves hit the wrist bones.

◎ Shoulder seams hang vertically from the notch where arm bone joins shoulder, or, in case of a drop-seamed shoulder, no more than an inch or two down the arm.

- ◉ Front button placket lies flat (no gaping whatsoever).
- ◉ Collar rests flat against back of neck.
- ◉ Darts do not pucker.
- ◉ Any bustline darts end at most prominent part of the breasts.
- ◉ Fabric lies smooth across bust and lower torso.
- ◉ If blouse is to be worn as a tunic, fabric drapes freely over backside and hips.

PROPER FIT – FEEL CUES

- ◉ You can stretch your arms comfortably over head and out to the side (when you put them back down, blouse sits properly in place).
- ◉ Any shoulder pads should rest snugly, not sliding forward, back or down arms.
- ◉ Top button can be done up without strain (even if you don't ordinarily button this high).
- ◉ Blouse does not balloon over waistband (meaning you can't grab a handful of fabric).
- ◉ Tails can be securely tucked in.

SKIRTS

PROPER FIT – VISUAL CUES

- ◉ Fabric drops straight down from the most prominent part of backside, rather than cupping the underside of the bum.
- ◉ Side seams hang straight.
- ◉ Hem hangs to same length in the front and back.
- ◉ Any pleats lie flat and are straight up and down.
- ◉ Pockets do not gape.
- ◉ Fabric does not mould over stomach, but falls straight down from waistband (don't forget natural pound-or-so of weight fluctuation over the course of the month).

PROPER FIT – FEEL CUES

◉ You can slide skirt on without wiggling.

◉ Waistband fits just tight enough to allow two fingers to slip in.

◉ You can sit without stress or strain.

◉ You can sit and cross your legs without yanking.

◉ Skirt does not circumnavigate waistline while walking.

◉ Skirt allows you to take normal strides.

TROUSERS/SHORTS

PROPER FIT – VISUAL CUES

◉ Fabric falls straight down bum rather than clinging to lower buttocks.

◉ Pleats lie flat and are straight up and down.

◉ Pockets don't gape open.

◉ Fly doesn't strain open.

◉ Standard trouser hems skim front of shoes, and fall about halfway to heel in back.

◉ Curve of your stomach isn't obvious from side view (exhale!).

PROPER FIT – FEEL CUES

◉ Trousers slip on easily over thighs.

◉ You can button without inhaling.

◉ Waistband fits just tight enough to let two fingers in.

◉ Seat isn't baggy (you can't grab a handful of fabric).

◉ Seat isn't painted on (you can pinch an inch or so of fabric).

◉ Crotch rides comfortably when walking.

◉ You can sit without stress or strain.

JACKETS

PROPER FIT – VISUAL CUES

◉ Sleeves extend to wrist bone.

◉ Armhole seam sits vertically rather than slanting towards body or arm.

◎ Shoulder pads are invisible, not hanging cliff-like over top of arm or puckering.

◎ All buttons close without gaping or strain.

◎ Fabric lies smooth against back.

◎ Collar lies flat against neck.

◎ Fabric falls gracefully over torso and waist.

◎ Back vents lie flat rather than gaping open.

PROPER FIT – FEEL CUES

◎ When you shimmy shoulders, you can't feel shoulder pads.

◎ You can move arms easily to the front and sideways.

◎ Your arms bend freely at elbow.

◎ You can bend at waist with buttons buttoned.

DRESSES

PROPER FIT – VISUAL CUES

◎ If it's button-front, the placket does not gape.

◎ Neckline does not strain or gape.

◎ Shoulders are in proportion with rest of fit, shoulder pads fit snugly and are invisible.

◎ Fabric does not mould to backside.

◎ Back drapes smoothly.

◎ If a belt is called for, it can be worn without sloppy-looking gathers above and below.

PROPER FIT – FEEL CUES

◎ Dress is easy to get into and out of.

◎ All buttons can be closed without strain or gaping.

◎ Waist sits properly, at your natural bend rather than too high or too. low (do a side bend if not sure where this is).

◎ Arms have full freedom of movement.

TOPS

PROPER FIT – VISUAL CUES

◎   T-shirts are neither too tight nor too baggy.

◎   Fabric falls smoothly at waist, rather than binding tight.

◎   Enough ease at bustline to prevent 'monobosom' look.

◎   Bra straps do not reveal themselves at neck opening.

◎   With sleeveless tops, you can lift arm without revealing bra.

◎   Long sleeves end at wrist bone.

PROPER FIT – FEEL CUES

◎   Top is easy to pull on.

◎   Shoulder seam falls at notch between arm bone and shoulder.

◎   Armholes do not bind.

◎   Tail generous enough to tuck in.

◎   Polo neck doesn't strangulate.

— Step 4: Alterations

Have you ever noticed how the clothes worn by shop mannequins are often pinned snug down the back? Think about it. If a *dress dummy* needs help looking good, we poor mortals have really got problems. But we do have an ally in our quest for perfection, and that is a great alterations person. Call this person a seamstress, a tailor, a dressmaker or what have you, she (or he) is one of the second-hand shopper's best friends. This kind of professional can often quickly dispatch small flaws that show up in the fit tests. These problems include:

◎   jackets or dresses fitting slightly too big over the back, bust, waist and hips

◎   sleeves (especially jackets) that are too long

◎   hemlines that are too long

◎   waistbands that are too loose
◎   backsides that are too loose

Bear in mind, though, that massive downsizing rarely works. Seams can be taken in here and there, but the proportions of a complete overhaul will never look perfect – you're better off leaving the piece on the rack.

Enlarging ('taking out') a slightly tight or too-short garment is another alterations option, but success hinges on having adequate spare fabric at the seam in question (usually more than one inch). Specific possibilities include:

◎   easing snug shoulders or back
◎   lengthening sleeves that are too short
◎   lengthening hemlines that are too short
◎   enlarging waistbands that are too tight
◎   gaining ease in backsides that are too tight

Here again (here especially), alterations can only be taken so far. If you are considering an undersized garment with the notion of having it taken out, take a good look at the amount of material at the seams, and consider getting a second opinion from the shop manager. Beware, too, that letting down hems may leave a **line of demarcation**. To tell, flatten the material to both sides of the hemline to see if the line is lighter than the surrounding fabric. If so, it may be diminished by dabbing with vinegar, but the results are unknowable at the buying stage, and you may be better off holding out for a less demanding piece.

What is the best way to find a great alterations person? First, seek the advice of friends and relatives. In so doing, avoid the temptation to go with Aunt Jean, who'd love a bit of practice on her new Singer. You need a professional – someone who not only knows her basques from her bobbins, but can advise you on fit and drape. Your favourite dress agency is a good source of information. Local boutique and department shops usually have seamstresses on call, but this entails buying at retail to make the connection. Many dry-cleaning operations have a sewer at the shop, but proceed with caution – likewise with people found through the Yellow Pages or the internet. Try all of them out with simple jobs first. You don't want to leave fragile vintage pieces or ball gowns to an untested stranger.

While alterations are a splendid thing, they require time and effort. Getting the clothes to the pro and paying the charge is, for many, a psychological hurdle. If you're buying clothes on the basis of getting them fixed, be *sure* that you'll get to it, otherwise the piece will sit unworn in a corner, making you feel guilty. If you're the kind of person who can't be bothered with one more chore, be sure your fit is great without extra help.

One final point about alterations: if you buy a vintage garment of extraordinary merit, for example a couture piece or mint-condition antique, be aware that alterations will sharply degrade its resale value. If you're buying it to wear, go ahead and alter. But if you're hem-haw-not-sure if you'll ever actually put it on, then have a hard think before messing with those seams.

— Special figure issues

Women who are unusually short, unusually heavy or pregnant are faced with particular challenges when it comes to getting flattering fit. If you're a member of one of the first two categories, a relationship with an alterations pro is particularly beneficial. Pregnant women need to do something rather different – envision their figure not as it is, but as it will be, allowing for flexibility yet maintaining style as the baby grows. All of these topics have been covered at length in purpose-written style guides. A bookshop, a resource like *amazon.co.uk*, or your local library are other excellent sources of information. Specialist magazines may also prove helpful. In the meantime, here are some points that apply specifically to these shopping challenges when buying second-hand.

THE LARGER FIGURE

Getting great fit has long been difficult for big women shopping second-hand, if only because the choice has been so limited. But better days are dawning. Mainstream manufacturers have finally woken up to the spending power and style desires of plus-sized women, and are now producing a solid range of fashionable clothing. There's always a time lag between retail innovations and the second-hand echo, so the dress-agency and charity-shop situation may need a while longer to improve dramatically. But it will.

Dress-agency owners are an invaluable resource for you. Call or, better yet, visit the shops in your area and investigate the kinds of garments they're getting. Be sure to inform the manager that you'll be a good customer for quality merchandise if the size is right, and leave her with your name, number and size details. This alone may spur her to find consignors who meet your criteria – creative matchmaking is what the business is all about. Charity shops won't be nearly as responsive, of course, but it still may be worthwhile to investigate whether your locals get donations of larger-sized clothing.

To find vintage pieces in larger sizes, you can't beat eBay for instant access, the downside being you can't see it or actually try it on. Here again, though, if you establish a relationship with given sellers they will keep you in mind (and if they're sharp, keep you alerted) when new pieces arrive in your size.

THE SHORTER FIGURE

Here again, second-hand shops tend to magnify the poor selection of styles available in the larger retail world. But don't despair. Many of the same strategies used by larger women can work for you, especially calling around and finding out what the dress agencies in your area are stocking. Again, your interest alone may encourage a savvy shop owner to seek out more petite consignments.

You should also take heart in the fact that you have it all over your bigger sisters when it comes to shopping for vintage clothing, especially if you're fond of the gorgeous delicacies of decades long past. Where today's average-sized women would split the seams, you can slip with ease into a muslin blouse, a flapper gown or amazing tapestry slippers. Take advantage of the styles that the rest of us can't get into.

THE PREGNANT FIGURE

Congratulations. No, for the other reason. Charity shops were made for your expanding waistline. Where else will you find drawstring trousers, blousy tops, jeans in all sizes and other fabulous gear for a mere fraction of the price at those wretched maternity shops?

Granted, specialised maternity clothes are the best way to go when it comes to business suits and swimming costumes, but, for everything else, second-hand rules. In charity shops, simply choose larger sizes as you grow bigger – at these prices, it won't matter if you only get a month or so of wear. In the last trimester, elasticised and otherwise expandable waistlines and billowy tops will do the job. In vintage shops, empire waistlines and trapeze cuts are made for you. Don't forget to key in the words 'vintage' and 'maternity' on eBay every so often – you might be charmed by a 1960s Mothercare top that'll have your prenatal class green with envy (or maybe that's morning sickness; either way, they'll admire your individuality).

The elements of personal style

In recent years, film actresses have become icons of chic, their images buffed to a degree last seen in the studio era of the 1940s. Since they're actresses, the stylishness seems as natural as breathing, but don't think for a second that they're going it all on their own. For camera-worthy events, a star will rely on an image guru, a stylist like Jessica Paster, who has dressed Minnie Driver, Cate Blanchett and Jane Leeves, among many others. A stylist slaves to ensure that the frock's colour makes the client's skin glow, the cut disguises any tiny flaws that remain in her figure, and the proportions add to the aura of elegance and grace. That's the Hollywood way to high style.

Interestingly, this can also be the Slough way to high style. Or Cork, or Aberdeen. Who needs stylists, anyway? Let's be our own gurus. We're two-thirds there as it is. Style begins with fabulous quality and carries through with great fit. The last part of the equation is buying clothes that celebrate the figure, colouring, and that certain inner something that makes you *you*. This chapter is all about pinning down what kinds of pieces those are.

Is it easy? On one hand, yes. With proper guidance and focus, it doesn't take very long to learn what kinds of cuts, colours and combinations look best. Yet the haphazard nature of second-hand shopping means we must search *that much harder* for pieces that fill our needs. Wonder clothes – the kind that fit and flatter and fall right in with the existing wardrobe – simply don't surface every day. In fact, world-class style is hard enough to achieve when money and other resources are limitless. Women attempting to be brilliant second-hand shoppers must be ruthless – able to say no to inappropriate pieces (no matter how cute or one-of-a-kind), willing to work through acres of also-rans, and patient enough to try again and again, until those few perfect items are found.

Frankly, most of us don't have the single-mindedness it takes to become a full-on icon. But if you want to ratchet up your style quotient by even a few degrees, read on. The smarts you gain will go a long way to making *your* dress sense the envy of others.

Note: this advice and much of what follows about crafting a personal style does not apply to girls under the age of twenty-five. If you're a teenager, a student, you're meant to experiment, try on looks, make big mistakes. Go crazy with clothes in your younger years, and take lots of photos to memorialise your style phases. By the time twenty-five (or so) candles are flaming on your cake, looking great consistently will start to make sense.

— The one true figure type: imperfect

Nobody thinks their body is perfect, even stars and supermodels (*especially* stars and supermodels). Short of plastic surgery, women have a choice. We can lie around and moan about the cruelty of fate, which cursed us with a flat chest, big feet and narrow shoulders (fill in your own blanks here). Or we can quit moaning and take control. Start taking steps to *manage* the figure we were born with. Not necessarily with diet or exercise, but with the garments we choose to adorn our body. The French have a special term for this, of course. It's called *mettre en valeur*, which roughly translates as 'putting your best forward' via clothes.

On Charting My Own Path
by Zandra Rhodes, fashion designer

My first vivid memory of women wearing wonderful
clothing was ballroom dancing – that's how my mother
and father met. I remember my mother sewing the
costumes and they seemed so exotic with the sequins and
yards of tulle . . . She taught fashion at Medway College
of Art and would put on dress shows, so this was
another early influence, but at the time I did not want to
pursue fashion; textile design was my true passion.
I never managed to get offered a job as a textile designer
when leaving the Royal College of Art, so in 1963 I first
did prints for other designers, then I started my own
business with Sylvia Ayton and the Fulham Road Clothes
Shop. I was convinced I could make beautiful clothes,
even without formal design training, so then I went on
my own. One important touchstone for me was Max
Tilke's compendium of peasant costume – those pictures
convinced me that my vision was on the right track and
I could be proud of having a different approach.
It didn't take long for me to get noticed and I took my
collection to Diana Vreeland, editor-in-chief of *US*

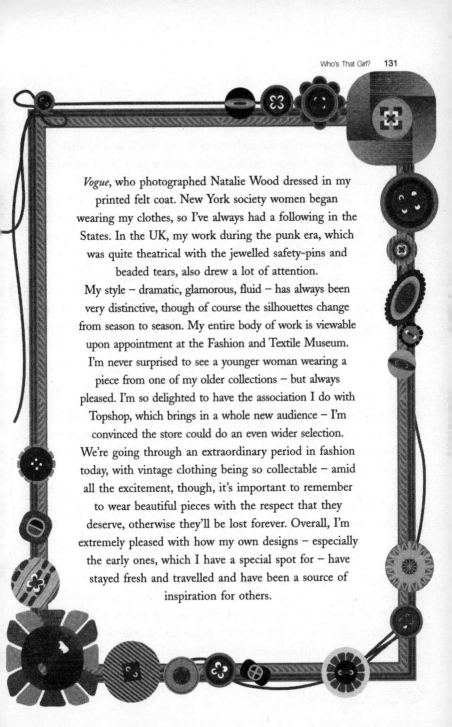

Vogue, who photographed Natalie Wood dressed in my printed felt coat. New York society women began wearing my clothes, so I've always had a following in the States. In the UK, my work during the punk era, which was quite theatrical with the jewelled safety-pins and beaded tears, also drew a lot of attention.

My style – dramatic, glamorous, fluid – has always been very distinctive, though of course the silhouettes change from season to season. My entire body of work is viewable upon appointment at the Fashion and Textile Museum. I'm never surprised to see a younger woman wearing a piece from one of my older collections – but always pleased. I'm so delighted to have the association I do with Topshop, which brings in a whole new audience – I'm convinced the store could do an even wider selection. We're going through an extraordinary period in fashion today, with vintage clothing being so collectable – amid all the excitement, though, it's important to remember to wear beautiful pieces with the respect that they deserve, otherwise they'll be lost forever. Overall, I'm extremely pleased with how my own designs – especially the early ones, which I have a special spot for – have stayed fresh and travelled and have been a source of inspiration for others.

Few traditions have as long and distinguished a history as *mettre en valeur*. There are quite a few books and perennial magazine articles written about dressing to enhance body type. While useful in a general way, providing an easy-to-grasp formula, along with the good advice come some drawbacks:

The advice can be over-generalised: 'Don't go strapless if you have broad shoulders.' This is sensible if you're a stocky 5 ft 3 in, but what if you're built like Elle Macpherson?

Sometimes it reinforces outdated values: Big bottoms, for example, are typically considered a curse. But in the real world, many observers find an ample bottom far more feminine and beautiful than, say, a swan-like neck. In the workplace, it's better to flaunt your accounting skills, but off-hours don't hide a spectacular asset under some loose drapey shroud.

Body type is fluid: Women gain and lose weight with perverse regularity. Exercise can make the scrawniest shoulder a thing of beauty. Childbearing does all kinds of colourful things to the figure. Ageing shortens the appearance of the torso (by encouraging breasts downward) and lengthens and flattens the backside. A formula that was letter-perfect a couple of years ago could be a disaster today. Buying a garment because it fits the former you won't do the current version any favours.

Body-shape guides try to fit an entire produce section into apple-, pear- and papaya-shaped compartments: Take, for example, the classic pear. According to the formulas, this woman has narrowish shoulders, an 'average' bustline and biggish hips. But have you seen how many kinds of pears there are in Tesco lately? Some breasts will be larger, some smaller, some waists narrower, some thighs shorter. While the guidelines may be accurate in a general way, they will never surpass what you determine on your own, with the aid of an unflinching eye and a good three-way mirror.

Which is where the next section comes in. It's a contemporary version of old-fashioned *mettre en valeur*. Rather than head-to-toe formulas for a limited number of body types, these are guidelines on how to downplay specific flaws, found on all kinds of figures. Once they're under the rug, you're free to emphasise what's best, be it slim ankles, a beautiful throat or womanly curves.

If you're unsure of your pluses and minuses, have a heart-to-heart with a good girlfriend, or the person who alters your clothes or your favourite second-hand professional. Resist the notion of asking your sister – she may be annoyingly eager to dwell on the flaws. Once you're armed with an accurate sense of the raw material, consult the guidelines below, remembering that they are guidelines only, not firm 'dos' or 'don'ts'. Let your own eyes make the final call. Also remember that at the quality level we're shooting for, designers routinely pull off miracles of cut and drape. A style that ordinarily makes you look like a brick house could turn out mighty mighty on your figure.

Finally, if a weekend afternoon comes along that sees you short on money but long on time, why not spend it in a great vintage or charity shop, trying stuff on, trying stuff on, trying stuff on? Cowl necks, polo necks, boat necks, scoops. Pencil skirts, rah-rah skirts, miniskirts, kilts. Nipped-waist suits, Ally-McBeal-long-jacket-short-skirt combos. Low-waisted flares, high-waisted mum jeans, wide-legged pyjama trousers. Dungarees. Bring your notebook and make a record of what suits and what doesn't. Pay careful attention to the effects of colour and trim while you're at it. You'll come away a thousand times smarter about your signature looks. And you thought you had nothing to do!

THE ROYAL COVER UP

A king was supposed to look and act his part. If nature did not endow him with a regal appearance, he felt that he had to make up for this deficiency by dressing for the part he was supposed to play. Any physical defect would detract from an imposing appearance and court dressmakers vied with each other in devising clever means of covering nature's deficiencies . . . Long skirts were brought into favour because the daughters of Louis XI of France had misshapen legs and feet. Charles VII adopted long coats to cover ill-shaped legs, and Louis XIII, who was prematurely bald, used a peruke [wig] made in imitation of long curls. Hoop skirts were said to have originated with Madame de Montespan to conceal defects produced as a result of an accident . . . Queen Elizabeth, in spite of the homely appearance which historians accord her, was exceedingly vain and ordered the court dressmakers to produce fashions which would cover up her defects and make the most of the good features

she possessed. One of her naturally good features was her small waist and in order to enhance it she used a corset to constrict the flesh to thirteen inches. Cloth proved to be too weak, so whalebone was used to reinforce it. The high neck ruff which is so characteristic of that period, was adopted by the Queen to cover up a long, thin and unshapely neck.

Mary Ellen Roach and Joan Bubolz Eicher,
Dress, Adornment and the Social Order

— Those very special parts of you

FEET

Unless you get regular pedicures, don't expect your feet to look divine in slinky sandals. Untended, most women's feet look like hell. A more discreet, covered-up look will be much sexier.

LONG FEET

Consider: A low-cut vamp (the part of the shoe that covers the top of the foot) and a slight-to-moderate heel. Matching hose colour to shoes will help disguise foot length.

Beware of: Two-toned shoes, T-straps and any footwear that is lighter than flesh (or hose) colour.

BROAD FEET/BUNIONS

Consider: Styles that emphasise the length of foot rather than the width (in other words, the main decorative elements of the shoe should run *down* the foot rather than *across* it). Matching hose and shoes will also minimise width.

Beware of: Straps that cross the instep, and shoes that are too tight across the instep. Wearing shoes too snug will *not* disguise a wide foot (ugly bulges will appear in the leather) and may cause long-term damage.

LEGS

SHORT LEGS

Consider: Elongating legs with monochrome shoes/hose/skirt or trouser combos, and slight-to-moderate heels. Slingback shoes, a low vamp and a pointed rather than rounded toe will also elongate the leg. If your legs are shapely, consider shorter skirts.

Beware of: Adding lots of width around the legs (with wide-legged trousers, full skirts), or super-skinny drainpipes that draw attention to the legs.

CHUNKY ANKLES (AMERICAN GIRLS CALL THEM 'CANKLES')

Consider: A low heel will be more flattering than flats. Matching hose to shoe colour will create a longer line. A low vamp will draw the eye down from the ankle.

Beware of: T-straps, mules, clogs, ankle boots or any other shoes that lure the eye up towards the ankle rather than down towards the toe. Ankle bracelets are not a stylish choice unless you're working a heavy seventies look.

THICK CALVES

Consider: Streamline legs by matching hose to shoes; slightly sheer hose will be more flattering than opaque.

ANOTHER FRENCH TRICK

Parisian ladies are unanimous on the subject: hose should match shoe colour, rather than the skirt or dress above. The reason? In that city of leg-worshippers, any visual technique that elongates the limbs is adopted *tout de suite*. Shoe/hose matching does just that, by creating an unbroken line from toe to hem.

Beware of: Very high heels and/or poorly balanced shoes (which cause calf muscles to bunch), flats, knee socks, knee-high boots, tight and/or light leggings, and light or patterned hose.

SKINNY CALVES
Consider: Textured and/or dark hose.
Beware of: Very high heels will emphasise lean calves; lower heels may be more flattering.

HEAVY THIGHS
Consider: Hemlines that fall below the knee. When wearing form-fitting trousers, pair them with a tunic or jacket that skims over thighs. Longer skirts with a slit to the knee are another stylish option.
Beware of: Any horizontal lines that fall over and therefore emphasise this area – either in a garment's pattern or from its own hemline.

CELLULITE/VARICOSE VEINS
Consider: If you favour short skirts, be sure hose has enough colour and support to smooth any irregularities.
Beware of: Light-coloured and/or skimpy stretch garments, which may mould to and emphasise bumps and ridges.

HIPS/BOTTOM
Wide hips and an ample bottom are feminine traits celebrated throughout civilization. But if nature was in a *very* generous mood, these tips can help.

BROAD HIPS
Consider: Tops and tunics with fabric that floats or drapes prettily over the hips. Choose garments with strong vertical lines or patterns. Long jackets and vests will draw attention upward, as will light or brightly coloured tops. Trapeze dresses and A-line skirts (wider at the bottom than at the top) can work well. Pleated trousers are usually more flattering than flat-front styles. If your waist is slender, draw the eye up with a beautiful belt. Emphasise neckline with scarves/jewellery. Consider small shoulder pads to balance proportions.
Beware of: Tops (including jumpers and jackets) that end on the roomiest part of the hips. Also, if your backside isn't toned, avoid stretchy or flimsy fabric that clings to this area.

JUTTING HIPBONES
Consider: Side pockets can minimise the prominence.
Beware of: Flat-front or size-zip trousers, and tight skirts.

HEMLINES

Most women buy skirts and let them hang where they may. Convenient, yes, but it passes up one of the simplest style improvements there is. Stylish women make hem length a personal trademark, revealing the legs to their best advantage.

To find your best drop zone, talk to your alterations person or enlist a friend with a good eye and steady hand with dressmaking pins. The goal is to have the hem hit a particularly attractive point of your leg. For 95% of us, it's where the limb curves inward: either a few inches above or below the knee, or below the widest part of the calf. For the sake of wardrobe flexibility, you may want to pick two target spots – one for long and one for shorter skirts. Some more hemline tips:

 Once past the age of twenty, the knee develops all kinds of knobs, fat pads and dimples that give it character but take it out of the running for the most attractive part of the leg. For this reason, skirts shouldn't ever fall right above or directly

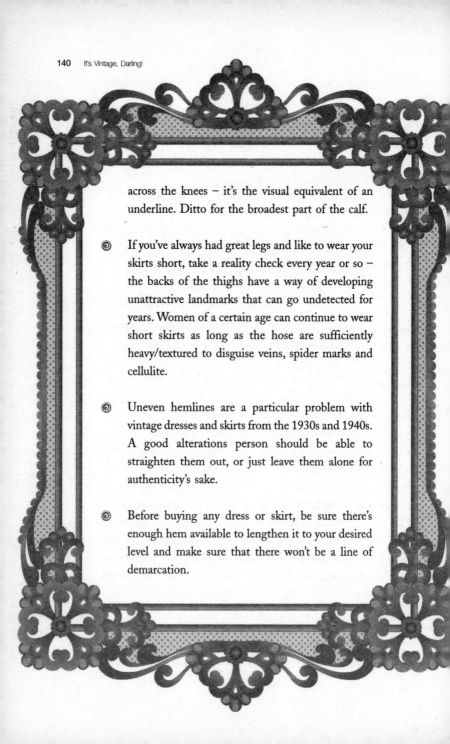

across the knees – it's the visual equivalent of an underline. Ditto for the broadest part of the calf.

- If you've always had great legs and like to wear your skirts short, take a reality check every year or so – the backs of the thighs have a way of developing unattractive landmarks that can go undetected for years. Women of a certain age can continue to wear short skirts as long as the hose are sufficiently heavy/textured to disguise veins, spider marks and cellulite.

- Uneven hemlines are a particular problem with vintage dresses and skirts from the 1930s and 1940s. A good alterations person should be able to straighten them out, or just leave them alone for authenticity's sake.

- Before buying any dress or skirt, be sure there's enough hem available to lengthen it to your desired level and make sure that there won't be a line of demarcation.

No hips
Consider: Low-rise, flat-front and size-zip trousers, as well as any trousers or skirts with gathers below the waistband. Pleated all-around skirts and kilts will also look good.
Beware of: Straight skirts that cling.

Big bottom
Consider: As with broad hips, above. Also, be sure knickers fit well to avoid frame-like panty lines.
Beware of: Bold patterns on trousers, long shorts and shorter skirts. Hot pants, needless to say, are out.

Flat bottom
Consider: Skirts and trousers gathered all around the waist can add fullness. Patterned trousers and skirts are another good option.
Beware of: Drawing belt too tight – this will place unattractive puckers above bottom.

Waistline
Do the terms 'short-waisted' and 'long-waisted' confuse you? Me too. If fashion writers would say what they mean – 'short-midriffed' and 'long-midriffed' – they'd spare us all a lot of puzzlement. What's being measured here is the stretch of torso between the bottom of the breasts and the natural waistline (where the body bends). If you can fit a hand span or more there, you're long-midriffed (long-waisted). If you can't, you're short-midriffed (short-waisted). We all go in one direction or another – at least until older age sets in, when, due to the southerly ramblings of the breasts, everyone tends to get shorter here.

Short midriff
Consider: Tops and buttoned jackets that skim over waistline and end near the hips are preferable to garments that are tucked into or end at the waist. Draw attention upward with scarves and jewellery.

Beware of: Thick belts, unusually high waistbands, and strong colour differences between top and waistband.

LONG MIDRIFF
Consider: If waist is slender, basques, chunky belts and high waistbands can be worn to flattering effect. Cropped tops are great on younger women, but on older ones (you know who you are) this look is hen-dressed-like-chick, no matter how toned your abs are.
Beware of: Low-rise and drop-waisted styles, which may look unbalanced.

BIG TUM
Consider: A top made of fluid, draping fabric will be more flattering than one of clingy material. Waistband with gentle gathers. Empire/high-waisted styles and trapeze tops are also excellent for this common figure problem.
Beware of: Styles where belts ride on the most prominent part of the stomach. Also avoid light-coloured stretch tops worn over stretchy skirt or trousers – this only emphasises curvature.

BUSTLINE
As with big bottoms, most style books urge you to 'normalise' very small or very large breasts. The truth is, either can be extraordinarily attractive (small-breasted women can wear slinky halters or other minimal coverage for evening; large-breasted women can work their décolletage). During the day, the right bra will do wonders to counter any visual imbalance. Otherwise:

LARGE BREASTS
Consider: Double-breasted jackets and V-necks, which will lay angles over the curves, minimising them. Tight-waisted jackets with a peplum (a little skirt of fabric running around the lower hem), which draw the eye down.
Beware of: Piped pockets or those with decorative buttons on breasts. Clinging sweaters. Busy or very light fabric may draw the eye to breasts.

SMALL BREASTS
Consider: Pockets and other trimming details on bust lend visual impact. Waistcoats are often very flattering. Attractive jewellery at base of neck will

draw the eye upward. Well-draped scarves are another option.

Beware of: Bulky shoulder pads that emphasise curves on shoulder to detriment of those below.

SHOULDERS

BROAD SHOULDERS

Consider: Halters, V-necks and scoop necks, which all draw the eye towards the neck.

Beware of: Shoulder pads, as well as any detailing along shoulder that draws the eye to this area. Very thin straps or no straps may be problematic, depending on your figure and the garment's other characteristics.

NARROW SHOULDERS

Consider: Small shoulder pads will help balance your lines, as will boat (wide-cut) necklines.

Beware of: Drop-shoulder styles, V-shaped and scoop necklines. Be particularly wary of long pendant necklaces that echo slope of the shoulders.

NECK

OVERLY LONG NECK

Consider: Stand-up or other high collars, scarves and jewellery at base of neck, dangly earrings.

Beware of: Collarless jackets or tops, scarves or jewellery that hangs very low.

OVERLY SHORT NECK

Consider: V-neck or scoop neck openings, long necklaces, collarless styles.

Beware of: High or stand-up collars, choker necklaces.

DOUBLE CHIN/WEAK CHIN

Consider: High (but not tight) polo necks, collars. V-necks and V-forming necklaces can also be flattering. Scarves draped around neck can be lovely.

Beware of: Round-neck styles, high-neck styles that squash skin under chin.

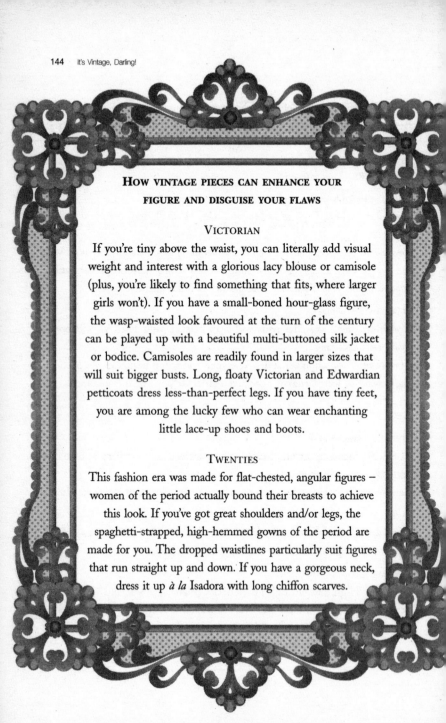

HOW VINTAGE PIECES CAN ENHANCE YOUR FIGURE AND DISGUISE YOUR FLAWS

VICTORIAN

If you're tiny above the waist, you can literally add visual weight and interest with a glorious lacy blouse or camisole (plus, you're likely to find something that fits, where larger girls won't). If you have a small-boned hour-glass figure, the wasp-waisted look favoured at the turn of the century can be played up with a beautiful multi-buttoned silk jacket or bodice. Camisoles are readily found in larger sizes that will suit bigger busts. Long, floaty Victorian and Edwardian petticoats dress less-than-perfect legs. If you have tiny feet, you are among the lucky few who can wear enchanting little lace-up shoes and boots.

TWENTIES

This fashion era was made for flat-chested, angular figures – women of the period actually bound their breasts to achieve this look. If you've got great shoulders and/or legs, the spaghetti-strapped, high-hemmed gowns of the period are made for you. The dropped waistlines particularly suit figures that run straight up and down. If you have a gorgeous neck, dress it up *à la* Isadora with long chiffon scarves.

THIRTIES

Girls with fabulous backs and bums are so flattered by the backless, trim-fitting 1930s styles. Bias-cut dresses will add seductive curves to slender frames, and a fabulous brocade or velvet opera coat makes for high daytime drama on larger figures. If you've got marvellous cleavage, a sparkly brooch pinned on a lapel is a super-subtle yet devastating way of drawing attention, while a slender belt with a gorgeous diamanté art-deco buckle will draw the eye to a lovely waist.

FORTIES

If you're on the petite side, the platform soles and ample shoulders of this era will add tremendous presence and style. An ample bustline can be downplayed with sharply cut lapels. Seamed stockings draw attention to gorgeous calves. If you feel even slightly self-conscious about your lower half, put on a cunning little hat. Guess where people will look.

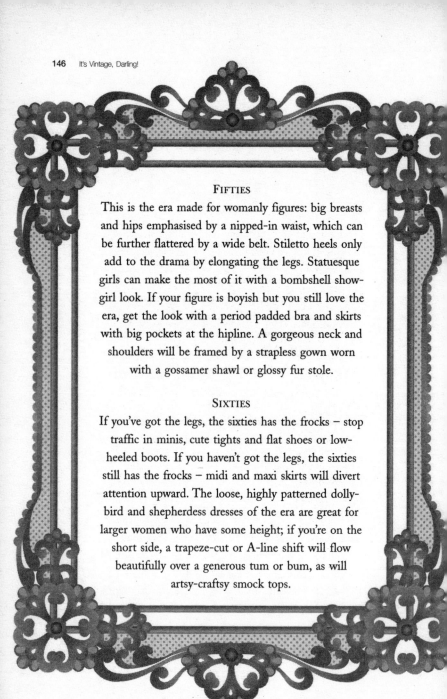

FIFTIES

This is the era made for womanly figures: big breasts and hips emphasised by a nipped-in waist, which can be further flattered by a wide belt. Stiletto heels only add to the drama by elongating the legs. Statuesque girls can make the most of it with a bombshell show-girl look. If your figure is boyish but you still love the era, get the look with a period padded bra and skirts with big pockets at the hipline. A gorgeous neck and shoulders will be framed by a strapless gown worn with a gossamer shawl or glossy fur stole.

SIXTIES

If you've got the legs, the sixties has the frocks – stop traffic in minis, cute tights and flat shoes or low-heeled boots. If you haven't got the legs, the sixties still has the frocks – midi and maxi skirts will divert attention upward. The loose, highly patterned dolly-bird and shepherdess dresses of the era are great for larger women who have some height; if you're on the short side, a trapeze-cut or A-line shift will flow beautifully over a generous tum or bum, as will artsy-craftsy smock tops.

SEVENTIES

The great trouser suits of this decade are flattering to a wide range of figure types, likewise the stretchy dresses. If you've got long, slender thighs, showcase them with a pair of striped leg-warmers. Shorter girls can get a leg-up with some Terry De Havilland platforms. Big busts can be concealed (or saucily revealed) with all manner of outtasight seventies waistcoats.

EIGHTIES

The styles of this decade swung back again to the waisted and woman-centric. Make an entrance in a drop-dead power suit that flaunts your cleavage and tick-tock walk. Black fishnets and glossy Doc Martens are alarmingly sexy on great legs; oversized slouch socks down around the ankles likewise emphasise wonderful pins. If you've got beautiful upper arms, don't forget the jolt of a Flashdance sweatshirt (try to find a gorgeous off-the-shoulder wool equivalent), and, lastly, if you've got nerves of steel and buns to match, consider hunting down some Alexander McQueen-style bumsters . . .

— What's your colour?

Colour Me Beautiful (*www.cmb.co.uk*) and rival programmes aim to help women find the best colours to wear near their faces. Whether based on 'seasons', or warm/cool theory, or some other principle, the systems exploit the fact that everyone has good and bad colours, based on a given hue's interaction with hair, eye and skin tone.

If you're unsure about your best colours, professional assessment can be helpful – as long as you find a pro who knows what she's doing. Like hair stylists, colour analysts have varying degrees of talent. It's always best to go with a personal recommendation from someone whose colour choices are always dead on. A less pricy route is the one to your local library, which will almost certainly have a few books to delve into. Easier still is following the guidelines below:

Knowing your best colours doesn't mean basing your *entire wardrobe* on these hues. For one thing, it's hard enough to amass decent basics in black and white, much less in pine-green or plum. For another, your two or three ideal colours might not mesh well with each other. A smarter strategy is to base your wardrobe on flattering neutral tones instead, reserving your best colours as **highlights** or **accents** (in the form of face-framing scarves, tops and necklaces). This strategy also counters the frustration of colour limitations when second-hand shopping. While you'll rarely find a lemon-yellow cardigan that is beautifully made and fits just right, a grey version is a decent possibility. Pair this with a lemon scarf or little top, and you've achieved the good looks without all the hassle.

The user-friendly nature of neutrals is old news for fashion readers. The reason is obvious: it vastly simplifies both shopping and getting dressed. When everything you own goes with everything else, your wardrobe stops being item-based and becomes outfit-based, a real blessing when the alarm clock goes off at 6:30 a.m.

SHORTCUTS TO YOUR BEST COLOURS

◎ Your skin tone is the most reliable clue. Everyone's skin is either warm-toned (with yellow-beige-brown-olive undertones) or cool-toned (with blue-rose-pink-purple undertones). Warm-toned women generally look best in clothes in the yellow-red-brown family; cool-toned women in the blue-green-purple family.

◎ In general, if there is a strong contrast between your skin/eye/natural hair colour (for example, light eyes/dark hair, or pale skin/dark eyes, hair) you can get away with punchy colours. If, however, your hair/skin/eyes are close to the same intensity, more muted shades will best become you.

◎ You are likely to look fabulous wearing any of the colours that are visible in your eye's iris (check under natural light).

◎ Believe it or not, some experts hold that the colours of your inner membranes (inner cheek, for example) are also flattering – why not give it a try and see?

◎ Ask your hair stylist or colourist what *they* think would suit you.

◎ Go through old pictures and pull the ones where you look great. Was it the colour you were wearing?

◎ Pick a stylish celebrity with colouring similar to yours and watch her choices (believe me, she's getting expensive advice on the subject).

Despite their soft-spoken nature, neutrals aren't boring – there's an entire hushed rainbow to choose from. If your accent colours lean towards bright, jewel tones, you might consider black, white, taupe, dark grey or navy as your base neutral. If you are flattered by more muted shades, black, cream, beige or light grey might be better options. Pick one or two neutrals and stick with them, at least from season to season. Life is so much simpler, and good style is so much easier, when colour matching stops being a big issue.

'It's beige! My colour!'
**Fashion designer Elsie de Wolfe, upon first sight
of the Acropolis**

— *More colourful tips*

◎ They say we can distinguish 10,000 different colours. Keep this in mind when trying to team separates, especially those made of like fabrics. Even if a skirt and jacket appear to be a close colour match in the dressing room, their differences will be obvious in sunlight, and you'll look clueless rather than chic. It's actually better to pair decidedly different textures or colours – say a black chunky-knit cardigan with smoothly woven wool trousers, or a cream jacket with beige trousers.

◎ The best tailoring in the world is worthless if the colour makes you look wan. Buy an off-colour item only if you will religiously wear a scarf or other intermediary piece to counter its effect.

◎ Bright, solid colours (say magenta and yellow) can work wonderfully together, but it takes an especially sharp eye to pull them off. For inspiration, check out the picture books on the great couturiers.

◎ Two different colours in one outfit often benefit from the addition of a patterned scarf or jewellery that picks up the tones of both. The accessory acts as a 'peacemaker', harmonising the contrasting aspects.

◎   Heightened make-up will let you go brighter than usual – but beware the fine line between heightened and clownish.

◎   If you're considering a garment with a multi-coloured pattern, hang it against a neutral background and look at it from ten paces away – the resulting colour meld might not be ideal for your complexion.

◎   Every so often, try on a shade you usually skip. Colouring changes slightly over time, and you may be very surprised by the outcome.

◎   Always check colours in natural daylight. Ask to bring a piece near a window or even outside to consider the hue (this will also highlight any stains).

—Proportion

Designers spend ages working out proportion when creating a suit or dress: widening a lapel here, downsizing a button there, trying to get it all balanced. Architects do the same thing when they draw a building, as do graphic artists when they develop a new logo. Good design makes it to the catwalks, into *Elle Deco*, onto a can of cola. Bad design, most of the time, ends up in the rubbish bin.

Unless it's home-grown. The kind that crops up when amateurs like you and I try to assemble outfits out of separate garment pieces. Unlike designers, we do not have a highly educated understanding of what lines and shapes work best together. As a result, it's rare to see a casual outfit that clicks brilliantly in all of its parts. Need it be said that the second-hand shopping mode doesn't help matters any. Our separates are *really* separate, sometimes even centuries apart.

Still, it's possible to create lovely proportions with a hotchpotch of pieces. The trick lies in knowing something about the innate rules of visual harmony.

Without doubt, the one that counts is the '**Golden Mean**'. Why is this one so special? Because its principles are practically hardwired into our brains.

When people are presented with a rectangle and asked to divide it into two parts, they hardly ever cut it in half, nor do they cut it into one very big piece and one very small. Instead, the dividing line falls somewhere at a point in between. This intermediate point is *so* attractive to *so* many people it was mathematically fixed thousands of years ago, by philosophers in ancient Greece. They determined that if the rectangle is 8 units in height or length, the dividing line will fall about 3 units along, leaving a second segment of 5 units. In honour of its popularity, they called the 3:5:8 ratio the Golden Mean.

The ratio was first put into formal design practice in the Greeks' temple to Athena, the Parthenon. Its appeal hasn't diminished with time – we continue to see it all over the place. On cereal boxes, for example, and paperback books, where the lettering typically falls about a third of the way down. It's not just visual designers who love the Golden Mean – scholars have discovered that creative minds as diverse as the Roman poet Virgil and the Hungarian composer Bela Bartok unconsciously used the ratio when setting up the structure of their masterworks. Nature, too, inclines towards the Golden Mean, causing trees to branch and rocks to fracture in patterns conforming to the principle.

This is the long way of saying that there's something about the Golden Mean that's innately pleasing to the eye. It makes sense to apply its principles when putting together an outfit of separates. In simple terms, *the pieces making up the whole should be just different enough in length and volume to create an eye-pleasing balance together.*

To clarify this, take a look at what happens when the Golden Mean is ignored. Remember those infamous 'dress for success' suits of the 1970s? Even back then they looked dowdy. Why? A boxy, hip-length jacket paired with an A-line, knee-length skirt results in components of near-equal (4:4) visual weight. Omigod boring zzzzzzzzz. Compare that to the sharper, unequal-yet-harmonious combos we see today and you start to understand what good proportion is all about. Here are some more examples:

◎   The eye appreciates harmonious differences in volume as well as in length. In general, roomy (and especially A-line) tops look better with slim trousers and skirts, while baggy or flowing bottoms tend to look ultra-smart with body-skimming tops. The recent trend of wearing dresses over trousers looked kind of cool if the wearer was tall and slim (i.e., Trinny), but for the rest of us the proportions were nearly impossible to work with.

◎   Likewise, separates don't look stylish when there's *too great* a difference between the component parts. There's a reason that clowns wear those teeny tiny hats.

◎   Imbalanced proportions are often seen with lapels – when a too-skinny blouse lapel or collar is placed atop a broad-lapelled jacket, the effect on the eye is uncomfortable. Here it would be better to tuck the blouse all the way under.

◎   Last century, the French architect Le Corbusier discovered that the human body is split according to the Golden Mean, with the head to the navel equalling 3 units, and the navel to the foot equalling 5. Therefore, any outfit that splits your body neatly at the waist (top and trousers, top and monochrome skirt/hose/shoe combo) is likely to fall into pleasing proportion.

◎   Ideally, the 3:5 relationship should echo throughout the outfit – with breast pockets proportionately smaller than those at the hips.

◎   Moreover, breast pockets appear slightly more refined if they sit about a third of the way from the shoulders to waist rather than exactly halfway.

◎   The 3:5 proportion also works upside down (think about traditional Asian garb). In Western wear this translates into tunics over slim trousers or skirts.

◎   The great designers consciously play death-defying balancing acts with the 3:5:8 and less-perfect ratios – it's wisest to leave this sort of thing to the professionals.

◎   Accessories fall prey to proportional problems, too. If you're wearing a wide belt over a blouse, be sure there's enough fabric showing below the belt to balance its visual weight.

◎   Colours and contrast also play a role in proportions. White and bright colours have more visual weight, a heavier punch, than black and muted colours. This is why long stretches of light-toned leg revealed by a short skirt can look girlishly overexposed, while the same legs look chic when dark-toned. It's also why a priest's white collar/black robe looks sharper than an oversize white sweater with a black turtleneck underneath.

◎   Shoes also play a role in the proportion equation. Generally speaking, the more delicate the fabric above, the more slender the heel, while heavier fabrics are better balanced by a chunkier heel.

◎   If a skirt or dress falls to the calf or lower, a mid-heel works best to balance it.

◎   When knee-high boots are worn with a shorter skirt, the slice of visible leg catches the eye and disrupts proportions. Unless that slice is *fabulous*, it's best to tone hose colour in with the boots.

◎   Familiarity plays a *major* role in the acceptability of certain proportions. What may look bizarre at the beginning of a season can look perfectly normal come final mark-down. Beware of trendy proportions at second-hand, however – by the time they hit consignment and charity shops, these one-season wonders can look hopelessly out of date.

Proportion is complex, even for professionals, but it does come more naturally with experience. If you'd like to build your sense of it, scour fashion magazines and catalogues to see how the experts put lines and shapes together. Try to be aware of proportions in your everyday world. And if you have a friend in a visually creative field like design or flower arranging or the fine arts, talk to her about how she does what she does – the added insight may be invaluable.

— Get up on the scale

There's one final visual element to bear in mind when putting looks together in a stylish way: the scale, or size, of the patterns and textures you favour. Some women (usually big of stature or personality) look great in loud patterns and gutsy textures – it suits their approach to the world. Other women (usually smaller in size and persona) feel more at home in more discreet patterns and surface qualities. Give scale some thought, if you haven't already, and decide what kind of volume level you prefer. Your personal style will be sleeker and more refined if you don't send out scrambled scale messages.

Of course, a number of you mix up scale and other style elements on purpose, going for a *totally* different look every day. This is particularly true of vintage-clothes lovers, who tend to have a heightened, more costume-y approach to getting dressed ('If it's Tuesday, I must be Mata Hari, if it's Thursday, Gwen Stefani.'). All in all, this a good thing – you bring zest and imagination to what is essentially a dull clothing world. You, however, will be bored rigid by the upcoming section, about crafting a cohesive look. This part of the chapter is addressed to women who, due to time limitations, professional constraints or personal taste, take a more conservative approach to getting dressed – yet yearn for a touch of your memorability.

— It's so your style

If you're idling somewhere in wardrobe limbo, getting to stylish can be a long haul. There are so many pieces to be had (*especially* if we compromise on fit and quality), the natural impulse is to buy buy buy, simply because it's so much fun fun fun. Which quickly leads to wardrobe overload – a collection of clothing that is 'eclectic', to put it kindly, and 'one big mish-mash', to put it not.

Does this sound familiar? Depressingly familiar? If you've had enough and are ready to make a break from sartorially schizophrenic to stylish, you'll need to begin with an entirely new shopping approach. Instead of random buying, make a sincere effort to build your wardrobe around two or three distinct looks. Initially, this may sound like a bore, especially if you enjoy sport shopping (bagging trophies just because they're new and different). But in the long run, you'll wonder why you ever did it any other way. In addition to revved-up personal style, a unified wardrobe brings these benefits:

- ◉ less decision-making early in the morning
- ◉ it's easier to look wonderful every day
- ◉ the money you save can be better spent on tango lessons or some other self-enhancing pursuit
- ◉ you can focus on buying the best, instead of scattering money on the mediocre
- ◉ you can wear the stuff again and again for years (try that with a sequinned catsuit)

SAMPLE MISH-MASH WARDROBE

Two cotton dress shirts * leather bustier * Vivienne Westwood tartan jacket (unworn as too valuable to wear) * Mexican wedding skirt * rayon bowling shirt * Gap skinny cardigan (bottom corner of wardrobe for past two years) * silk cheongsam dress embroidered with lucky dragon * fringed suede trousers * angora shrug * wool culottes (they looked adorable on SJP in *Sex in the City*) * pinstriped trouser suit * satin hip-hop puffa . . .

— *Finding your best look* . . .

The designer Betsey Johnson and the late fashion editor Diana Vreeland exemplify polar opposites of personal style. On the minimal end was Vreeland, who, despite having the fashion world at her fingertips as an editor at *Vogue* and *Bazaar*, was said to limit her daytime wardrobe to black cashmere polo necks, grey wool trousers and special handmade shoes replicated over and over again by Manolo Blahnik. Now, myth was as powerful as reality in this fashion doyenne's life, and the severity of her garb may be an exaggeration. But the basic point is clear – Vreeland knew her look, and wasn't going to follow the whims of fashion just because her magazines told everyone else to.

At the other pole is Betsey Johnson, who was once reported in a magazine article to own 300 pairs of shoes, and claims to buy six of everything, 'wearing neon orange Mongolian sheepskin, and embroidered peasant coats, over her own tight, stretchy dresses'. Her style, she says, is 'spontaneous and uncontrived. But I do try hard to make my uncoordinated look work.' While at first this may seem a classic case of mish-mash, it's not really. There's probably not a single conservative piece in that closet, making her look eclectic, but still of a piece.

In their own ways, both women are icons, sharing two characteristics that define their wardrobes (and those of every woman who achieves great personal style):

CONSISTENCY
Even if Vreeland woke up one morning and felt like throwing on the chicest bo-peep blouse ever, she knew better. Part of her image rested in the iron control of her look. If she compromised that, her very identity as a style sibyl would begin to chip away. Likewise, Johnson wouldn't be caught dead in a boring old suit, because this counters her own persona as an avantgarde, free-spirited designer. Which relates to:

STYLE AS AN EXPRESSION OF ONE'S INNERMOST SOUL
We've all seen ladies whose individuality is hidden under a swarm of designer logos. True style doesn't work when it's simply put on. It has to emanate from within. If your spirit feels most at home in delicate lace, you will never be (or look) totally comfortable in corporate armour until you mould it into your own image (perhaps with frilly camisoles underneath, or an array of beautifully detailed lace pocket squares). In a world that revolves around designer whims, true style comes from charting one's own course.

> 'Know, first, who you are: and then adorn
> yourself accordingly.'
> **Epictetus,** *Discourses*, **2nd century**

— Nailing down style

It's not necessary to go to Vreeland's or Johnson's extremes in charting a course to personal style. But they do point the way towards the destination. If your style focus is murky, grab a pencil, find yourself fifteen minutes or so of quiet time, and give some serious thought to the following questions:

What sort of looks do you love for:

1)   work/school
2)   casual time (summer and winter)
3)   going out

Now jot down some of your style icons – women who wear these particular looks amazingly well. Flip through magazines, tear out pages, but for goodness sake don't limit yourself to *OK!* and *Hello!*. If you love looks of a particular past era, spend a morning in a library with some old magazines, pattern books, picture books (don't tear here, obviously; photocopy). Rent a stack of films that are glorious for their costumes (more on these in Chapter 13). Watch old sitcoms on telly and see who looks good in what. Inspiration is all over the place . . . your job is to find it.

Finally, think hard about whether the looks are realistic for you, given how much money and time you have to shop, and also given the realities of your figure and lifestyle (if you have a young baby, for example, the beaded cashmere sweaters will have to wait a year or so).

If everything is a go, you will have three **style templates** upon which to base your wardrobe. The next step is to acquire ensembles that fit these templates, and then, when considering additional pieces, buy only if they act *in support of*, rather than *in conflict with*, these central outfits. In this way you'll develop a theme and variations – an efficient, streamlined, yet highly wearable selection of clothes.

How much you develop each of the three sub-wardrobes depends on how much time you devote to each area of life. Those with stay-at-home responsibilities will weight casual clothes differently from those who are working an all-encompassing sales job; just as those who go clubbing every weekend will have different needs from those who spend their free time seeing fringe theatre.

Shopping takes on a whole new aspect once you have some style templates to work with. Now, instead of randomly buying whatever seems to work, you're *collecting* within a fairly tight framework, as a connoisseur does. You may find it very helpful to keep a running list, either written down or in your head, of any major gaps within your categories. Having three or four pieces on an ongoing **needs roster** (glittery evening jacket, black cotton cardigan, calfskin belt) will quash the devilish temptation of non-essentials.

It will take a fair amount of shopping time to build your wardrobe up to the kind of consistency that marks personal style. In the meantime, here are a few shortcuts to reinforce it.

CLASSICS

You've surely heard it before, but the reminder never hurts – you can't go wrong investing in pieces of absolutely irreproachable classic style. The truly stylish, truly beautiful pieces will cost a small fortune (even second-hand), but will pay you back by wearing well for years:

1) Monochrome, clean-lined trouser suit in impeccable lightweight wool

2)   Hand-stitched slip-on shoes

3)   Midheel courts in alligator or calfskin

4)   Little black dress (again, as simple as possible, but in deluxe fabric)

5)   White button-down blouse, in Egyptian cotton or silk

6)   Wool dress trousers for winter

7)   Linen-blend trousers for summer

8)   Perfect white T-shirt

9)   Dark wool skirt, hemmed to flatter your legs best

10) Cashmere sweater in a neutral colour

11) Beautifully made trench coat

12) Great handbag

13) Small collection of top-rate scarves

PERIOD LOOKS

One of the many irresistible siren calls of vintage shops is the variety, and the possibility of indulging in seven different decades at a go. But if you're older than, finger in the wind, twenty-five, and you don't have huge stretches of time in which to get ready in the morning, you're far better off finding a favourite period and sticking with it, at least for a year or two. Your look will be of a piece, your accessories have a hope of chiming with new acquisitions, and you'll be working with a familiar family of cuts, fabrics and proportions so you can mix new and old without a huge amount of faffing and despairing in front of the mirror.

TRADEMARKS

These are the unique markers, the points of interest, that women adopt to distinguish themselves from the herd. A fashion trademark is not only fun to devise and collect, it also piques the inner life of those around you (what kind of pin will she have on *today*)?

FASHION BLACKOUT

Less a style than a way of life, wearing black makes for easy matching and

– in its casual incarnation – implied creative depths. It also seems to be the de facto uniform for ladies working in the City or for estate agencies. Black has the major disadvantage of being dull and unflattering (fixable, though, with cleverly chosen accessories). While many women wear black to get away with cheap fabric and make, don't follow their lead – when fabric and make are all you've got, you've really got to go for the best possible.

DESIGNER-SPECIFIC

One final way to hook into style is to borrow it altogether, limiting your selection to a single designer. This is an extremely demanding option for second-hand shoppers – most of us don't have the time or wherewithal to hunt down every last Hussein Chalayan within a hundred-mile radius. But if you're in an urban centre replete with the look you love, or if your favourite dress agency happens to have a consignor who shares your size and taste, then you may get lucky.

> 'Only God helps the badly dressed.'
> **Anonymous Spanish quotation, 19th century**
>
> 'The expression a woman wears on her face is more important than the clothes on her back.'
> **Dale Carnegie**

So who's right? They both make a good point. The question of how much importance to attach to personal style is one that has flummoxed women throughout history. How you resolve it is your business. Do try to remember that valid choices lie to either side of the divide. Stylishness is neither foolish vanity nor the mark of a real woman – it's simply one way (of many) to express yourself.

Flaws – the not-so-bad, the bad, and the very, very ugly

Once you've discovered a promising item – one that looks great, fits and meshes with the rest of your wardrobe – take a deep breath and get as far away from the till as possible.

Given the worldliness of second-hand garments, they're subject to a wide range of flaws. Some are so easily fixed they are easy to forgive (the not-so-bad). Others require additional spending and/or effort, possibly overwhelming any bargain factor (the bad). Still others are beyond hope (the very, very ugly) and are grounds for instant rejection.

We all have individual standards. You and I will differ on what is problematic and to what degree. At one extreme are perfectionists who only buy contemporary pieces that are or look brand new, and vintage garments that are in mint or museum-quality condition. More easy-going souls accept minor booboos like missing buttons, knowing that quick work with a needle and thread will turn another woman's cast-off into a treasure. And then there are the buccaneers who don't mind challenges like grit and grime, and are willing to attack with detergent and muscle power to bring garments back to their former glory.

You may quibble with the following categorisations. That's fine – healthy dissent makes for an interesting world. More important is knowing exactly which flaws *you yourself* will tolerate, so you don't make a purchase you'll later regret. Being a connoisseur means knowing exactly what you're getting yourself into.

> **Connoisseur's Tip:**
> Never buy an item before checking every last inch for spots, holes and other signs of wear.

— The not-so-bad

This type of flaw may put off retail shoppers, but it by and large leaves us serene. The problem is either so minor it can be fixed at home, or it can be dispatched inexpensively by a professional sewer. By the way, it's a good idea to ask your alterations person for a price list of routine alterations such as letting down hems, zip repair, relining and other chores you wouldn't do yourself. This way, you can accurately calculate the true end cost of a garment that needs a little attention before it blooms into full glory.

WRINKLES

As we saw in Chapter 7, tension wrinkles indicate how a garment sits on the body. The other type of wrinkles – the plain old un-pressed kind – may interfere with the all-important fit check, but are otherwise no big deal.

Un-pressed garments rarely show up in good dress agencies, whose policies mandate dry-cleaning. If you do find a crinkly piece, ask the owner – diplomatically – if the item was indeed cleaned prior to consignment (if not, you may be able to haggle on price). Next, see if a steamer can be brought out to get the article hanging straight and true.

If you find a wrinkled garment in a charity or a vintage shop, bear in mind that it may have been in that state since the Thatcher years. Don't rush to buy until you've made sure that the crimps and crevices are free of discolouration or fading.

IF YOU MUST HAVE IT

Carefully determine the type of fabric and its ironability. If it can be pressed and there are no visible stains, buy it and have a go, being sure to use the correct iron temperature (see Chapter 12). If the item is silk or wool, a hot steam in the bathroom may be a better alternative. If neither approach yields great results, take the piece to a dry-cleaner for professional pressing.

MISSING BUTTONS

While buttons gone missing mean spending a few more quid to replace them and require some of your free time, they are a minor fault, provided you know how to attach them yourself (a skill every diehard second-hander should master).

IF YOU MUST HAVE IT

Take the garment to your local button purveyor. See if you can match the missing round. Can't do it perfectly? Then find replacements for *all* the buttons (look for real beauties), and sew them on while watching telly. It's important to do this chore as soon as possible – otherwise the garment will languish in the to-do pile and you'll feel like a lazy so-and-so every time you look at it. Telly time is perfect for minor repair work, because two mind-less activities somehow add up to a gratifyingly productive evening at home.

'I am forever changing the buttons on my clothes, usually for the same reason that I correct a drawing or shift colours around in my paintings: it sharpens the total effect and creates harmony.'
Jim Dine, American artist

OFFLINE HEMLINES

Most people don't pay enough attention to trouser length. Fashionistas do. Make no mistake – these women hem their trousers down to the *millimetre*. The precise fall of fabric over the front of shoes or boots, and where it hits the heel, makes the critical difference between elegant and *not quite cutting it, darling*. If you don't have an eye for this sort of thing, the fabric should hang about three-quarters of the way down the back of the heel, and should slouch ever so gently over the front of the shoe or boot, without wrinkles. The fabric should not sweep the ground. (There's some leeway with length if you're wearing skinny-legged trousers with flats; Kate Moss herself has been seen showing a bit of ankle.) Most hemlines are easy to shorten when too long and *sometimes* can be lengthened if too short. Ill-fitting sleeves are a more serious problem. But, for a price, a good tailor may be able to work wonders.

IF YOU MUST HAVE IT

◎　Raising hems on trousers: As long as the trousers are of a sturdy material, you can do this yourself, following the instructions in a good home-sewing book (helpful for a connoisseur to have handy). Basically, it involves measuring carefully, pinning the fabric in place and making sure the stitches catch only a few threads at a go.

◎　Lowering hems on trousers: Before purchase, turn the hem inside out to see if there's enough extra fabric to drop to the right length. Allow for at least a half-inch to be hemmed back up inside afterwards. Also, take a good look at the current crease line. Cotton, velvet and suede tend to get lines of demarcation that can be tough to eliminate once the repair work is done.

◎ Adjusting hems on skirts: Unless you're an experienced seamstress, leave this to a professional, because uneven work can result in an unattractive hemline. Bear in mind that a slit on the back or side will become an odd little flap if the fabric is taken up too high. If a skirt has pleats, a tulip-style front opening or another kind of curving hemline, don't hold too many expectations for success-ful alteration – hemming these can be a nightmare, even for a professional.

◎ Adjusting sleeves: For professionals only. Shortening, for them, is fairly straightforward. Lengthening is probably possible if it's only a matter of a half-inch or so, but note that the expense may hardly be worth it.

BROKEN ZIPS

> 'Is there anything more deadly than a zip
> that turns nasty on you?'
> **Agatha Christie,** *Come, Tell Me How You Live*

Agatha Christie was exaggerating – a bad zip is annoying but hardly lethal. A good home-sewing book (try Eithne Farry's *Yeah, I Made It Myself*) will offer instructions on how to replace a worn or broken zip, but most of us are happier to leave this to a professional.

IF YOU MUST HAVE IT
As long as the construction of the garment is straightforward and you're willing to pay for the repair, go ahead and buy. After consulting the alterations person, you may wish to purchase the zip yourself to ensure the best colour match and quality.

HAIR
While it's repellent, hair – human or animal – on a garment is harmless, unless you are prone to allergies. If you find a hairy castaway at a dress agency, alert the owner – dry-cleaned garments shouldn't carry any hair. (Though it could have shed off a previous customer.)

IF YOU MUST HAVE IT
If the garment is otherwise perfect, wash or dry-clean it and don't give the hair a second thought.

TORN LININGS
Vintage clothes often have torn or frayed linings, as do winter coats of every era. What with all the inning-and-outing, the underarm areas undergo a great deal of wear and tear, and if the coat is long the lining is also vulnerable to errant heels.

IF YOU MUST HAVE IT
Put the item on hold. Your alterations expert can tell you the approximate cost of replacing the lining, as long as she knows the size and style of the garment. If you decide to go ahead and it's in keeping with your personality, pick out a replacement fabric with real dash.

> There was a young belle of old Natchez/Whose garments
> were always in patchez/When comment arose/On the state of
> her clothes/She drawled 'When ah itchez, ah scratchez.'
> **Ogden Nash**

—The bad

STAINS

In dress agencies, where dry-cleaning is mandatory, any visible stains are likely to be so long-entrenched you can count on living with them forever. Paradoxically, stains on clothing from charity shops may come out more easily, simply because nobody's ever given them a real go (not true of old underarm stains, which are not only gross but incredibly stubborn, see pages 230–233).

If you see a stain yet still love the garment, take a harder look. Do you see any evidence of a cleaning attempt (in other words, is the mark shadowy and greyish rather than crisp)? If the stain looks like it's been through a laundering, your chances of eliminating it are poor. Many stains set forever once they have been washed at high heat.

If, on the other hand, the stain has some colour and texture, for example make-up on a collar, it may be fresh enough to offer hope of removal. One way to test is to carry some wet-wipes in your bag. If you see a stain, bring the garment to the counter, ask permission of a member of staff and dab lightly with the wipe (do not try this on silk or on vintage pieces, as damage may result). If the colour lifts or fades, odds are good that the stain will come out.

> 'Out, damned spot; out I say.'
> **Shakespeare,** *Macbeth*

IF YOU MUST HAVE IT

The best (if priciest) option for removing stains on contemporary clothing is the dry-cleaner. With at-home attempts, the appropriate product can work wonders on fresher stains (see Chapter 12). But be warned – none of these options is guaranteed.

ODOURS

One of the worst old clichés about second-hand clothing is that it smells. On the rare occasions when it's true, this can be very, very ugly. All the same, it's not a reason to reject clothing outright, for some odours are fairly easily eliminated. It all comes down to the source. Old perfume usually responds well to dry-cleaning. Embedded perspiration usually does not. Mustiness due to storage in less-than-ideal conditions often eases after a good airing. If the odour lurks in the lining of a coat or jacket, replacing the lining may do the trick.

Sometimes, too, clothing smells because of its nature. Waxed waterproof country coats do a terrific job of keeping out the rain, but are quite smelly due to the natural oils impregnating the fabric. Heavy woollen fisherman's sweaters, when wet, develop much the same kind of aroma, due to the activation of the lanolin coating the hairs. There's no good way to get rid of the smell of such pieces, and you really wouldn't want to, for this would render them ineffective against rain. Some stuff is just meant to be worn outdoors. Besides, with a couple of shot grouse in the back pocket or a cod or two hanging from your neck, the smell of the outerwear isn't nearly as noticeable.

IF YOU MUST HAVE IT
Again, a good relationship with your dry-cleaner will pay off. Put the garment on hold and give him or her a call. Describe the fabric, its age, the location of the odour. Try to describe it. Is it musty, like old newspapers? Pungent like a gym locker? Faintly sweet, like L'Air du Temps? If you give your cleaner regular business, you should get the straight dope on getting the smell out.

> 'As a perfume doth remain/In the folds where it hath lain/So the thought of you, remaining/Deeply folded in my brain/Will not leave me: all things leave me/You remain.'
> **Arthur Symons**, *Memory*

BOBBLING
Knitted wools and fuzzy synthetics have the unpleasant habit of bobbling when they're rubbed the wrong way. Opinion varies over whether this relates to the quality of the piece – all I know is, every cashmere sweater I've ever owned eventually developed a few fuzzballs. Constant abrasion lifts the fibres up, they become entangled, and then, under the continued force of abrasion, roll into little balls that cling tight to the surface of the knit. While not repulsive, they do indicate age and wear.

IF YOU MUST HAVE IT
Bobbles can be removed successfully. Not by pulling them off – that's the worst thing to do because it draws out more fibres, leaving them vulnerable to further pilling. Instead, stretch the sweater flat over a pillow and

carefully clip pills off with nail scissors, or buy one of those bobble shavers from a gadget shop or catalogue. By trimming the bobbles, you can dramatically freshen the look of a jumper; but remember – they always come back.

MOTH HOLES

Moth holes are devilish – they often go unnoticed until you've got the item home and are trying it on again, then . . . *$%^&!!!* This is why, before you purchase anything made of wool, you need to go over it meticulously. Especially a sweater that otherwise looks pristine – the very reason it's second-hand could be because a peckish moth got to it first. The most effective (if a bit mad-looking) way to inspect is with a mini-flashlight in a dark corner, running the light up the insides of the sleeves and legs. If you see pinholes of light, gotcha.

Actually, it's not the moths themselves that do the damage but their offspring, caterpillars, especially those of the breed *Tineola bisselliella*. The little buggers thrive on the protein keratin, found in wool fibres (they also require generous side orders of food stains and perspiration, one more argument for keeping and storing clothes in a scrupulously clean state). About four generations can breed in one year, wreaking untold havoc in your closet.

IF YOU MUST HAVE IT

If you find a moth-eaten garment in a dress agency, alert the owner and remind her where it was hanging. Any live animals could seriously eat into her profits. For your part, if you can live with the holes, the first thing to do, before letting that piece anywhere near your own precious clothes, is get it to the dry-cleaners to remove any lingering eggs or (yes) larvae. A somewhat less reliable but much cheaper wipe-out technique is to hang the garment in bright sunlight for an entire day (the dark-loving larvae literally die away in the rays). Be sure to open out any pockets, unfold any creases and turn the garment inside out at least once, then brush vigorously. Once the item is all clear, take an extra-fine needle and wool thread in an identical match, and loop the hole closed. In some cities there are even professionals (called 'reweavers') who will do this for you, but the price is likely to be high.

— ... and the very, very ugly

Here are the flaws that should make you drop the garment and move smartly along – possibly right out of the shop. Nobody needs this kind of aggravation, even if the piece started out as a couture wonder. Go ahead, be a snob; these clothes deserve it.

CRITTERS

While moth holes rest on the border zone of acceptability, other kinds of bug infestation, meaning the small, grey, pinhead-sized egg casings that house lice – or, worse, the animals themselves – are repulsively different. Please note that clothing carrying body lice is unlikely to *ever* make it past a shop's sorting and tagging operations, because typically it was worn day in and out for weeks without being washed (i.e., it will be *rank*). If the staffers were asleep at the wheel, you won't be. Immediately alert the shop owner or manager if you come across an infestation, and strongly consider alerting your local health authority.

> 'He can see a louse as far away as China but is
> unconscious of an elephant on his nose.'
> **Malay proverb**

BUCKLED SEAMS

On a less drastic, but still reject-worthy note, puckering along seam lines happens for a variety of reasons. Every now and again, designers deliberately work them in (for example, in cargo pants or in certain makes of preppy-slovenly shirts). Nine times out of ten, though, it's the unhappy result of ill-chosen materials or shoddy assembly. Who needs more wrinkles?

WASHED-OUT KNITS

Cotton knit jumpers are lovely to have in the wardrobe, especially come cool summer evenings. Unfortunately, one accidental spin in a hot dryer and their good looks will simply fade away. Racks and racks of washed-out jumpers can be found in every charity shop in the land. They're not worth good money – newer, brighter versions are also plentiful and will look good much longer if given proper care.

BOILED WOOL

Like faded cotton knits, this flaw indicates that the previous owner had little clue about how to care for her clothes. Amateur boiled wool (as opposed to Austrian loden coats, which are purpose-boiled by experts) has a hard, tight feel that is extremely unpleasant. It's said that these pieces can be brought back to life with a second round in the washer, but perfect re-incarnation is not guaranteed. This is another case where passing is the smartest shopping decision you can make.

OVERSTRETCHED KNITS

Like their boiled and washed-out cousins, knits that droop at the neck, cuffs and waistband do your appearance no favours. There's absolutely no reason to purchase an underachiever like this when there are so many beauties awaiting discovery. Put a clamp on your wallet and wait for the best.

'SHATTERED' FABRIC

'Shattering' describes the breakdown of fibres in a very old fabric, especially silk. The telltale signs are slight tears that run with the grain. Pulling at the fabric even slightly will cause it to rip, meaning it is practically useless as a wearable item. As beautiful as it may be, give it a pass, unless you want the item for display purposes only.

BAD ALTERATIONS

There are a lot of well-meaning but completely incompetent people wielding a needle out there. Unfortunately, once mis-stitching is done, little can repair the damage. Signs of bad alterations include: sloppy, oversize or irregular stitching at the seams; jagged hemlines; uneven trouser or sleeve lengths; odd bunching at the waistline. It's particularly important to check inner seams – you can see the mischief before you try on the garment.

FRAYING

While a frayed lining can be replaced, a frayed cuff or collar is another story. Even the slightest hint of fringe means the piece is on its way to the rag bin.

YELLOWING

Sometimes yellowing occurs after a garment has done many tours of duty in the laundry, or after only one mistaken go-round with coloured items. Other times the fault lies not with the consumer but with the dry-cleaner. If instructions are not carefully followed, a white item can yellow in the dry-cleaning process. Careful bleaching may restore sparkle to off-tinged items, but it can also result in greying, which is just as bad. Always examine clothing in natural sunlight, where any off-tint will be evident.

SWEAT AND BLOOD

Old biological stains are not only disgusting, they're the devil to get out – the proteins lock into cloth at high wash temperatures. Certain clothes-care advice books recommend removal by dabbing with vinegar or even a solution of crushed aspirin, but is this the kind of project you really need? Think hard. If not, give this stuff a pass and a good riddance.

GORGEOUSLY FLAWED

Broad patches of missing beads, trailing sequins, frayed gashes, clusters of pinholes from the daily affixing of a cameo brooch at the neck . . . these are flaws every vintage lover knows all too well. The most decrepit of these garments sit on the rails, unbought, unloved, or are picked up by a specialist for study purposes. But if you're daring . . . and you've got the confidence . . . and you've got the event, wearing such a piece makes an amazing fashion statement. How many absolutely stunning period homes are decorated with tattered old oils? Take that same concept to a personal level and dare to wear a vintage ruin. But there are some clear rules . . .

1) It must be intact enough not to fall apart midway through the occasion.
2) It must be flattering in the usual ways: colour, silhouette and fit.
3) Everything else about you must be absolutely immaculate – hair, make-up, other clothing.

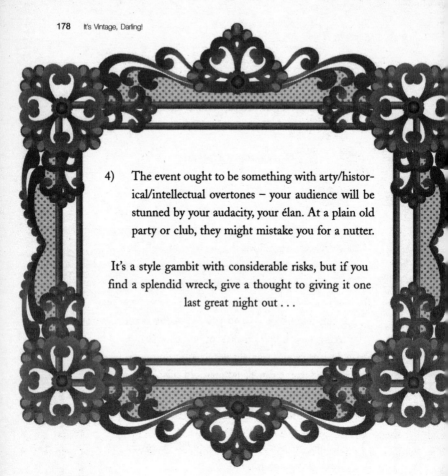

4) The event ought to be something with arty/histor-
ical/intellectual overtones – your audience will be
stunned by your audacity, your élan. At a plain old
party or club, they might mistake you for a nutter.

It's a style gambit with considerable risks, but if you
find a splendid wreck, give a thought to giving it one
last great night out . . .

SHININESS

Certain tightly woven fabrics, particularly those that contain synthetic materials, develop a sheen when they've been pressed at too-high heat or rubbed
constantly over the course of long wear. Seats, elbows and lapels are the
usual locales. A shiny suit is a suit that's past its wear-by date. If there's
one in your wardrobe, you may be able to temporarily restore it by gently
stroking the spots with fine sandpaper or dabbing them with a vinegar solution, but this won't fool anyone for too long. Don't buy anything this worn
– it's not worth the money.

10

Glorious accessories

Looking great makes a difference. *Not looking beautiful*. Looking put-together, polished, what the French call *soignée*. Doors open, you get attention rather than attitude, you're treated like a somebody because you *look* like a somebody, a woman who takes pride in her presence.

If this reaction doesn't ordinarily come your way, you're probably wondering what sort of tiresome preparation is necessary. Actually, it couldn't be simpler. Wear accessories. As often as you can, not just for dinners out and job interviews. Jewellery, scarves, cute shoes instead of trainers or uggly boots, the finishing touches to a fine outfit.

As advice goes, this may sound straight out of the Football Wife manual but, honestly, it works. Accessories have this weird power. Once upon a time, charms and amulets were worn to guard against evil and to signal status in society. The shiny bits and bobs we hang on our bodies, even today, may inspire an ancient, reflexive respect. Beyond the anthropological explanation, accessories are nice to look at, plain and simple. Back when women dressed up for a trip to the corner shop, little extras were standard: earrings; matching shoes, gloves and bag; a cunning hat. But as the decades passed, strict codes of public appearance disintegrated. Looks that were once hidden behind closed doors, like torn T-shirts and velour sweatpants, became fashion statements. These days the old codes are gone altogether. Never mind Page Three girls parading to grade-z parties wearing little more than four coats of mascara, far more offensive to the discerning eye is the spectacle of grown people of both sexes routinely dressing like toddlers – to the theatre, in nice restaurants, on the streets of the most sophisticated cities of the world. Needless to say, accessories (apart from bum bags, baseball caps and marshmallow 'athletic' shoes) are missing in action.

Given this, eye-catching refinements carry great force. Wearing lovely accessories is a form of public beautification, like a clean-swept pavement. Onlookers are chuffed to have something lovely to look at, and old-fashioned courtesy is their way of saying thanks in return.

—Looking good = feeling good

Let's not kid ourselves – wearing heels instead of flip-flops does mean a trade-off in comfort. But it doesn't mean buying into the false premise that women have to suffer for good looks. Leave that to the supermodels, who get paid for it. Any discomfort *you* feel dressing well should be low to nonexistent, as long as you:

◎ acquire pieces that fit, made with great fabrics
◎ wear well-made shoes that cushion your feet
◎ think about your posture so that slouching doesn't artificially tighten clothes' grip
◎ adjust jewellery so that it hugs rather than pinches

Accessories shouldn't cause much financial pain either, because second-hand offers such reasonable prices. Sure, a Hermès scarf will set you back £100, but a lovely no-name copycat may be tagged at £3. Earrings routinely turn up for less than £5. Astonishing belts are there for the grabbing because other shoppers don't recognise their allure. Build a great accessories collection and you effectively double your wardrobe. And with prices like these, it only makes sense to go for the best.

—*Keep it clean*

As with all matters of style, there's a fine line between looking done and looking overdone. Accessories are like the flicks of a brush an artist uses to bring interest and depth to a portrait. If they go on too thick, in glaring colours or in poorly judged combinations, the sitter is overshadowed by the special effects. Keep this in mind if you choose to wear a stand-out accessory, such as a beautifully bold necklace. It should be the star of a relatively simple outfit, with other pieces playing a supporting role.

It's all too easy to overdo or under-do it with accessories, because none of us were born knowing how to wear them. If you'd like inspiration on how to put subtle looks together for work or special occasions, the *What Not To Wear* series by Trinny Woodall and Susannah Constantine are wonderful references.

If a younger, more exuberant vibe is what you're after, then spend an afternoon or two in Topshop (or your closest local equivalent) analysing how the cool girls do their look. Be insanely bold and ask to take their photos for a style book you're putting together; they'll likely be flattered enough to say sure.

If your style ideal is a more pampered *bring on the bling*, benefit from a few hours on Bond Street (or your poshest local parade). If this is unpromising or impossible, browse through the glossy retrospective books on Yves Saint Laurent, Christian Lacroix or John Galliano (on the Fashion/Design shelves in good bookshops). Especially at the haute-couture level, these designers go all out to dazzle the eye. You will find countless images to set your imagination racing – looks that may be directly applicable for parties and clubs, and, with careful editing, for daytime wear as well. To see fab vintage ensembles on real people, check out the special outings and events listed in Chapter 13.

One more general tip on accessories: colour-matching your bag, belt and shoes sometimes works wonderfully and other times doesn't, depending on the colours and textures. If they're all the same low-key shade (black, brown, grey, cream), a two/three-way match usually looks great, especially if the textures are different. But, if the colour is offbeat, like lavender, yellow or even white, perfect matching will look very 1980s – possibly not your intention at all.

— The last word on shoes

The saleswomen in ritzy boutiques always check out incoming customers' shoes. They read them as an index of buying power, and before you can say Louboutin platform (LOO-boo-teh PLAT-form), they've got the customer pegged. Yes it's superficial, but it also makes sense. The well-heeled shopper is clearly willing to spend top-to-toe on her appearance. She's not going to settle for second best. That describes you as well, no? The difference is, instead of putting thousands into footwear, you'll invest cunning, good taste and patience.

New, well-made shoes regularly turn up at dress agencies. As they are invariably some other woman's mistake, when you find them proceed with caution. Be sure they're there because they didn't fit their former owner. A more diabolical problem, like a rough inner seam or an unusually narrow arch, is going to haunt you as well.

New shoes are easy to detect because their soles are as smooth as a baby's bottom. With *slightly broken-in footwear*, you'll see moderate abrasion of the soles and heels and some erasure of the print on the insole. No matter how easy-going you are about mileage, you don't want to buy *goners* (roughed-up toe, dinged heel, leather as wrinkled as a Shar-pei puppy). Why?

- ◎   They're not going to look any better on.
- ◎   They've absorbed more perspiration than you care to know.
- ◎   They're probably at the tail end of the most recent style cycle, and nothing looks more over than last year's shoes.

As bad as worn-out shoes are, ill-fitting ones are worse. When it comes to buying shoes, lots of women temporarily go dead from the ankle down (and the neck up). Let's stop the madness right now.

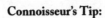

Connoisseur's Tip:
Never buy shoes that rub the wrong way. By the time the blisters heal, the season will be half over.

QUALITY CONSIDERATIONS

- ◎   The very best dress shoes are made entirely of leather, right down to the heels. This is designated on the sole with a hide-shaped insignia bearing the words 'vero cuoio' (Italian for real leather), 'cuir' (French for the same thing), or the English variation, 'all leather'.

- ◎   Shoes of the next-best quality consist of leather uppers (the part above the sole) with a synthetic sole and heel. Here, again, the content is stamped on the sole of the shoe, usually as 'all-leather uppers'.

- ◎   Synthetic uppers run a poor third. While they're fine as foul-weather shoes, they make feet smell even on the driest days.

◎   Fabulous shoe leather feels plump and yielding when pinched, like a ripe cherry. Cheap shoe leather feels thin and stiff like cardboard.

◎   The finest court shoes have no seam at the instep.

◎   The leather in fabulous shoes is stitched together. Further down the quality scale, the leather is glued. Stapling is grounds for instant dismissal.

◎   The shoe should flex back and forth easily at the point at which the big toe would flex away from the foot.

◎   The interior of a fine shoe is perfectly smooth – no ridges, seams, bumps or bulges. All visible seams should turn inward.

◎   Patent leather holds its own against rainy weather but it can dry out easily. It requires regular care with patent-cleaning polish (though in a pinch, a good rub-down with some petroleum jelly will bring back its lustre).

◎   If heels, outer and inner soles are worn down, they can be replaced, but be sure to factor this work into the total cost of the shoes. Also, be sure that there's enough life left in the upper to make the time and investment worth it.

◎   Boots with exposed zips may snag hose or the linings of your clothing. A narrow flap covering the zip is a sign of superior quality.

◎   Vintage shoe leather is dry, and therefore delicate. Even a pristine sole may crack under the stress of wear.

> 'To kiss, pretty Saki, thy shoes' pretty tips, is better than
> kissing another girl's lips.'
> **Omar Khayyam**

FIT CONSIDERATIONS

◎ Shoes should allow a half-inch between the big toe and the end of shoe. You should be able to flex your toes.

◎ Your heel should be gently cupped. If it's shifting, buy an insert.

◎ Knee-high boots should fit snugly at the ankle and at the top of the calf.

◎ Walk around the entire shop a few times before buying a pair of shoes. If the shoes feel tight, for heaven's sake throw them back.

◎ Remember that feet swell towards the end of the day, and this is when trying on is most accurate.

◎ The smaller the total surface area upon which you stand (in other words, the tinier the shoe's footprint), the more unstable you'll feel. Skinny sandal straps only add to the precariousness. Unless you're a practised wearer, or these are intended to be car-to-bar shoes only, go for wider heels and platform soles.

> Women today 'experience four times the number of foot
> problems as men due to high heels, poorly fitting footwear, or
> other abuses in the name of fashion.'
> **Temple University's School of Podiatric Medicine**

SOME OF THE MOST EXCLUSIVE NAMES IN WOMEN'S SHOES, SOLD
FIRST-HAND IN BOUTIQUES OR DELUXE DEPARTMENT STORES:

Alaïa

Alberta Ferretti

Anya Hindmarch

Bottega Veneta

Celine

Cesare Paciotti

Chanel

Charles Jourdan

Christian Louboutin (note
    lipstick-red soles)

Emma Hope's Shoes

Georgina Goodman

Gina

Giorgio Armani

Gucci

Guiseppe Zanotti

Hermès

Jimmy Choo

Lambertson Truex

Lanvin

Loewe

Lulu Guinness

Manolo Blahnik

Maud Frizon (vintage)

Moschino

Paco Gil

Pierre Hardy

Prada

Rickard Shah

Robert Clergerie

Rochas

Roger Vivier (vintage)

Rupert Sanderson

Salvatore Ferragamo

Sergio Rossi

Stephane Kelian

Stuart Weitzman

Susan Bennis/Warren Edwards
    (vintage)

Terry de Havilland

Tod's

Vivienne Westwood

Yves Saint Laurent

MORE TOP-RANKED NAMES, USUALLY FOUND IN SIGNATURE SHOPS OR
THE DESIGNER SHOE DEPARTMENT OF BETTER DEPARTMENT STORES:

Amalfi	Fratelli Rosetti
Bally	French Sole
Bruno Magli	Patrick Cox
Casadei	Richard Tyler
Delman	Si di Sandro
Donna Karan	Sigerson Morrison
Fendi	Sonia Rykiel
Fortuna Valentino	Walter Steiger

COMING IN AT A SLIGHTLY LOWER PRICE ARE THE DESIGNERS'
DIFFUSION SHOE LINES, AS WELL AS HIGH STREET FAVOURITES:

Caressa	Kurt Geiger
Cheap & Chic	L. K. Bennett
CK	Marc Jacobs Look
D&G	Nine West
DKNY	Office
Donald Pliner	Pied a Terre
Dune	Ravel
Enzo Angiolini	Russell & Bromley
Hush Puppies	Sacha

SHOE-CARE TIPS

◎   Try to find shoe trees at a charity shop near you. These help restore
and preserve the shape of shoes after a hard day's wear. Rolled-up
socks are a second-best substitute. Rolled-up newspaper inserted vertically to mid-calf will help prevent knee-high boots from sagging.

◎   It's worth investing in a good shoe-shining kit (with appropriate
brushes and polishing cloths) to help keep footwear in top form. The
kit will last a lifetime – and your shoes will last longer, too.

◎ Shoes should be polished with cream or wax shoe polish on a regular basis. This not only helps them look great but protects against splashes and grime.

◎ Restore the lustre of patent leather by rubbing it with a dab of petroleum jelly. Be sure it is thoroughly wiped clean before wear.

◎ Marks on suede can usually be lifted with a clean white pencil eraser. If that doesn't work, try gentle rubbing with a bit of fine sandpaper.

◎ Try not to wear the same shoes two days in a row. Feet sweat a great deal, no matter what the time of year, and shoes require adequate time to air out.

◎ Be stringent about maintenance. Have your shoe repairer attach heel and toe guards as soon after purchase as possible – this costs less than replacing an entire heel later on. Also, try to buy shoes just large enough to accommodate a cushiony insole. This will protect the interior against wear, keep shoes smelling fresh and improve your chances of reselling the shoes later on.

— Belt it out

A great belt, properly cared for, is one of the most enduring pieces in a woman's wardrobe, easily lasting for a decade or longer. Since belts hang around for so many years, it only makes sense to buy the absolute best, even if it means spending more than you're used to. In dress agencies, the finer belts are usually showcased under glass. In charity shops, they're found on a rack at the back of the shop, sportily mixed in with the vinyl cheapees.

QUALITY CONSIDERATIONS

◎ The maker's name, and occasionally the type of leather, are printed or stamped on the inner side. Names to watch for are the same as for fine bags and shoes.

◎   The inner side is a key checkpoint of an excellent belt. Leather belts should be lined with leather whose quality and attractiveness matches that used on the outside (it may be a different colour). If the interior is raw suede or vinyl, the belt is of inferior quality.

◎   The best belts have a buckle and fittings made of solid metal (these feel more substantial than the cheaper hollow or metal-plated versions). If you detect a silver buckle with tiny hallmarks stamped onto its surface, congratulations: the metal in question is sterling.

◎   Great belts are sewn together (with tiny, tight stitches). Cheap belts are glued.

◎   Alligator, crocodile and snakeskin belts are actually more durable than those made of calfskin (the finest belt leather).

◎   In the best belts, the holes are punched clean as a whistle.

◎   There should be no cracks running from the holes on the inner side – this means the belt is at death's door.

◎   Studded belts fly in and out of fashion. Don't spend a lot of money on one (unless it's Hermès).

◎   If you find a gorgeous buckle on a worn-out belt, it's possible to replace the strap – a good shoe repairer should be able to do the job. Unfortunately, the work will probably cost more than the belt itself.

◎   Don't forget to the check men's and boys' areas of second-hand shops, which often hold wonderful well-made belts.

FIT CONSIDERATIONS

◎   Never buy a belt without trying it on. It may be too *long*, which is as bad a problem as being too short.

◎   If the belt only buckles on the very last hole, remember that weight gain or bulky tops may make it a useless dust catcher.

◎   New holes can be punched by a shoemaker, but be sure the extra measure of strap will go through your belt loops and/or won't droop.

◎   Be sure that the belt's width works with the loops you currently own – even the greatest belt doesn't deserve its own wardrobe.

◎   To keep your belt gleaming, supple and crack-free, treat it every so often with a good leather cream.

— Hey, bag spender

Handbags are major markers of personal style. Some women go for broke with Balenciaga lariats, Mulberry reptile or whatever is this season's designated arm ornament. Others prefer the more discreet (but no less luxurious) offerings of Delvaux or Bill Amberg. Still others like the classic lines and sweetie-jar hues of Furla, or the extravaganza of styles possible with vintage. No matter what *your* carry-on preferences, you can't go wrong with a beautifully made bag that complements your overall look.

While it's admirable to have a wardrobe of bags to match different outfits, changing them daily is beyond the budget and the fashion discipline of most of us. That's why it makes sense to spend heavily on a few really great bags that match the main neutrals in your wardrobe. Bag switches are made easier, by the way, by regularly clearing out debris and keeping make-up in its own holder.

Formal evening events are the one occasion when a bag switch is mandatory. A day bag, no matter how nice, will sabotage your gala look. Even if you don't go formal very often, it's worth investing in a simple satin or velvet number that will carry you through such events for decades.

How a Touch of Vintage Leads to Bags of Style
by Lulu Guinness, designer

I discovered vintage at the age of sixteen and it's been my style ever since. All my friends – somehow they were always very tall and very blonde – looked great in jeans but I'm short and have a small waist so I really suit the clothes of the 1940s and 1950s. I just took to them. In Portobello back then you could buy dresses for 50p and an entire wardrobe for £5. I created my own style – crêpe de chine tea dresses, stretchy belts that really cinch the waist, red lipstick – and this is still what I love to wear today.

The women in my mother's family were always tiny, neat and immaculately groomed. My grandmother had six or seven couture suits – I was the only granddaughter who was at all interested in them. One was by Hardy Amies, when he a director at Lachasse. I just had it restyled and wore it to the British Fashion Awards. My grandmother also used to give me her evening coats – I especially loved one in shocking pink with a dramatic cowl neck.

My passion for vintage unexpectedly influenced my direction as a designer. My first bag was a briefcase with interior transparent pockets, for your Raybans and what have you. It was meant for businesswomen in the 1980s, fun but sensible. But when I took it round to buyers they said, 'Why don't you do bags more like *you*?' That was a turning point. I've always loved the visual trickery of the Surrealists – it inspired my florist-basket bags, for example. And the collectable evening bags I've done in limited editions: a miniature version of the famous lobster dress by Elsa Schiaparelli, a chocolate-box bag topped with brown felt bonbons . . .

My autumn/winter 2006 bag collection was influenced by the wonderful things I saw at the Dalí museum in St Petersburg, Florida – the clasp is a surrealist eye within a jewelled starburst. I also love Jean Cocteau, and all those marvellous French fashion advertisements from the 1950s. The first thing I want people who look at my designs to think is, 'Oh, isn't that charming?' I adore embellishment, embroidery, the look of old tortoiseshell. If people don't always catch the visual references, it doesn't matter, but the lineage is there for people who do . . .

I think it's absolutely possible to gauge something about a woman's personality by the kind of bag she carries. One of my favourite places to do this is in airport queues where you see so many people, and there's really nothing else to do. I admire anyone who is carrying a vintage bag, because I think the thing is to create a unique style. Dita von Teese, for example, she does it so well . . . Whenever I see someone wearing vintage I know she'll be interesting, and that I could have a good conversation with her.

QUALITY CONSIDERATIONS

◎ Top-quality leather bags have several layers of padding and support in between the interior and exterior, giving the leather a plush, cushy feel (see the description of Leiber bags, below).

◎ As with a great suit, the interior of a top-of-the-line bag is as beautiful as the exterior. The best examples are lined in fine suede or silk. Lesser bags are lined in nylon. At the lowest end, they're unlined.

◎ The surest give-away of an inferior bag is cheap hardware. Make sure all buckles, clasps, zips and bolts are solid metal rather than cheap moulded or plastic substitutes, *especially* on hot-name fabric bags, which are easy to counterfeit.

◎ Finer bags often have magnets helping clasps grip.

◎ The clasps on great bags usually 'thunk' together in a heavy, satisfying way, while on cheaper bags the attachment is flimsy.

◎ The finest framed bags (those designed to keep their shape no matter what) often have four rounded metal 'rests' on the underside.

◎ Real leather takes a tiny scratch (do this discreetly on a hidden part) and smells like leather. Vinyl resists scratching and smells like nothing.

◎ Straps should be stitched together rather than glued.

◎ All stitching (unless decorative) should be tiny and regular.

◎ If you opt for a straw bag, select one with a distinctive pattern and tight weave, with all raw edges carefully bound.

◎ Beaded and sequinned bags are so common at vintage it makes sense to hold out for perfection. Metallic mesh is a sturdier alternative.

◎ Fabric bags should show the same kind of seaming and overall workmanship seen in fine clothing.

STYLE CONSIDERATIONS

◎ How will you wear the bag? Over the shoulder, clutched in hand, slung over a wrist? Will you be happy carrying the bag all day, or do you prefer your hands free? These questions should be carefully considered *before* purchase.

◎ If your wardrobe leans towards crisp lines, go for a geometric bag. If your look is softer, a scrunchier bag is more on target. If you're a vintage queen, you have the widest range of all.

◎ Petite women can get shoulder straps shortened (by a good shoe-repair shop) so that the bag hangs at a comfortable spot.

◎ Beware of a bag with flimsy straps. It's easy pickings for a purse-snatcher.

◎ The quickest way to downgrade the look of a great bag is to overstuff it. Bag volume is *always* smaller than it looks.

◎ Rucksacks kill the lines of a good suit, but stylish ones are great at weekends.

◎ Nothing downgrades a great look faster than a sensible totebag, which people *do* notice, even when it's at the end of your arm. If you need to transport bulky papers to and from the office or school, get yourself a stylish carry-all.

◎ New mothers: there's no rule that says you *have* to carry one of those cartoonish nappy/toy/catch-all baby bags. A roomy nylon bag in a sleek shape is light and waterproof, and looks ten times smarter.

◎ Be aware that designer initials turn off as many people as they impress.

GREAT NAMES IN BAGS

If a given design house is famed for the beauty of its footware, odds are high it will make gorgeous bags as well. Many appear in the previous shoe section.

THE MAKING OF A JUDITH LEIBER HANDBAG

... the first operation consists of cutting a paper
pattern and then cutting every part of the bag,
completely by hand, in whatever material is being
used. After that, the skins or fabric are gathered,
folded, shirred, quilted or trapunto-puffed before
marriage to their interlinings and later attachment to their frames. Whenever a pattern
requires bending or stitching, the leather is
skived, or thinned, to the necessary degree. If a
fabric is used, particularly a tartan, each section is
carefully matched.

A latex machine, similar to one utilised in shoe
factories, is used only for putting interlinings
together. The interlinings are one of the truly
hidden secrets of a Leiber bag, with as many as
seven in a single design. Among the interlinings
used are paper, muslin, flannel, horsehair, foam
rubber, canvas and wadding. All of them go into
some bags and at least several go into every bag.
The soft bags usually take an extra layer of a
stiff material.

Once the interlinings are put together, they are
cemented to the outside material by hand and
the various parts are sewn together. Many
operations – shirring is one – that theoretically
could be done by machine, are done by hand
so that the leather remains soft. Machine work
for such details can work well but the outcome
is more chancy, a risk Mrs Leiber is not
prepared to take. If the bag is a soft one, it is
piped, turned over, and the lining – silk or
leather – is dropped in, not quite literally but
almost. Backed by the multi-interlinings, the
lining is, to a great degree, what makes the
difference between a sleek bag and one without
distinctive form.

Enid Nemy, *The Artful Handbag*

OTHER BAG SPECIALISTS TO LOOK OUT FOR:

Asprey	J & M Davidson
Balenciaga	Hermès
Bill Amberg	Longchamps
Bulgari	Luella
Celine	Mulberry
Chloe	Philip Treacy
Delvaux	Smythson of Bond Street
Furla	Tanner Krolle
Jamin Puech	

— *Marv scarves*

There are almost as many styles of scarf – square, oblong, pocket, shawl, muffler, wrap, bandanna, kerchief – as there are ways to tie them. They're unusual accessories in that the best ones easily make the jump from casual to professional and even to formal wear, which is why you can hardly have too many. It's good to mix them up in terms of fabrics and styles. Silk and cotton are the usual suspects, synthetic metallic are great at night, and there is nothing more luxurious in chilly air than a cashmere shawl (which sadly costs a fortune, even at second-hand).

QUALITY CONSIDERATIONS

◎   The best dress scarves are made from ultra-heavy silk. Hermès, Ferragamo, Gucci, Tiffany and Versace are some of the names to watch out for.

◎   The designs on most silk scarves are screen-printed, which means that every single colour requires a separate procedure to put it there. The more colours in a printed scarf, the more complicated the production, and the higher the intrinsic value. Hermès scarves are among the most colourful, featuring up to twenty-five different hues.

WOMEN WHO COULD REALLY TIE ONE ON

Salome
Lady Hamilton
Amelia Earhart
Gloria Swanson
Audrey Hepburn
Ava Gardner
Grace Kelly

◎ With printed silk scarves, the colouration is usually less intense on the reverse side, but if there's a major difference, be on alert. Silk absorbs colour brilliantly, rayon less so – and this may be a sign that the scarf is counterfeit.

◎ The finest silk scarves have hems that are rolled and sewn by hand. Hermès is so proud of the beauty of its hem it is meant to be worn facing outwards.

⊚ A hand-sewn hem should be slightly puffy rather than flat. If it is flat, the scarf is either fake or has suffered callous pressing. This detracts from its value.

⊚ Dry-cleaning and pressing kills the lustre of silk, which is best washed by hand in a gentle detergent, then steamed wrinkle-free.

⊚ Carefully clip the label off a scarf – it's unattractive when left in place. But if the make is excellent, keep the label handy in case you eventually choose to resell.

⊚ With wool/cashmere/other animal fibre scarves, be on the lookout for moth holes.

> 'A heavy shawl called a "manto" was worn on the head and shoulders in sixteenth-century Spain, as widows and young women were allowed to show only one eye.'
> **Alice Macknell, *Shawls, Stoles and Scarves***

STYLE CONSIDERATIONS

⊚ Pick your knots carefully. The *scout neckerchief* works fine with sweaters and tops, but with button-down blouses a high knot can look fussy – a looser, lower knot may be more appealing. The *choker* works with almost every type of open collar, but may look odd with a dress, and isn't right for women with short necks. Avoid knots that turn scarves into *droopy loops* – another turn around the neck usually prevents this, or tethering with a carefully placed pin.

VINTAGE TIES

With a few flicks of the wrist, a large, square silk scarf can conjure an entire era. It's all in the way you wear it.

TWENTIES STYLE

Fold square into a triangle, then roll scarf down starting at the peak until it's long and skinny like a snake. Knot it Isadora Duncan-style at the neck, long ends trailing, but steer clear of open-top roadsters.

THIRTIES STYLE

Make the snake into a loop and drape around neck. Pass loose ends through the loop and draw tight, then pass one end behind the loop from above and another from below. Twist the ends around each other once, then knot together at the back of the neck to form an imperious choker, à la Wallis Simpson. This looks particularly lady-of-the-manor under a starched white blouse, with pearl earrings.

FORTIES STYLE

For a Land Girl look, drape the triangle into a
kerchief on your head and knot it behind your ears
(knotting under the chin is for members of the Royal
Family and/or women going walkies with the corgis).

FIFTIES STYLE

Make a snake and, doubling it up if necessary, knot it
around your neck, tying the ends in a tiny, pert bow,
à la Audrey Hepburn driving down the Italian Riviera.

SIXTIES STYLE

Wear the snake as a headband, with the ends trailing
loose in your hair.

SEVENTIES STYLE

Make a triangle, draw the long-side corners under
your arms, and knot at back to make a bandeau.

EIGHTIES STYLE

Make a Prince-style foulard to wear with a ruffled
blouse. Make a triangle, bring the long ends around
your neck and back to the front. Finish with a knot.

— Batty for hats

> 'People still see hats as an old-fashioned accessory. I disagree.
> Hats are a form of expression and people love a hat whether
> they are a connoisseur of fashion and style or not.'
> **Philip Treacy**

Few items in the wardrobe carry such drama. Whenever you shop second-hand, don't overlook the hats. Whether they're sporty, demure or dashing, wearing them provides great pleasure to onlookers, and it's a rare hat that goes unappreciated.

QUALITY CONSIDERATIONS

◎ Felt hats are made from wool or, in superior-quality toppers, a wool-rabbit fur blend. The latter are much softer and finer-feeling, rather like velvet.

◎ Great felt hats, like great clothes, are substantially constructed. Cheap versions are flimsy and easily crushable.

◎ Tip-top straw hats are made with so-called Panama or Manila straw, which is very fine and glossy, or Italian (also called Leghorn) straw, which consists of strands braided, then woven, together. At the lowest end, straw hats are made with recycled paper fibre.

◎ The finer the straw and tighter the weave used in a summer hat, the better the quality. Authentic Panama hats are so well constructed they can be rolled up as tight as a cigar and will instantly pop back into shape.

◎ The quality of the label used in a hat is an excellent overall indicator.

◎ Flowers and other doodas can add greatly to the charm of a hat. Examine these extras carefully. Cheap plastic flowers are a minus; unusual feathers add value.

◎ If you're inclined to wear all-fur hats, be vigilant for thinning patches and other signs of wear.

◎ To restore a battered felt hat, hold it over a steaming kettle and brush vigorously. Steaming also lets you change the shape of the crease or brim – be careful not to burn your fingers.

◎ Be wary of a hat with a fraying ribbon band – it's probably not of high quality.

FIT CONSIDERATIONS

◎ When considering a hat, keep it on your head for at least five minutes. If it's even slightly small, it will begin to itch or otherwise irritate your forehead.

◎ For fitting accuracy, it's best if your hair is styled as it would be while wearing the hat for real.

◎ Know your hat size (there are many measuring keys on the internet), but be aware that the size may vary depending on the style and period.

◎ A slightly large casual hat can be cute. A slightly small one will be a torment.

◎ If you love a hat but you're worried about other people's germs/bugs/what have you, relax – you're more likely to catch them off the back of a cinema seat, and you don't worry about that, do you? You *do*? Then buy the silly thing, put it in a plastic bag, stick it in the freezer for a couple of days, defrost and give it a good brush inside and out.

◉ Never buy a hat without checking it out first in a full-length mirror. Some women can't carry really big ones, others can't carry really small.

◉ To tighten a too-large hat, or to keep an irritating crown away from the forehead, get some adhesive-backed Velcro tape, cut a few inches and stick it on just where your forehead hits, keeping the hook and loop parts of the tape attached together.

> 'Hats are the most unnatural of all items of clothing; they are the least necessary but most powerful.'
> **Colin McDowell,** *Hats: Status, Style and Glamour*

STYLE CONSIDERATIONS

◉ A man's hat, especially a fedora or trilby, looks smashing with trench coats, and is often of better quality than similar models made for women.

◉ After trying on a hundred hats, you'll know which shapes work best for you. That's why it's always worthwhile to spend a minute or so sampling, even if you're not in hat-buying mode.

◉ Generally speaking, the lines of the hat ought to complement the lines of the outfit. A clean-cut overcoat will look best with a crisp hat, while a curvier jacket can take a scrunchier chapeau.

◉ If you're wearing a hat to complement a dress or suit, keep other accessories fairly quiet.

◉ 'Hat head' is the one downside of wearing a topper. The best way to minimise it is to style hair smooth and straight back from the forehead.

◉ There are few occasions, apart from funerals, when dark veils can be carried off successfully. But if your destination is sophisticated, your outfit is chic, and you have the nerve, why not? Interesting men adore a touch of mystery.

SOME GREAT NAMES IN HATS:

Borsalino	Marie Mercié
Carlos Lewis	Patricia Underwood
Cosmo Jenks	Philip Treacy
Frederick Fox	Philippe Model
Gabrielle Cadet	Stephen Jones

World-class names in hats do occasionally show up at second-hand shops, but you're more likely to come across the work of local hat makers. Millinery (to use the formal term for the art) is undergoing a renaissance. Wildly creative and technically impeccable examples pour forth from these artisans, who may only distribute to a few neighbourhood boutiques. If you're a hat lover, it's worth getting to know the local all-stars, so you'll recognise the names when they crop up in your favourite shops.

— Jewellery, jewellery, jewellery

Discovering fine gemstones second-hand is a high-risk pursuit, best backed by training in gemology. Gold, silver and other precious metals are a slightly safer bet, but you still can't be sure of authenticity – even items with all the right stamps could well turn out to be bogus. The point is, don't splash out on jewellery because you're bewitched by the carat count – do so because you're dazzled by the piece. That way you'll never be disappointed.

AU-INSPIRING

Gold works hard for its sparkling reputation. According to Fleming and Honour's *Dictionary of the Decorative Arts*, this most precious of metals is so easy to tool it can be hammered to a mere four-millionths of an inch thick, yet so heat-resistant it won't start to melt until temperatures climb over 1000ºC. Gold's miraculous properties, along with its beauty, led the Aztecs – better known for human sacrifice than for poetry – to call it the 'excrement of the gods'.

Pure gold (otherwise known as **24-carat** gold) is too soft to make durable jewellery, so it is always blended with copper, copper and silver, or platinum. When the blend reaches half gold, half another metal, it is called **12-carat**. The highest-quality pieces are generally **22-carat** or **18-carat** gold. In some countries in Europe, such as Italy and France, any alloy below eighteen can't be called gold at all.

By law, all gold jewellery must have the content stamped somewhere on the piece. On rings, it's usually inside the band; on necklaces, on the flat oblong loop near the catch. Sometimes, instead of a carat designation, you'll see a numeric symbol:

916 indicates 22 carat
750 indicates 18 carat
585 indicates 14 carat
375 indicates 9 carat

But, again, don't count on any stamp if you see one that is second-hand – to get a 100% guarantee, you should limit purchases to reputable jewellery shops.

HI-HO, SILVER!

Like gold, pure silver is too soft to be easily worked and worn – it is usually alloyed with copper for increased strength. The percentage of silver varies depending on the time and place of manufacture. **Sterling**, the best quality, is generally somewhere around 93% pure. The number **958** or **925** is occasionally used to designate sterling. There's also another method – hallmarks. These are the tiny stamps silversmiths use to designate a piece's origin. To learn more about a specific hallmark, see if your local library has a guide. One other way to tell silver from lesser metals such as pewter or nickel is the presence of tarnish – a result of a reaction between its molecules and oxygen. But lesser-quality **silver-plate** will also tarnish (see below).

GOING PLATINUM

The rarest of precious metals, platinum has been used as a setting for precious stones since the early part of last century. But in recent decades, it has emerged from a supporting role to become a star in its own right. The number **950** or the letters **plat** stamped on a light silvery metal should indicate that a piece is of platinum, but at the risk of sounding like a broken record, don't bet the farm on its authenticity if buying second-hand.

PRECIOUS METAL JACKET

Both gold and silver looks can be produced on the cheap by a process known as electroplate. Here, laboratory fiddling enables base metals such as copper or nickel to be coated with a thin layer of gold or silver. With time, the coating wears away, revealing the metal underneath. Before that happens, your skin can be a better bogus detector than your eye. If skin near the piece starts turning green, you've got a case of electroplate-itis. Don't worry, it's harmless and will go away shortly after the jewellery is removed from the spot.

COSTUME PARTY

Where second-hand jewellery really shines is in the costume department. At charity shops, extraordinarily fun stuff can be had practically for pennies, especially ethnic-style beads and those wonderfully fake paste starbursts from the 1950s. A sharp eye can often detect pieces of real value as well, jumbled together with the junk. Vintage shops offer an even more bountiful array of faux baubles, from the marcasite-and-silver combos so popular at the turn of the twentieth century to 1970s-era mood rings. The prices at vintage will surpass those at thrift, reflecting the pieces' age (some are true antiques, over 100 years old) and collectability (there is a thriving market for period jewellery of all kinds and quality levels). Dress agencies, for their part, tend to specialise in big-ticket contemporary costume – the stuff usually found under the pricey counter at department stores. If you're shopping for a big night out, this may be exactly the place to find the perfect finishing touches for your outfit.

According to Deanna Farneti Cera's excellent reference *Costume Jewellery*, the rise of these adornments closely follows the evolution of clothing in the twentieth century. She categorises faux pieces as follows:

Bijoux de couture (couturier's jewellery): At the richest end of the costume scale are the limited-edition pieces commissioned by haute couturiers, meant to be worn with specific outfits from their collections. Coco Chanel was the great pioneer of this kind of adornment, and this house's pieces still carry a lot of cachet. Other classic names in couturier jewellery include Schiaparelli, Balenciaga and Dior – their early pieces are among the most coveted. The tradition of couturier jewellery continues today. Sporadically before the 1950s and consistently afterwards, such pieces have been 'signed' (in fact stamped) with the name of the commissioning couturier.

Costume jewellery: Produced in greater volume than the models above, this group tends to follow fashion rather than set it. Still, the level of craftsmanship is often superb. Certain path breakers from the past, such as Miriam Haskell, Fulco di Verdura and Jean Schlumberger, produced pieces that are as sought after today as the best of the couturier baubles. Other makers, such as Napier, Butler and Wilson, and Kenneth Jay Lane are collected at an equally avid rate. Like the couture pieces, ready-to-wear also tends to bear the signatures or marks of its manufacturers.

Inexpensive costume: Also called trinkets, these pieces were and are produced in the hundreds of thousands to be sold inexpensively as light-hearted adornments. Riding the fashion tide, the styles appear in department stores, markets, mail-order catalogues and the like. They disappear just as quickly, washing up sooner or later under the glass cases of vintage and charity shops. Rarely signed, they are usually not worth much to collectors, but that's not the important thing. If you love something and will put it to good wear – that's what counts.

Countless women accumulate jewellery like magpies, only to hide it away in the box or a drawer. One of history's most striking examples is memorialised at the Royal Museum in Edinburgh, Scotland, in the jewellery collection of an ordinary woman of the earlier part of last century. Like some of us, she spent most of her lunch hours out shopping, scouring her favourite shops and second-hand shops. She was an avid and meticulous collector, carefully noting the origin and price of every piece. But instead of ever wearing the jewellery, she kept it all squirrelled away. Even her closest friends were astonished when, after her death, the hundreds of treasures were revealed. You can't help but think how much brighter her life might have been with some of that razzle-dazzle at her neckline and wrists.

The lesson? Don't wait for special occasions to wear your accessories. When you start dressing as though life were occasion enough, special times will come right along with it.

Tender Loving Clothes Care

11

The well-tempered closet

Ah, the ambiance of a packed second-hand shop – some of us love it so much we have a home version in our very own closet. But what a disservice this does to beautifully made clothes. To look their best, blouses need to breathe, trousers need leg room, garments need personal space. In James Wagenvoord and Fiona St Aubyn's book *Clothes Care*, Elise Gaubert, a lady's maid, recalls how she 'once looked after a woman who had enough closet space to leave six inches between each garment. Nothing was ever crushed . . . which reduced the need for pressing, ironing and cleaning.' *Six inches*. For most of us, this is about 5⅞ inches beyond our wildest dreams. Still, when times get tight in the wardrobe, there are steps we can take to make sure clothes hang properly.

Here's a simple test to tell when your closet has reached maximum capacity. Will a blouse stay hung even if its hanger isn't touching the rail? If so, it's time to clear the decks with a full-scale storage overhaul. Admittedly, this is a chore only a domestic goddess could love, but the end result is worth the half-day of effort. Why?

◎   You'll be able to dress faster in the morning (in other words, an extra five to ten minutes of sleep).

◎   Your clothing won't need as much maintenance and repair.

◎   According to the principles of feng shui, the less mess in the closet, the clearer and happier the mind.

Done right, an overhaul consists of three parts:

1)   Emptying and cleaning the closet and drawers.

2)   Sorting through the clothes to weed out substandard and little-worn pieces.

3)   Reorganising the wardrobe in an orderly and pleasing way.

Doing the whole job in one go is the smartest tack, for it gives you an overview that helps you streamline and unify. For the same reason, a systematic approach like the one outlined in the following pages is better than diving in unprepared. To get you started, here's a look on the bright side: you've been nosing through your closet so often as part of your quality research that you've subconsciously done a lot of the groundwork already.

Before you begin, read through this chapter once to get an idea of the steps involved and what you can do to prepare. If you share your closet with someone else, consider doing the closet clean-up as a team. Finally, check out a housewares shop or catalogue to learn about storage options and equipment. You may find a container that revolutionises the way you keep order.

—Stage 1: Closet clear-out

TO PURCHASE/PREPARE AHEAD OF TIME: Household cleaners, cedar blocks/mothballs, fragrant sachets/potpourri, shelf liner.

THE PLAN: First, clear any non-wardrobe items off the flat surfaces in the bedroom – you're going to need all the space you can get. Then throw the doors open and start in. Every hanging item should be draped on the bed (it's easier if you keep clothing on the hangers, but beware of snagging neighbouring garments). Dressers, bureaus and any other repositories should also be emptied on the bed. Finally, shoes, belts, scarves, etc., should be brought out in plain sight.

Once the closet and drawers are entirely empty, they must be cleaned. Dusted, vacuumed, shelves wiped down, old mothballs, potpourri flakes and what have you swept up (wear rubber gloves for the mothballs), burned-out light bulb changed, old love letters reread, etc. If you are extremely motivated and have the space to temporarily stash the clothes elsewhere, you might consider repainting the closet's interior.

Once the closet and drawers are spotless, strew mothballs (but not if there are young children in the house) or nail up cedar blocks. These and the mothballs should not come in contact with the clothing – the mothballs are toxic and cedar oils could cause yellowing. Apply fresh contact paper and toss in the lavender, taking pleasure in the thought of all those fresh smells that soon will infuse your clothes.

— Stage 2: Survival of the chicest

TO PURCHASE/PREPARE AHEAD OF TIME: Decent hangers (wood, padded or well-shaped plastic; avoid wire). The best hangers for skirts have rubber-dipped metal or plastic clips (those with hinged flip-up crossbars crease waistbands and are a bore to use). If you have the room to hang trousers full-length, hangers with clips are also a good option. If you need to hang trousers folded, hangers with a crossbar are your best bet. For dresses, look for hangers with notches for dress loops. If space is very tight, think about buying multi-tiered hangers for trousers, shirts and skirts. For long-term storage, look for heavy plastic garment bags (not the clear ones used by dry-cleaners, which are terrible for your clothes), old suitcases/trunks, etc. If you have delicate vintage pieces, consider purchasing some acid-free boxes. Also get a fresh roll of rubbish bags for discards.

THE PLAN: At this point, the pile on your bed would strike fear in the heart of a skilled Sherpa guide. Don't be daunted – you can conquer the mountain all on your own, doing it step by step. Start by separating the items (shoes and accessories included), into four separate piles, according to the following guidelines:

1) DISCARDS. These are the clothes, shoes and other accessories that you know, in your heart of hearts, have come to the end of their useful life. Typically, they have one or more of the following characteristics:

◎   the quality now makes you cringe
◎   the flaws are so bad even a starving moth won't touch it
◎   your style has moved on
◎   the fit no longer meets your standards
◎   it's been two years since you've worn it

Put the stuff of low desirability (in other words, charity shop-bound) straight into a rubbish bag. Don't include anything truly nasty – you deplete the shop's manpower with items they have no hope of selling.

If you're thinking about consigning the better clothing to a dress agency (and you should be), weigh the cost of dry-cleaning against the profit you could realistically earn (see Chapter 15 for more on reselling clothes), then set these clothes aside as well.

> 'There comes a time when you have to let your clothes go
> out into the world and try to make it on their own.'
> **Bette Midler**

2) DEEP STORAGE. These are the items that you probably should throw out but, for various reasons, ranging from the fairly rational to the border-line psychotic, don't want to. They include:

- ethnic garb picked up on vacation that you may need for a fancy-dress party someday
- anything you haven't worn for a full year
- perfectly good clothes that are one size smaller than the current-model you, if you're taking steps to lose weight
- athletic clothes, if you're not actually sporty
- old T-shirts reeking of nostalgia or an ex-boyfriend's Lynx
- ski and any other clothing that requires an air ticket
- ball gowns (if your prince isn't coming through with steady invitations)

Before storing the clothes, take them off the hangers and assess. Do they need to be washed or dry-cleaned? It may seem bothersome to go to the trouble, but when you unearth them in the fullness of time, you'll be glad you did. Once the clothes are ready for deep storage, carefully fold them and place into appropriate holders. These can be suitcases, trunks, heavy-duty garment bags – even cardboard boxes, but remember that the latter contain acids that will eventually have an adverse affect. Be sure to add mothballs or other critter-preventatives such as bay leaves (in bags so they aren't in direct contact with the clothes). Finally, polish and bag to-be-stored shoes (will they really be stylish in another year or so?) and accessories and put them into containers as well. Before shoving the motley assembly into the darkest reaches of your living quarters, quickly jot down the contents on a piece of paper and tape it to the outside. This will spare you lots of hassle if that fancy-dress party ever comes through.

3) MENDERS. Meanwhile, back on the bed, this pile contains everything you ought to be wearing but aren't, because the zip's stuck, the hem's not

right, a button's gone, etc. As soon as you can face another round of domestic detail, stock up on supplies and get to work on fixing this stuff, or bring it to your alterations person and let them worry about it.

4) KEEPERS. These are the pieces that make you proud. Carefully re-hang them on appropriate hangers, and refold the ones that will go back into the drawers (have a look at the storage tips on pages 220 and 221). As you do this, be sure to give the items a quick once-over to be sure they don't require any cleaning or mending themselves.

Now that you're through sorting, what's left to do? Apart from organising your hanging space, little except dropping a couple of bagfuls of clothing off at your favourite charity shop, consigning a few items, and figuring out what to do with all the left-over wire hangers. In the spirit of recycling, gather them together and take them to the one place they'll be warmly welcomed: the dry-cleaner.

—Stage 3: Organising and how to do it

Different people have different notions on how to organise a closet. Some believe arranging clothes by colour is best. Others insist on hanging ready-made ensembles. Still others recommend grouping clothing by type. How you do it is a matter of taste and needs. If you're uncertain, the following rundown of advantages/disadvantages may help you make up your mind.

ORGANISING CLOTHES BY SEASON: A few experts recommend grouping clothes according to the time of year that they're worn. For example, all winter skirts are in one corner, all summer tops in another.
CONCLUSION: Seasonal segregation seems a lot less apt now than it did a few decades ago. Today, we're a lot more flexible about what colours are

right when, and many fabrics span three seasons of wear. Still, if you have a huge wardrobe and storage capacity (i.e., a walk-in closet), this method can help bring order to your abundance. Just beware of overlooking wardrobe possibilities (such as wearing a T-shirt under winter wool) due to over-categorisation.

ORGANISING CLOTHES BY COLOUR: Some women like to open their closet and see a rainbow of hues. Yellow pieces moving through to oranges, then to reds and beyond. In this system, the colour rules placement, so a skirt might hang alongside a dress or a pair of trousers. Besides pure aesthetics, there's a theory at work: when clothes are arranged by colour, matching is easier.

CONCLUSION: While it makes for a pretty closet, the method has its short-comings. Valuable space is often wasted when short and long items are mingled together (since there is no room for a second hanging bar below). Also, just because clothes are the same approximate hue doesn't mean they will match – style and proportion also count for a great deal. In any case, the best match is often between colours that are at different ends of the spectrum.

ORGANISING CLOTHES BY READY-MADE OUTFIT: Advocates believe that tops and bottoms that work beautifully as a team should be hung together (with appropriate accessories slung over the same hangers). They say the method streamlines the process of getting dressed.

CONCLUSION: This is a great way to guarantee consistent good looks, because the outfits have proven themselves already. And it gives women with very large wardrobes another way to get to grips with their possessions. Those with a limited number of pieces, however, may feel too tightly locked in. Moreover, some of us secretly enjoy the semi-panic that sets in when trying on combination after combination before getting it exactly right. Finally, as is the case with the colour method above, arranging clothing in this manner may encourage space inefficiency, as pieces of different lengths must be hung next to each other.

ORGANISING CLOTHES BY GARMENT TYPE: Here, skirts are hung with skirts, trousers with trousers, etc., progressing from one end of the closet to the other. There's a vague 'scientific' air to this arrangement, as it is the one promoted by the closet-organising companies.

CONCLUSION: Closet companies like organising by type because it makes maximum use of minimum space. It also allows for high flexibility in putting outfits together and makes it possible to detect wardrobe gaps. However, with the freedom comes danger – poor matches may occur because it's so easy to throw any two pieces together.

Ultimately, you know best how you want your clothes to hang. Pick one of the systems and try to stick to it – at least until the next closet overhaul (most experts recommend twice a year).

A FEW LAST STORAGE TIPS

- Knit dresses should be folded just like jumpers.
- Trousers can be folded or placed on shelf, or hung two to a hanger, facing opposite directions.
- Never fold a jumper lengthways – the crease will take forever to fall out.
- Blouses can be hung or folded.
- When buying hangers, be sure the hook is big enough to fit your bar.
- If you must use wire hangers, wrap elastic bands around ends to prevent garments from sliding.
- A fishing tackle box is an excellent jewellery holder.
- Wine racks are good for storing shoes.
- Alternatively, store shoes in boxes with the ends cut out so you can see what's inside.

◎   To prevent cracking, belts should be coiled or hung straight, not left in garments.

— Expanding your storage capabilities

There's never enough room, is there? Even after the closet is organised to the last inch, overflow may still be a problem. What to do? Forget about hanging items from the shower rail. The following fairly instant, not-very-expensive methods are lifesavers. Besides keeping stuff out of sight, they'll upgrade the style quotient of your living space.

HATBOXES
Whether antique or brand new, these are a marvellous way to add room to your room. It doesn't matter if you never wear hats. You surely wear tights, T-shirts, scarves and gloves – all of which fold flat and are perfect candidates for tucking away. These containers stack up in a corner or on top of a wardrobe and look great, plus they are light enough to fling around when you're looking for an item one holds. Be sure to line the box with tissue paper before adding clothes. Hatboxes are often found at charity or vintage shops, car-boot sales, and, best of all, in relatives' attics.

RATTAN TRUNKS
Also lightweight and fairly inexpensive, a rattan trunk can hold a couple of seasons' worth of sweaters within easy reach of the rest of the wardrobe – or jeans, puffa coats or other bulky pieces that don't merit a full-time parking space in the closet. Spray-painted a great colour or with a pretty throw on top, they're a lovely addition to all manner of decor. The best place to find them is at funky, lower-priced furniture shops.

ANTIQUE LUGGAGE
A bit pricier are the gorgeous leather pieces that huddled in the hold while their owners sipped champagne at the captain's table. Stack these up against

some underused wall space and you've not only got instant storage but inimitable transatlantic style. Pieces with Louis Vuitton's initials are particularly covetable. The less expensive trunks are usually pretty beaten up but can be redeemed with some tender loving polish and strategic positioning to hide damage. Antique luggage can be found at vintage shops, antique shops and fairs (here you'll pay big), relatives' attics and charity shops.

SCREEN/CLOTHES RAIL

I once lived in a bedsit that didn't have a single closet. The solution? A rolling garment rail, hidden behind a pretty folding screen. Voilà, instant walk-in closet. Household organising shops should be able to supply the rolling rack. The screen can be had from import shops, car-boot sales, or even made with some plywood, hinges, fabric and a staple gun.

With a little ingenuity and some careful combing of your favourite second-hand haunts, you'll not only detect fabulous finds, but also fabulous storage aids to hold them. And even if your own lady's maid is out of the question, nobody will know it from looking at you.

Caring for your clothes

In the past, people were famously less fussy than we are today when it came to keeping their clothes clean. The same garment would be worn for weeks (if not months), pressing was infrequent, stain removal was haphazard at best. But before rushing to judge, it's only fair to consider the circumstances. If you think a full hamper is one of life's torments, consider the fluff and tumble of laundry years ago.

—Rub a dub dub

The very first washing apparatus was simplicity itself: a pair of hands or feet, a river and a nice big flat rock. When clothes were beaten against the hard surface, dirt and oils would loosen and drift down the current. If this original version of stonewashing was tough on clothes, it was even tougher on the washerwomen's limbs. The introduction of tubs and paddles didn't help. According to Una Robertson's *Illustrated History of the Housewife*, women worked 'with their coats tucked up . . . and this not only in summer, but in the hardest frosty weather, when their legs and feet were almost literally as red as blood with the cold . . .'

In many parts of the world, plants (especially those in the *Saponaria* family) helped get clothes clean. When pounded, their stems released a lathery froth, the forerunner of soap. In the fifteenth century, the first true soaps were fashioned from plant or animal fats blended with ashes and sodium bicarbonate. By the nineteenth century, soap-making was a world-wide industry. Even so, it wasn't standard at laundry time, for two reasons. Firstly, in certain countries and eras, it was highly taxed, making it prohibitively expensive. Secondly, this primitive soap would only dissolve in hot water, and so wasn't always practical in the days before electricity. This is why washerwomen from ancient Rome up to nineteenth-century England turned to another natural product to get clothes clean and bright: stale human urine. Though this may sound like a bad Monty Python routine, it's actually not that far-fetched. Urine contains ammonia, one of the best natural cleaning and brightening agents around. Something else in its favour – it was a cleaning supply that never ran low. Many households had troughs in the backyard especially for collecting the raw material. This pungent chapter in laundry history drew to a close when laundry soap as we know it entered the scene at the beginning of the twentieth century.

The saga didn't end with the final rinse – pressing was one more reason women dreaded washday. Before the introduction of specialised tools, clothes were literally pulled or trampled flat, or hung on a line to dry straight (and board-stiff) in the breeze. Heavy irons simplified the job, but what with all the heating and reheating, scorched fabric and fingertips were inevitable. In the eighteenth century, a contraption called a mangle appeared in wealthier households. Clothes were set on rollers underneath a weighted box, which, as it was cranked over them, flattened the items and pressed out most of the water. Since the box could be up to six feet long and was filled with heavy stones, the mangle could hardly be described as a labour-saving device, though it did lighten up in later years.

So the next time your laundry duties start getting you down, cheer yourself up with some snapshots from the past – chilblains, aching back, burned fingers and swishing around in what amounted to a full toilet. The contemporary version – sorting, loading, folding and ironing, all in the space of two hours or so – is, by comparison, low agitation.

— *New improved formula*

In fact, it's so easy to do laundry these days that lots of us slide by with half-measures. You know what I mean. Cheating on sorting, flinging stuff into machines without adjusting the controls, leaving minor stains to take care of themselves, blithely ignoring temperature recommendations. While most of today's clothing is tough enough to withstand the occasional shortcut, doing laundry sloppily with any regularity is certain to increase fading, wear, permanent stains and the outright ruination of favourite items. Spending an extra five or ten minutes to do it right points to a woman who truly values her clothes, one who knows that a little virtue come laundry time brings more than its own rewards.

◎   Drying clothes for the recommended time means they need less ironing.

◎   Dealing with stains before they set means fewer visits to the dry-cleaner.

◎   Keeping an eye on laundry temperatures means colours stay brighter.

◎   Doing it all right means your precious investment endures.

Connoisseur's Tip:
Great clothing only stays that way with careful upkeep.

—Separated, but equal

In the laundry kingdom, there are three broad classes of clothing:

1.   machine-washable items
2.   hand-washable items
3.   items that must go to the dry-cleaner

The breakdown depends on the type of fabric involved and its reaction to water, heat and agitation. To sort out what's what prior to cleaning, it's best to check the garment's care label. Predictably, though, second-hand clothing throws in a few wrinkles. The care tags are cut out, for example. Or written in Armenian. Or, due to the clothes' age, were never there in the first place. Not to worry. As long as you know what kind of fabric the garment is made of, you can proceed with confidence. Here's a rundown of the typical care requirements:

Acetate: Dry-clean, or machine or hand wash at cool temperature. Do not wring when wet or put through spin cycle in washer. Hang or dry flat (do not tumble dry). Iron while damp at cool temperature.

Acrylic: Machine wash. Hang or dry flat. Iron at cool temperature.

Corduroy: Wash as per material (usually cotton), turning inside out. Tumble dry. Leave inside out for ironing.

Cotton: Separate lights and darks, and machine wash. Whites may be washed very hot, colours warm. Tumble dry, but remove while still a bit damp or wrinkles will set fast. Iron on hot.

Denim: Wash as per cotton, but the first time all alone so that dye does not stain other clothing. Turn inside out to discourage fading. Hang to dry to avoid shortening and shrinkage.

Leather: Send to specialist dry-cleaner. Spray with protective product once back.

Nylon: Wash by hand or machine at cool temperature with like colours. Nylon's natural hue is greyish and it will revert if mislaundered. Special nylon whiteners can be purchased at the supermarket. Iron cool.

Rayon: If washing instructions are missing, dry-clean only.

Silk: Dry-clean or hand wash in cool water with Stergene or similar gentle product. Do not rub or a chalky bloom may arise due to broken filaments. Hang or dry flat. Take care with spot cleaning, as this may leave rings. Shirts and blouses should be steamed or ironed on cool on reverse side.

Spandex content: Wash at cool temperature. Hang or dry flat, or tumble dry at cool temperature. Iron cool.

Suede: Dry-clean only. Spray with suede protector once back from cleaner.

Wool and cashmere: Dry-clean or hand wash. Wool may be damaged by traditional soaps and detergents – better to use Stergene or baby shampoo. Put wool through washing machine or tumble dryer only on settings specifically designated for this fibre. If wrinkled, hang dry woollens in steamy bathroom.

If the garment is older or delicate vintage, see the specific care instructions on page 242.

— *Your partner in grime*

Sometimes, due to the nature of the fabric or the delicacy of construction, you simply can't go it alone. Here are the main reasons to take an item to the dry-cleaner:

- you don't know what kind of material it is
- the garment has interfacings and/or linings
- the garment is made up of two or more kinds of fabric
- the garment is beaded
- the garment has metallic thread
- the fabric is otherwise very dressy, like velvet or taffeta
- lord only knows what that stain is
- the laundry care tag tells you to

Whether you dry-clean clothes once a year or twice a week, try to work with the best outfit in town. Yes, it'll be more expensive, but ultimately it's worth it. In choosing dry-cleaning professionals, remember that those with equipment on the premises come out ahead, for three reasons. Firstly, the personnel are more knowledgeable, since they're the ones doing the job. Secondly, you can make any complaints directly, without having to go through a middleman.

Thirdly, it cuts down on the chances of items being lost (exasperatingly frequent, in my experience). Something else to seek out: specialisation in cleaning wedding dresses and formals, for these people will be comfortable with a gamut of fabrics.

DRY-CLEANING INSIDE SCOOP

- Only dry-clean cotton and linen if shrinkage is a real worry – otherwise detergent and water do the best job. What's more, some believe these fibres retain whiffs of dry-cleaning solution.

- If you must dry-clean jeans, be aware that the pressed crease down the front will soon bleach in permanently.

- Work with your cleaner. Point out any stains, describe the source if you can and mention any special dry-cleaning requirements (it *is* their job to check, but the nudge never hurts).

◎   Garments are ironed in one of two ways: entirely with specialist pressing
    equipment (faster and less expensive) or finished by hand (pricier,
    better results). The following signs of careless machine-pressing mean
    the garment should be redone (and if you specified hand-pressing,
    they are signs that you're being ripped off; get your money back and
    don't return).

- Lapel squashed flat against the front of a suit jacket (it should
  gently curve inward instead).
- Trousers turn-ups pressed so hard they leave an indentation
  against the side of the ankle.
- Cuffs and collars wrinkled or otherwise distorted (French cuffs,
  the kind that require links, are routine victims).
- Cuffs pressed so hard buttons leave an indentation on the fabric
  below.
- Buttons broken, chipped or pitted from the heat of the iron. By
  rights these should be replaced by the dry-cleaner. If it's a
  gauntlet button, make sure they use a smaller one than those at
  the cuffs.

—Into every life, a little stain must fall

We're all only human, and stains are nature's proof. When it happens to
you, don't lose your cool. Most will vanish if you treat them as quickly as
possible. Even if it means excusing yourself from the table – you'll look
much more composed after some quick work in the Ladies' than with mari-
nara sauce all over your blouse. The point is to do as much as you can before
laundering, because washing, drying and ironing, especially at high temperatures, often locks the mark in for good.

Effective stain removal depends on two things: the fabric's care requirements and the culprit. **If the garment is dry-clean only**, try to remove as
much of the offending stuff as possible with a white paper towel (being

careful not to rub it in), then get it to the cleaner pronto. (Some clothes-care experts recommend tackling the stain yourself with a shop-bought dry-cleaning product, but unless you have total confidence in your abilities, it's best to leave it to the experts.)

To treat stains on washable clothing, there are three options.

1. If it's just a spot, attack it directly with a store-bought pre-wash product, then launder as usual.
2. If it's a bigger, nastier stain (and the item can go into the machine), run it through the pre-wash cycle.
3. Or, soak the garment in a basin or sink (if it's silk or wool, use only cleaners safe for those fabrics and never soak for longer than a few minutes).

If the item is badly or very stubbornly soiled, the soaking and pre-wash techniques are preferable because they prevent gunk from getting trapped in the washer and being re-deposited on the other clothes. If the stain is biological in origin, such as blood, egg or grass, bio pre-soak cleaners are helpful. Note, though, that they will eat away at animal fibres such as wool and silk.

Before using any stain remover, test it on a hidden area of the garment, blotting after a moment with a white cloth or paper towel to see if the dye lifts. Also be sure to use the appropriate product. All-purpose stain removers work best on machine-washable fabrics, while solvent-based products are intended for dry-cleanables. If you can't get your hands on an all-purpose stain remover, baby shampoo, clear washing-up liquid or even hand soap will do.

If there's one thing that regularly blots our reputation, it's food. Such spills usually don't happen where reference books are at the ready, so it's a good idea to memorise these general treatment rules:

For non-greasy stains: Rinse in cool water as soon as possible. Apply a pre-wash product, stain remover, clear washing-up liquid or soap. (If you're not sure how the fabric will react, test first.) Gently press suds through – rubbing may damage fine fabric. Rinse under cool water or flush soap through with spray water bottle. If you're out of the house, press dry with paper towels, or, keeping fabric well away from the heat, hold for a few minutes under a bathroom hand-dryer. As soon as you can, launder garment as usual.

For greasy stains: If feasible, use an absorbent such as talcum powder to soak up the stain, let it sit for twenty minutes, then gently brush off. Next apply a stain/grease-removing product (testing first on unpredictable fabrics). If greasy stains come your way with pathetic regularity, consider carrying a pocket-sized stain-remover stick in your bag. Follow manufacturer's instructions (you may need to repeat several times). As soon as possible, launder in the hottest temperature that the fabric can stand.

For combination stains (chocolate, dairy products, gravy): Treat as for greasy stains first. If stain persists, treat with all-purpose product. Launder in the hottest temperature that the fabric can stand.

The methods above are good general remedies for emergencies. There's also a roster of at-home techniques to deal with more specific spots and spills. Many have been used for generations, well before the advent of specialised laundry-care products. If you know the source of your stain and are green-minded, you may want to try one of these first, as they are a gentle and responsible way to treat your clothes. Then, if they don't work, move on to the stronger stain-busters.

Alcohol: Even if the alcohol was colourless, the stain will turn brown if untreated. (If you remember anything at all the morning after, try to remember this.) Sponge several times with white vinegar diluted 1:1 with warm water. Launder as usual.

Ballpoint ink: Flush immediately with cold water, then treat the stain with hand soap (which is more effective on inks than laundry soap). Rinse and repeat if necessary. Traditional alternative method: soak stain in sour milk. If you can't wait for milk to sour, try spraying with alcohol-heavy hairspray, then rinse with cool water.

Blood: Soak as soon as possible in cool, heavily salted water, then dab on liquid laundry soap; rinse. Launder as usual. If stain remains, consider soaking in bio pre-treatment (check that fabric will not be harmed first).

Candle wax: Put item in plastic bag in freezer for an hour. Peel solid wax off fabric; lift any remaining stain with solvent-based product. Launder as usual.

Coffee and tea: rinse in warm water, then wash in warm soapy water. On wools and silks, first apply glycerine (available at a good chemist's or hardware shop); let stand; rinse with warm water.

Egg: Scrape off any solids with a dull knife or spoon edge. Turn garment inside out and place towel between layers, then sponge cold water on fabric (never use hot, which will set the stain permanently). If stain is stubborn and item is not silk or wool, soaking in enzyme cleaner is the next resort.

Grass: Treat with liquid soap rubbed into stain, followed by sponging with denatured alcohol, if the stain is persistent (test rubbing alcohol on inconspicuous area first!). Treat with a bio product, if necessary, or dry-clean

Mildew: Leather stored under damp or humid conditions is especially prone to mildew. After testing on inconspicuous area, apply antiseptic mouthwash on cottonwool ball; dab gently.

Mud: Let dry completely first. Remove dry mud with brush or cloth. Presoak if fabric allows, then launder.

Pencil: Rub gently with a soft, white eraser.

Perspiration stains: If the stain is on cotton or linen, sponge old stains with 1 tbsp white vinegar in one cup water. Alternatively, apply paste of 1 tbsp cream of tartar, 3 crushed aspirins and water. Leave on for 20 mins. Rinse well.

Rust marks: On white cottons and linens only, stretch stained fabric tight over pan of boiling water and sprinkle lemon juice on top. After a minute, rinse well and repeat, if necessary. Or, again with these fabrics only, spread stain with cream of tartar; hold over steaming kettle. Rinse immediately.

Scorch marks: Try rubbing with the edge of a 10p coin. If this doesn't work, resort to dry-cleaner. Note that bad scorches probably won't come out.

Toner: Do not wet. Try vacuuming powder out; otherwise take to dry-cleaner.

Watermarks: Hold marks over steaming kettle. Remove from steam, dab mark gently with cloth.

—A brief word on bleach

Bleach is a valuable cleaning aid in certain situations – namely with all-white cottons and linens, where it helps lift stubborn stains and boost brightness. But with coloured items and other fabrics (silk, wool, rayon and permanent-press cotton), bleach could out and out ruin your clothes. Always check care labels before using such a product, and be sure it is well-diluted according to the label's instructions. For coloured clothing, non-chlorine bleach formulations are a safe alternative.

— Symbol logic

Doing laundry right means having a firm grasp of the lingo. In the old days, this meant knowing your permanent press from your gentle cycle. But today, it's more a matter of telling your 🧺 from your. 🧺 Increasingly, in the name of simplification, the clothes-care business is turning to icons in the place of words.

Cleaning clothes without knowing the symbols is like driving in a land with unfamiliar traffic signs. Most of us can manage to do so without an ugly accident, but it is safer all round to be prepared. All the more so since, as of 1999, clothes manufacturers are no longer obligated to provide written instructions along with the icons on care labels. In other words, you could be faced with a bunch of symbols and no other guidelines whatsoever. That's why it makes sense to check these symbols as often as you can. Just as with road signs, the more frequently you see them, the more routine they become.

As ever, second-hand garments add a few extra curves to the symbol-reading process. If your garment was made before June 1997, any care symbols present will look slightly different, as they may if they're of foreign origin. The following table should sort it all out. Currently, all don'ts are represented by an X through the icon. If you see this, pay attention; they're not kidding.

🧺 Machine launder, normal: set washer to 65–85ºF/30ºC (With this and all wash settings, older and/or foreign garments may show the recommended Celsius temperature rather than dots.)

🧺 Machine launder, normal: set washer to 105ºF/40ºC

🧺 Machine launder, normal: set washer to 120ºF/50ºC

⊞ Machine launder, normal: set washer to 140ºF/60ºC

⊞ Machine launder, normal: set washer to 160ºF/70ºC

⊞ Machine launder, normal: set washer to 200ºF/95ºC

⊡ Machine launder, permanent press (Any dots indicate same temperatures as those above.)

⊡ Machine launder, delicate/gentle cycle (Any dots indicate same temperatures as those above. In foreign garments, a single broken underline may be used instead of a double underline.)

⊞ Hand wash

◎ Tumble dry

⊖ at high temperature

⊙ at medium temperature

⊙ at low temperature

◎ Tumble dry, permanent press

◎ Tumble dry, gentle

▥ Drip dry

⊓ Hang to dry

⊟ Dry flat

⊠ Do not wring

⊿ Iron

⊿ High: set iron to 390ºF/200ºC

⊿ Medium: set iron to 300ºF/150ºC

⊿ Low: set iron to 230ºF/110ºC

⊿ Do not use steam

○ Dry-clean

⊗ Do not dry-clean

Ⓐ Dry-clean with any solvent

Ⓟ Dry-clean with any solvent except trichloroethylene
Ⓕ Dry-clean with petroleum solvent only

✖ Do not bleach
⚠ Do not use chlorine bleach
△ Use any bleach when needed

—Another load off your mind

Now that you're fluent in the care symbols, let's move on to the heavy equipment. As mentioned earlier, there's a right way and a wrong way to feed the washing machine. The wrong way is to throw it all in come what may. Do this and your clothes will soon resemble the charity shop bargain-bin items you ordinarily reject out of hand. Taking a few more seconds to do it right means gaining months, if not years, of increased wear.

Sorting: Once upon a time, I divided clothes between coloured and white (and took pride in being so fastidious). Then I met my beloved, who, as it happened, broke them down further into greens, greys, permanent press, towels, each bundle getting a separate turn in the wash. Wow, that's exacting, I said when we shared our first hamper (but in truth had another word in mind). Now, though, I've come around to his way, because sorting this specifically does make sense. For one thing, it lowers the risk of colour tainting. For another, it maintains the life of certain fabrics, like permapress, delicates and synthetics, all of which require cooler temperatures. Likewise, heavy items like towels do best all together, since they shed a lot of lint.

Checking: Before putting anything in, run through pockets to remove any coins, paper or, God forbid, pens. Also snap snaps and do up zips prior to washing, which will prevent snags and damage to other items in the laundry.

Loading: Smaller loads are much easier on your garments than gargantuan piles, and will help keep the washer repairman at bay. With front-loading machines, fill the drum three-quarters full.

Choosing your settings: Follow instructions on the care labels, or, if these are missing, the general care advice provided for different fabrics on pages 226–7.

Washing-machine inside scoop

◎   If you use coin-operated machines, you may be reluctant to waste money on many small loads. Consider doing your laundry with a friend if it will help get you into the habit.

◎   If you send your laundry out, the clothes will be washed all together unless you do a sub-sort beforehand. If you buy a couple of different sacks for this purpose, the process will be automatic.

◎   To clean detergent build-up from your own machine (a good idea every few months or so), run an empty load, putting a quarter-cup of white vinegar into the soap dispenser.

◎   Using more detergent than recommended will not get clothes cleaner. Heavy suds do not mean a better wash. In fact, any excess detergent remaining in the fabric will actually attract dirt later on.

◎   Try to get wet clothes out of the machine as soon as they're done – this will help reduce wrinkling in the dryer.

◎   Safety pins or special sock clips can combat vanishing sock syndrome.

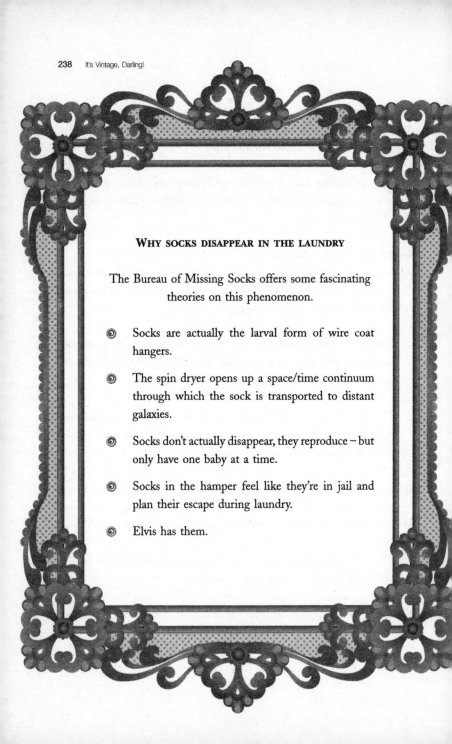

WHY SOCKS DISAPPEAR IN THE LAUNDRY

The Bureau of Missing Socks offers some fascinating
theories on this phenomenon.

- Socks are actually the larval form of wire coat
  hangers.

- The spin dryer opens up a space/time continuum
  through which the sock is transported to distant
  galaxies.

- Socks don't actually disappear, they reproduce – but
  only have one baby at a time.

- Socks in the hamper feel like they're in jail and
  plan their escape during laundry.

- Elvis has them.

—Hand-washing

Putting hand-washables in a net bag near the hamper keeps them safely away from the rest of the load, and acts as subtle reminder to do it. I prefer to hand wash at night, so I'm not stepping over (on) the drying items.

◎   When the instructions say use only warm or cool water temperatures, they mean it.

◎   Make sure soap has dissolved completely before adding clothing.

◎   Don't rub at grime, especially if it's on silk. Gently press suds through instead.

◎   Don't keep stuff soaking forever – try to remove clothing as per time instructions.

◎   Rinsing hand-washing is easier and faster in the bath than in the sink. Put in the plug and fill a few inches with cool water. Immerse garments, swish around well, drain and repeat. (Adding a tbsp of white vinegar will help get rid of the soap).

'Dry flat only' is the method recommended for most wool sweaters. Why? Because machine-drying will shrink them, and hanging will stretch the arms and torso. To flat-dry properly, first roll the garment up in a towel to remove excess moisture. Then lay the sweater flat (ideally on a glass table, but any even, dry surface will do – use a dry towel as a barrier on floors and carpets). Try to position the garment in same shape as desired when dry. Martha Stewart's *Living* magazine once recommended measuring the garment before washing to ensure the proper length when laying out to dry. This sort of attention to detail is why so many Americans love Martha Stewart, and also why so many rejoiced when she was sentenced to jail.

If cuffs or ribbing have become stretched, use wool's shrinking properties to your own advantage. Dampen these sections, then blow-dry on hot to shrink back to shape.

If you have minimal floor space and the garment is almost dry, you can get away with hanging if you do it like this: grab an old pair of tights and feed through the arms of the sweater. Clip the hose ends to a line and hang.

If a garment can be hung, do so outdoors if you can, for nothing beats the smell of line-dried clothes. Also, sunlight is an excellent natural bleaching agent for dingy-looking whites. Remember, though, that it will have the same effect on coloured items, so it's best to hang these in the shade. If hanging clothes indoors on hangers, don't use uncoated wire or stained wooden ones, for they may leave a residue on clothing.

— Going for a spin

When it comes to reading dryer settings, a lot of us are functional illiterates. Still, if you've gone to all the trouble to sort clothes for the laundry, it only makes sense to keep up the good work on the back end. Remember that synthetics always do better on cool temperatures than warm. Also, if a care tag specifies hang-dry, don't cheat. Putting it in the machine might strip away special finishes, and leave the piece looking miserable.

DRYER INSIDE SCOOP

◎   Give each item a good shake before putting it in. This will prevent wrinkles, and gives you a last chance to rescue non-dryable items from the load.

◎   Don't over dry (it's especially easy in laundrette machines). Better to remove garments when the tiniest bit damp – the wrinkles won't be as fierce and the clothes will last longer over the long run.

◎   Machine-drying causes cotton knits to fade and fuzz up much faster than drying naturally. I always try to hang them instead. They may dry a bit stiffer, but the pay-off in added wear is worth it.

—Press for success

There's a difference between ironing and pressing – with the latter, a cloth is used between the iron and the fabric to reduce the possibility of damage. Actually, it's always a good idea to use a pressing cloth routinely (any clean white pillowcase will do), for it prevents damage to delicate fabrics, keeps the iron from over-flattening the garment, and reduces the risk of raising a shine. You can further protect an item by turning it inside out. Most ironing is simplified if the clothes are slightly damp – keep a mister handy for this purpose.

IRONING INSIDE SCOOP

◎ Start by ironing at coolest setting first (silks) and progress towards warmest (cottons).

◎ When ironing blouse collars, always move from the tips to the centre.

◎ Don't use the steam setting on silk – if your iron should spit, watermarks may result.

◎ When ironing pleats, hair grips can help keep them in place. But avoid running the iron over the pins.

◎ Never put a freshly ironed garment onto a wooden chair – the polish may transfer onto the warm cloth.

◎ Always empty steam irons after use so that vents stay clear and mildew doesn't develop. Strictly speaking, distilled water should be used for ironing, to prevent the build-up of minerals or other contaminents in the vents. Scented water specifically intended for use in irons is available at large supermarkets. If you like, add a drop of cologne (just *one* drop, and alcohol-based only) to tap water to add a delightful scent to pressed clothes.

◎ Never iron across buttons or zips; iron around them instead.

—Caring for delicate vintage clothing

Gentle treatment with a Dustbuster (with the nozzle held well away from the cloth and the garment placed in a fine-meshed nylon net to prevent accidental sucking away of any beadwork or delicate threads) may be the best method of all for very old or very worn garments. White cotton and linen items can be gently hand-washed. Coloured items must be tested before washing (blot with a damp white cloth) to ensure that the dyes won't run. To wash, place the garment in a fine-meshed nylon net bag, use warm water and an extremely gentle washing agent, like Stergene, well diluted. With a small sponge, press gently on fabric to push through suds. Rinse with distilled water. The garment should be dried flat and not ironed. With items such as vintage rayon, a good dry-cleaner will be able to offer the best advice and care. A classic Hawaiian shirt (which is always made of rayon) may shred in the machine!

—Keeping up appearances: general clothing care

◎   Always hang just-worn items out overnight so that air can circulate, drying residual perspiration.

◎   Hanging clothes also allows gravity/the residual heat of your body to gently act on wrinkles, pulling them clear.

◎   Heavier garments, such as wool jackets, trousers and jeans, should be whisked with a good clothes brush to remove dust after wear. If it's allowed to settle in the creases, it will literally grind your clothes apart, fibre by fibre.

◎   Don't leave clothes in a steamy bathroom hamper for weeks on end. Mildew and perspiration will begin to rot them away. If an eternity passes between your laundry loads, keep the hamper someplace dry.

◎   Lint, dust, dandruff and hairs can be removed with a piece of masking tape wound several times around the hand, or with one of those shop-bought dust-removal rollers. If none of these are handy, a damp sponge will work at a pinch.

◎   If you've never read the back of a laundry soap box or the manual that came with your washing appliances, consider taking a look. While they won't beat a good thriller, they will take a lot of the mystery out of doing your laundry.

Hitting the Shops

13

The vintage advantage

I find vintage the most fascinating – and challenging – mode of second-hand shopping. Added to the usual considerations of quality, fit and suitability are wearability, fragility and over-the-top quotient, making for a tumbling flurry of purchase factors. What's more, the secret history of these pieces lends them a mystique that fresh-off-the-factory-floor clothes utterly lack.

Two types of people pursue vintage clothes. The first (not us) are the collectors. They wouldn't dream of exposing their antique treasures to excess handling or, worse, actual wear. Instead, they seek to preserve specimens under museum-quality conditions, as though they were works of fine art. The alternate approach (us) is, in contrast, more hands-, arms- and thighs-on. Our tastes may be as refined and our knowledge as keen as our preservationist sisters, but we feel a garment doesn't come into its own until it's worn on a living, breathing human being.

— Old beginnings

Ironic but true: countless girls who were disposed to sleeping through history class could score A-levels in past-era fashion. Why? It offers originality, exceptional construction and arresting style. Following the trend, costume history, once the rather dusty realm of a handful of specialists, is now a glamour field. Christie's auctioneers holds biannual sales of twentieth-century vintage clothing, joining the old-line New York house of William Doyle and Paris's Drouot, which have been in the game since long before it became ultra-fashionable. Such sales not only draw costume curators and the preservationist wing of the vintage crowd, but also fashion-conscious (and well-funded) girls looking to pump up their wardrobe.

Vintage can cost the moon, but the prices are more likely to be very down to earth – somewhere in the double or triple figures. Even at this level, you don't need a degree in costume history to find marvellous items. Women who don't know a bustle from a barn door can browse purely for the pleasure of it, and learn as they go along.

Beyond gran's attic

Where are the best places to find vintage clothes? It's funny speaking with shop owners, who merrily chat about all aspects of their business – except this. Ask them where they source their pieces and all of a sudden they shut tight as clams. And who can blame them, given the competition, and the tooth-and-nail jostling for steady supply at the vintage equivalent of the wholesale level?

— Jumble and car-boot sales

As for us, while it's still (remotely) possible to unearth pieces in (remote) charity shops, finds of true quality on the cheapy cheap are scarce.

Other iffy, but not altogether hopeless, sources are car-boot and jumble sales. No less a glamour hound than Judith Krantz, the novelist who pioneered the beach-book formula of shopping, sex and more shopping (*priorities*, darling!), praised jumble sales in this memorable passage from *Princess Daisy*:

> Her buys all came from London jumble sales in church halls. There she specialised in unearthing English and French couture originals, preferably over forty years old, clothes that had been made in the great dressmaking decades of the twenties and thirties. She researched them after she had brought them back in triumph, for nothing she owned had cost over thirty-five dollars.

OK, so this is a starry-eyed take on the potential of jumbles, which in fact are the second-hand equivalent of playing the lottery. You just have to strike at the right time (the second they open) and be having an especially lucky day. But you never know. To maximise your chances of finding choice goods, keep these other factors in mind:

◎ Location: Wealthier neighbourhoods tend to have better-quality merchandise.

◎ Regularity: When churches and schools hold regular sales, participants save their closet clean-outs for those dates, boosting the likelihood of high volume and good quality.

◎ Early bird = worm: You'll have plenty of rival shoppers who *live* for these things. Their expertise quickly wins them the best buys. Get there early, bring plenty of cash, and don't let the competitive buzz override good manners and a sense of humour. If you do arrive after the clothes have been fairly well picked over, don't give up – there's always accessories, where true treasures often linger.

— Vintage exhibitions

Far more fail-safe indeed are specialist vintage fairs and exhibitions, which bring together tens, even hundreds of vintage purveyors under one roof. You'll have to pay admission to gain entry (generally under £10), but the merchandise and variety and learning opportunities are well worth it. Since these are regular affairs, make a point of stopping at the information booth to get show schedules and be put on the mailing list. Since exhibitions offer such a dazzling array of goods, it makes sense to go in with a game plan, to avoid premature burn-out or budget-blowing.

— Markets

Antiques and street markets are fantastic opportunities to find many vintage purveyors within paces of each other. The Portobello Road market is the most famous, a streetwise emporium with all the historical and sociological significance of the grand old department stores, except instead of dowdy old dames substitute browsers like David Bowie, Stella McCartney, Erin O'Connor . . . Vintage and more recent-era retro sellers tend to cluster in market areas, where street traffic and keen buyers are steady. At stalls, expect nothing more than a flap of canvas to serve as the dressing room. Also, count on paying in cash – many dealers are not equipped to handle credit cards and don't like the rebound potential of cheques. If you find a dealer and merchandise you like, get the card and some directions so you can find your way back easily the next time you visit, and do try to do so on a regular basis. Always make a point of speaking with the owner about the kinds of clothes she specialises in, what else she may have to your liking (the stock might not all be present on a given day) and where else she sells.

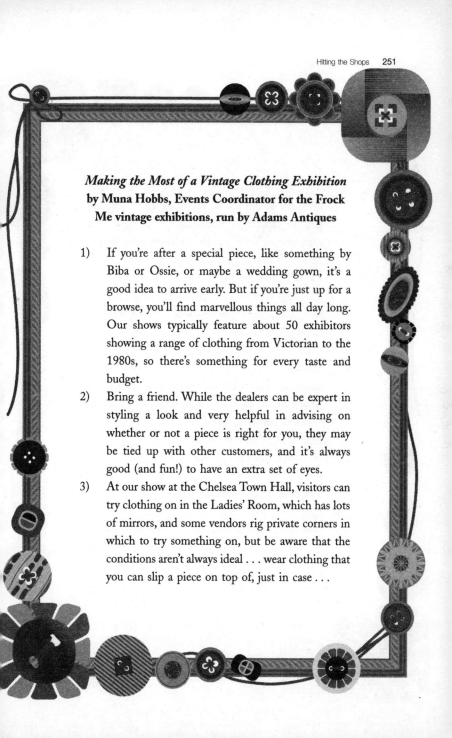

Making the Most of a Vintage Clothing Exhibition
by Muna Hobbs, Events Coordinator for the Frock Me vintage exhibitions, run by Adams Antiques

1) If you're after a special piece, like something by Biba or Ossie, or maybe a wedding gown, it's a good idea to arrive early. But if you're just up for a browse, you'll find marvellous things all day long. Our shows typically feature about 50 exhibitors showing a range of clothing from Victorian to the 1980s, so there's something for every taste and budget.

2) Bring a friend. While the dealers can be expert in styling a look and very helpful in advising on whether or not a piece is right for you, they may be tied up with other customers, and it's always good (and fun!) to have an extra set of eyes.

3) At our show at the Chelsea Town Hall, visitors can try clothing on in the Ladies' Room, which has lots of mirrors, and some vendors rig private corners in which to try something on, but be aware that the conditions aren't always ideal . . . wear clothing that you can slip a piece on top of, just in case . . .

4) Most visitors like to have a look around first, get their eye in and see what's available, before shopping in earnest. As the stalls are arranged in no particular order, it's a good idea to pick up business cards as you go and make a quick note of what might interest you . . .

5) The biggest crowds are right before lunch and right after. You never know who will show up: we've had Julien Macdonald, John Rocha, Alber Elbaz, Lucinda Chambers of *Vogue*, and many others . . .

6) Plan on spending a minimum of an hour at the show, you'll probably want more time once you see what's here . . . you can grab lunch in the exhibition hall before jumping back into the fray.

7) One thing vendors really don't appreciate (apart, obviously, from people manhandling the clothes!) is a potential buyer who puts something on hold and then never comes back, preventing a possible sale.

8) You can pretty much count on finding something you'll love at an exhibition; even I can't resist and I've been running these for several years now. What can I say, I'm a girl . . .

— Vintage on the internet

Meanwhile, over the road in bandwidth, the past decade has seen an explosion in the number of internet sites carrying vintage clothing, complete with detailed descriptions, high-quality scans, and owners willing to provide service on a par with bricks-and-mortar operations. If you're stuck at a desk with a good broadband connection this is a highly gratifying way to pass the time (not that I'm encouraging skiving off at work, oh no, no, no). Many of the sites are filled with great information and links about fashion history, details about specific garments and periods, insiders' buying tips, how to measure heads and hands for hats and gloves, chat rooms, you name it. The downside of internet vintage buying is not being able to see or try on the garments, but, if you find an honest trader (and most of them are scrupulous), can wield your measuring tape with accuracy and are willing to take a flutter, you can acquire phenomenal stuff. One more very cool thing about the internet – it opens the doors internationally, for most sellers are willing to ship overseas. Just be sure to account for postage and potential customs duties in your buying calculations.

Connoisseur's Tip:
Overseas packages sent via courier are invariably snagged by Her Majesty's agents and it's quite likely you'll pay duty on the item. Items sent via airmail, on the other hand, often breeze through with no added charges. There's a trade-off between trackability and paying duty, which you'll need to give some thought to.

The Road from Portobello to Topshop
by Emily Bothwell, founder of Peekaboo Vintage

I remember visiting charity shops at the very young age of
fourteen and being fascinated with them. My friends would
laugh and refuse to go in. But I would buy items and take
them home and customise them.

I was on course for a very good career in the music
industry, but my future husband (who now runs the men's
side) and I were obsessed with Portobello. Eventually
I thought I could run a stall selling clothes. I gave up my
music career and one week later started at the market.
I did very well on my first day but had not really thought
about how hard it was going to be to restock. So it took
me a couple of years to establish myself as one of the
biggest vintage sellers at Portobello. I nearly gave up
many times but I really do have an absolute love for it,
which saw me through.

We have a lot of the same customers at Portobello and
Topshop. Stock always changes as we try to follow trends –
for example I may see some gorgeous hippy summer
dresses but I wouldn't put them in Topshop this

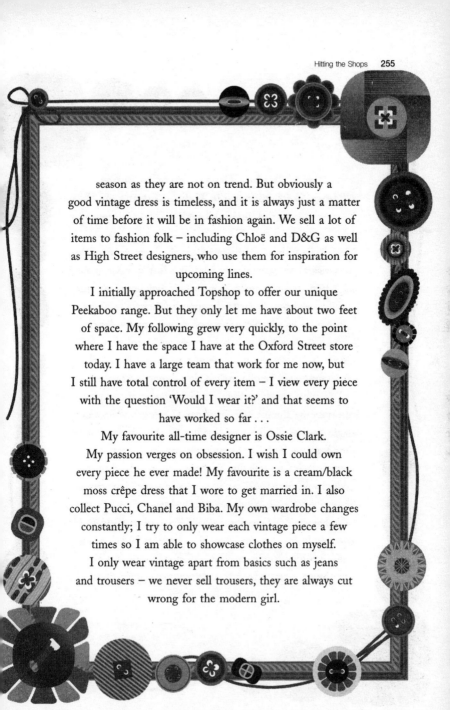

season as they are not on trend. But obviously a
good vintage dress is timeless, and it is always just a matter
of time before it will be in fashion again. We sell a lot of
items to fashion folk – including Chloë and D&G as well
as High Street designers, who use them for inspiration for
upcoming lines.

I initially approached Topshop to offer our unique
Peekaboo range. But they only let me have about two feet
of space. My following grew very quickly, to the point
where I have the space I have at the Oxford Street store
today. I have a large team that work for me now, but
I still have total control of every item – I view every piece
with the question 'Would I wear it?' and that seems to
have worked so far . . .

My favourite all-time designer is Ossie Clark.
My passion verges on obsession. I wish I could own
every piece he ever made! My favourite is a cream/black
moss crêpe dress that I wore to get married in. I also
collect Pucci, Chanel and Biba. My own wardrobe changes
constantly; I try to only wear each vintage piece a few
times so I am able to showcase clothes on myself.

I only wear vintage apart from basics such as jeans
and trousers – we never sell trousers, they are always cut
wrong for the modern girl.

How to Acquire a Design Legend at Auction
by Patricia Frost, Specialist in Textile, Costume and Fans,
Christie's London

Many believe that auctions are the exclusive preserve of the
very rich or very expert buyer, but this isn't the case at all.
Our March and September sales of twentieth-century fashion
and accessories are fantastic opportunities for younger
collectors to see, handle, assess and acquire spectacular pieces
of real historical import – for hammer prices as low as £150.
Given that the equivalent amount is easily spent on a High
Street spree, we offer incredible and enduring value.

Our most recent auction featured a range of costume
encompassing the most brilliant names of twentieth-century
design: a topaz silk dress by Fortuny weighted with Venetian
glass beads, a 1960 Dior wedding gown, a silk jersey Pucci
dress, a ladies' trouser suit by Biba, a cheesecloth bondage
shirt by Vivienne Westwood. The accessories included a
cherry-red crocodile Kelly bag and an Ossie Clark silk stole.
In many ways our viewing room is like a mini-museum of
costume history, and many fashion students and designers
visit for this very reason. But unlike museums, if a piece
catches your eye and you're a determined bidder, you'll be
able to take it home.

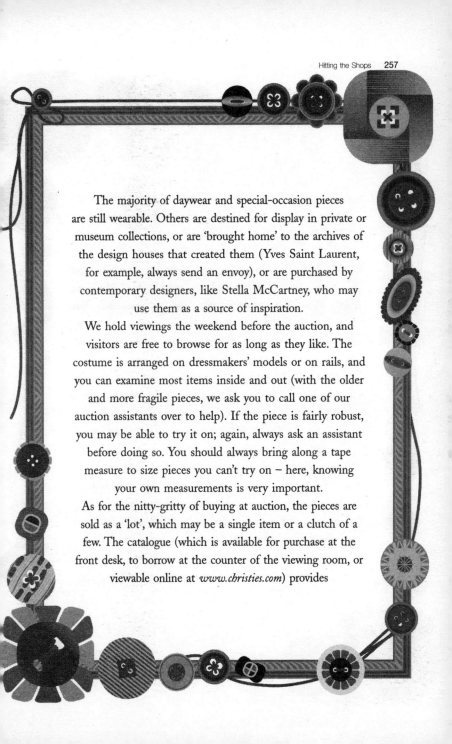

The majority of daywear and special-occasion pieces are still wearable. Others are destined for display in private or museum collections, or are 'brought home' to the archives of the design houses that created them (Yves Saint Laurent, for example, always send an envoy), or are purchased by contemporary designers, like Stella McCartney, who may use them as a source of inspiration.

We hold viewings the weekend before the auction, and visitors are free to browse for as long as they like. The costume is arranged on dressmakers' models or on rails, and you can examine most items inside and out (with the older and more fragile pieces, we ask you to call one of our auction assistants over to help). If the piece is fairly robust, you may be able to try it on; again, always ask an assistant before doing so. You should always bring along a tape measure to size pieces you can't try on – here, knowing your own measurements is very important.

As for the nitty-gritty of buying at auction, the pieces are sold as a 'lot', which may be a single item or a clutch of a few. The catalogue (which is available for purchase at the front desk, to borrow at the counter of the viewing room, or viewable online at *www.christies.com*) provides detailed descriptions, as well as estimates to guide you to your winning bid. You can also obtain a written description of a piece's condition from our department prior to the sale.

Come auction day, upon filling out our registration form and providing a bank or credit card, you will be issued a bidding paddle. When your lot comes up, make your intentions clear to the auctioneer by waving clearly – scratching your nose really doesn't count as a bid. Alternatively, if you can't attend, you can either leave a bid online the day before the sale, bid by phone, or leave a bid with the house on the auctioneer's book. If yours is the winning bid, expect to pay a buyer's premium of 20% of the hammer price immediately after the sale. Once you have paid, you can collect your purchase right away or at your convenience later.

Currently our most sought-after pieces are by Ossie Clark and Vivienne Westwood. Her older pieces (particularly from the Seditionaries and SEX collection) are increasingly rare, as the idea was that you wore them until they literally fell apart; you did not wash and mend them. If you'd like to see – or possess – clothes that are the fashion triumphs of the twentieth century, come along to our next viewing.

—Auctions

If you're serious about collecting first-rate vintage clothes, you'll find the ultimate goods at auctions – the haute-couture marvels, the pieces every fashion museum in the country hopes to add to their collections. As these garments are valued as art objects, trying-on is not always allowed. Auction houses issue catalogues providing information about each piece, which includes the history of the garment, including its designer, season and construction details. Fast, furious and a true social phenomenon, auctions offer a wonderful education in crème-de-la-crème clothes.

— eBay

And then there's eBay, the internet auctioneer that has so enriched its founders (and its visitors, for the buying opportunities and chance to interact with truly knowledgeable sellers, though at the end of the day wallets might be somewhat the worse for wear . . .). I happen to be an eBay fanatic even though, like many others, I've been burned. I find that the proportion of transaction success runs something like this: a third of the buys are stupendous, with the merchandise easily surpassing what I envisioned. Another third of the stuff is just fine – I got what I paid for, fair enough. And then the last third are disappointing in some way or another – the fit isn't great (usually my fault), the piece isn't as nice as it appeared in the scans, it reeks of smoke, or there's some flaw or other that the seller neglected to mention. Most of these problems were preventable, if I had been a bit more scrupulous about making enquiries and checking. You can learn from my mistakes – here are some more insider's tips.

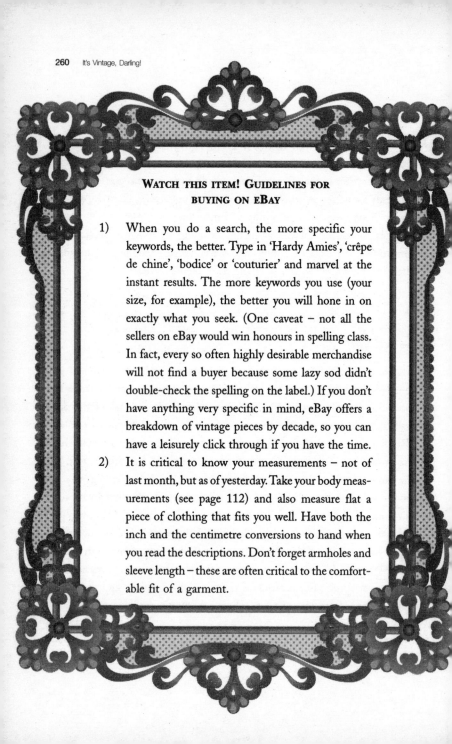

WATCH THIS ITEM! GUIDELINES FOR BUYING ON EBAY

1) When you do a search, the more specific your keywords, the better. Type in 'Hardy Amies', 'crêpe de chine', 'bodice' or 'couturier' and marvel at the instant results. The more keywords you use (your size, for example), the better you will hone in on exactly what you seek. (One caveat – not all the sellers on eBay would win honours in spelling class. In fact, every so often highly desirable merchandise will not find a buyer because some lazy sod didn't double-check the spelling on the label.) If you don't have anything very specific in mind, eBay offers a breakdown of vintage pieces by decade, so you can have a leisurely click through if you have the time.

2) It is critical to know your measurements – not of last month, but as of yesterday. Take your body measurements (see page 112) and also measure flat a piece of clothing that fits you well. Have both the inch and the centimetre conversions to hand when you read the descriptions. Don't forget armholes and sleeve length – these are often critical to the comfortable fit of a garment.

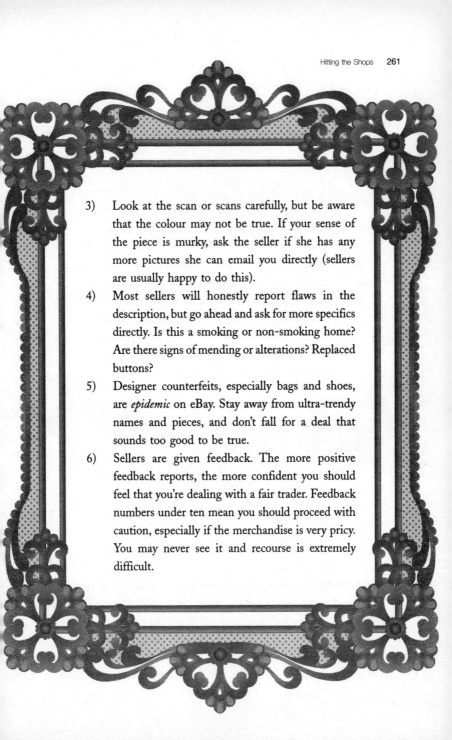

3) Look at the scan or scans carefully, but be aware that the colour may not be true. If your sense of the piece is murky, ask the seller if she has any more pictures she can email you directly (sellers are usually happy to do this).

4) Most sellers will honestly report flaws in the description, but go ahead and ask for more specifics directly. Is this a smoking or non-smoking home? Are there signs of mending or alterations? Replaced buttons?

5) Designer counterfeits, especially bags and shoes, are *epidemic* on eBay. Stay away from ultra-trendy names and pieces, and don't fall for a deal that sounds too good to be true.

6) Sellers are given feedback. The more positive feedback reports, the more confident you should feel that you're dealing with a fair trader. Feedback numbers under ten mean you should proceed with caution, especially if the merchandise is very pricy. You may never see it and recourse is extremely difficult.

7)   If a seller has lots of great stuff in your size (always check 'seller's other items' to see), let her know that you'd love to have an ongoing relationship. Likewise, if a dealer has proven especially helpful and her merchandise especially nice, you can add her to your 'favourites' list in order to track and get word of her new listings.

8)   If you really know and love more obscure labels, you can do wonderfully on eBay, for most bidders are dead set on snagging only the best-known names. Try typing in Emmanuelle Khanh, Galanos and Goldpfeil, for example, and see what lesser-known treasures you'll find.

— Vintage boutiques

Last but far from least are the stand-alone shops. Many offer a broad selection from the past hundred years of fashion history. Garments post-dating the 1980s (eek!) are increasingly available in retro shops, though a few more years may need to pass for our eyes to adjust to the charms of high-waisted mum jeans.

Besides the general vintage shops are those devoted to a particular type of merchandise or era: 1950s bombshell attire, Edwardian lingerie,

Hawaiiana, 1970s boogie outfits. For hard-core aficionados these are not so much stores as ways of life, one-stop shopping outlets for the wardrobe, home furnishings and personality.

What awaits in vintage shops

Above all, expect volume. The square footage runneth over with clothes, accessories and assorted bric-a-brac, making for an environment in which abundance often triumphs over shopping ease. It's hard to fault the poor owner, who may aim to satisfy a century's worth of tastes. Besides, she probably started the business to offset her own collector's passions, so naturally the stock piles up. As it begins to encroach on every corner, dressing rooms and lighting may suffer. The funky attic atmosphere is definitely part of the vintage experience, and is best accepted with a cheerful shrug. Every so often, you may come across a gallery-like store, with a great deal of light and air between the objects. While merchandising of this sort makes shopping easier, it also cuts into sales volume, reflected in the high prices of the garments.

As for the store owners, they tend to be delightfully offbeat, and are happy to share knowledge with enthusiastic novices. Get them talking about their favourite periods, and you'll come away so much the wiser.

Off and on

When dressing to shop, the goal is to get in and out of street wear as quickly as possible. This means slip-on shoes, tops and trousers – clothes you won't mind getting a bit dusty if the try-on conditions are less than ideal. Also keep in mind the following special considerations (applicable to all second-hand try-ons but *especially* important at vintage):

◎   Older clothing – especially that made before the 1940s – probably won't have a size label and, if it does, it may be irrelevant to present-day figures. Ask the owner's help in finding appropriately sized pieces.

◉   Do all try-ons at half speed, and don't ever force a piece on or off. Call for help instead.

◉   Think twice about trying on delicate pieces that you're not really interested in or can't afford to buy. The less this stuff is handled, the longer it lasts.

◉   Your own jewellery, hair ornaments, belts and other jagged items may snag and tear delicate fabrics. If you damage a piece, you are obliged to let the owner know, and if she's a toughie, she may insist that you pay for it. Better to avoid the whole unpleasant scene by leaving the accessories at home (this time!).

◉   Leave off smudgy make-up, especially lip gloss. Perfumes and especially scented oils are another no-no.

SHORT-CIRCUITING SHORTCOMINGS

Careful flaw-checks (see Chapter 9) are imperative with vintage clothing. A good once/twice-over not only helps you decide whether a piece is immediately wearable, it also indicates whether it will endure. Most of these garments have spent much of their life packed in storage, and are susceptible to moth holes, long-ignored stains, damaged material and a host of other faults. The 'shattering' of silk and satiny fabrics is a particular problem with older clothes (see page 175). If you're unsure of your flaw-spotting abilities, by all means ask the owner what, if anything, is wrong with the garment. It's in her best interest to be honest, and she's probably factored any flaws into the price. If problems exist, she can advise on the surest means of repair. On most occasions, by the way, there will be *something* wrong – given the age of the clothing, imperfections are a matter of course.

HOW TO GET A FREE EXPERT OPINION ON
YOUR VINTAGE PIECES

If you're new to collecting vintage clothing, you may
not have heard of the Victoria and Albert Museum's
Opinions Service, a resource offered to the general
public at no charge. The curators of the individual
departments hold these sessions on the first Tuesday
of every month, from 2.30 until 5 p.m. In the
twentieth-century costume department, the curator
aims to place your mystery pieces (up to six at a time)
into historical context – much as the experts do on
Antiques Roadshow – giving an opinion on the
approximate age, style influences and rarity. She
cannot give a valuation on a given piece, but she can
give you insight into its past life.

The department specialises in Western dress of the
twentieth century. According to Sonnet Stanfill,
department curator, all sorts of things come in for
evaluation – from a 1920s dress from eastern Europe
with elaborate art deco-influenced embroidery to
High Street pieces from the 1960s.

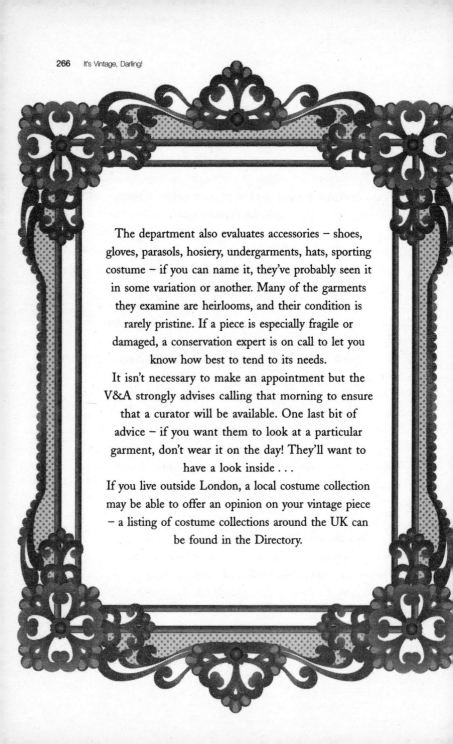

The department also evaluates accessories – shoes, gloves, parasols, hosiery, undergarments, hats, sporting costume – if you can name it, they've probably seen it in some variation or another. Many of the garments they examine are heirlooms, and their condition is rarely pristine. If a piece is especially fragile or damaged, a conservation expert is on call to let you know how best to tend to its needs.

It isn't necessary to make an appointment but the V&A strongly advises calling that morning to ensure that a curator will be available. One last bit of advice – if you want them to look at a particular garment, don't wear it on the day! They'll want to have a look inside . . .

If you live outside London, a local costume collection may be able to offer an opinion on your vintage piece – a listing of costume collections around the UK can be found in the Directory.

WEARABILITY ISSUES

Before laying down any cash, give a few moments' thought to how you intend to wear the item. Vintage pieces are frequently less comfortable than modern garb. Fabrics from the mid-century may feel stiffer and scratchier than today's sophisticated blends. There's a hot, sweaty reason why 1970s polyester leisure suits aren't widely worn today. All these factors need to be carefully weighed when considering a piece's overall appeal. You'll also need to factor in the general soundness of the garment and how it will withstand intended wear. A cobweb-light Edwardian lawn blouse may be perfect for a brunch outing, but exposing it to the slings and arrows of a full day in the office is probably more risk than the fabric should bear.

HOW PRICES ARE SET

Vintage stores generally purchase items outright from individuals and dealers. When the owners set prices, many variables come into play (rarity, condition, size, current trends and what they paid the supplier). This makes it difficult to pin down exactly what a given item 'should' cost. In the end, it comes down to the owner's judgment and experience. Two things to count on: haute couture and well-known designer names will be much pricier than mass-manufactured pieces, and stores in larger cities will be more expensive than their small-town counterparts. One way to get a notion of average and/or estimated prices is to refer to price guides, eBay completed auction listings, and auction house catalogues.

IS IT BETTER TO BARTER?

Yes and no. *Yes* if you can justify it – you know your stuff and the item's price seems too high, or if there are serious flaws, or you are making a sizable purchase. *No* if you're a stranger to the shop, don't really know what you're on about, and are doing it simply to knock a couple quid off for drinks later on. Stallholders will be more open to bartering than those with brick walls. Remember, most vintage professionals are in the game for love rather than money and price the merchandise just high enough to stay afloat.

Yesterday's news

Making sense of the welter of styles and periods is one of the biggest challenges of shopping for vintage. If you don't have time to immerse yourself in a full course of fashion history, this capsule guide covering key trends from the Victorians to Versace should help clarify the periods and predominant styles.

— The Victorian and Edwardian spirit

Diaphanous and demure, white lace and black satin, floaty and cinched – the clothes of the Victorian and Edwardian periods are a delightful contradiction in terms. Nobody is suggesting you attempt a head-to-toe reprise involving shift, corset, multiple petticoats, bodice, skirts, jacket and shawl – this is way too costume-y and encumbering for a girl who needs to beat the sliding doors on the southbound Bakerloo. But as individual elements, these pieces can add an unexpected, piquant freshness to every look.

Here are some simple definitions to help you get started:

Bloomers/Pantaloons: Floaty cotton undergarment, knee-length or longer, usually white, often decorated with lace or embroidery, to be worn under skirts or petticoats. Inseam may be left open down to cuffs.

Blouses: Frequently high-collared, of cotton, linen or silk, often embellished with embroidery or lace, with mother-of-pearl or glass bead buttons.

Bodice: A garment (or part of a dress) that fits from shoulders to the waist, i.e, the top part.

Bolero jacket: Short jacket ending at mid-torso, Spanish-influenced originally, often highly embellished.

Bustle: Padding, small cushions or a frame device used to lift a skirt away from the bum. The skirt on top may be pleated, draped, be-bowed or otherwise embellished for an even more bootylicious look.

Camisole: Cotton or silk top worn over or under the corset.

Chemise: Also known as a shift, this is a simple, sheer, unwaisted garment that was the first item Victorian women donned for daily dress.

Corset: Usually made of heavy cotton, sometimes of silk, a waist-cincher that did its job thanks to steel or whalebone stays (strips) inserted vertically around the garment. Victorian, Edwardian and later examples open with hooks and eyes at the front and are laced tight at the back.

Corset cover: Simple top layered between corset and bodice or blouse.

Crinoline: Heavier underskirt, often framed, made of net or buttressed with horsehair, to add volume under a skirt.

Gowns: Ranging from relatively simple day dresses to incredibly ornate presentation gowns, made of deluxe fabrics including velvet, silk, satin, taffeta, and beaded, bowed and otherwise embellished.

Petticoats: Lightweight underskirts, often of white cotton, worn under a skirt to lend modesty and shape.

Spencer jacket: Tight-fitting day jacket ending just below the bust.

While many of the pieces of this era have succumbed to the ravages of time, underwear – floaty, wispy shifts, camisoles, petticoats and pantaloons – is still fairly easy to find in good condition and reasonably priced. Beautifully adorned with lacework or eyelets or embroidery, the pieces are typically so sheer you can read through them. How to wear them? Do as the Victorian belles did – layer up (though not to the same stifling degree!). A petticoat worn all alone can be immodest even in our day, but one atop another delivers all of the beguilement without visible panty line as distraction.

Another way to dip into Victoriana is to slip on bits and pieces as accents – a gorgeous lace collar worn as a scarf, a frilly apron atop a floral skirt, knit gloves peeking out of a jacket pocket . . . or, most dramatically, a gorgeous velvet opera cape worn to keep out the wind's chill.

Meg Andrews, an expert in Kashmir shawls and the British imitations made throughout the nineteenth century, believes that these paisley-patterned forerunners of the pashmina can add period dazzle to any ensemble. 'They're not well suited to clubbing or wild parties,' she says of the often spider-web-delicate printed silk versions, 'but they could work wonderfully at more low-key events.'

Sexy then . . . and now

Channelling an exquisite 1939 Horst photograph of a model in a Mainbocher corset, Madonna immortalised back-laces for the MTV generation in her video, *Vogue*. Less visibly, an entire subculture is devoted to the whittling effects of the steel and whalebone stays (read all about 'tightlacers' wasp-waisted exploits on *www.corsetted.com*). Vintage-shop corsets are usually found in white or peach, but they also occasionally surface in black and racy red. Corsets range in shape from a minimal waist-cincher to an armour-worthy shaper of hips and bust, bedecked with lace, ribbonwork and intricate embroidery. A proper Victorian or Edwardian lady would never dream of wearing a corset against bare skin – she would slip it on top of a chemise or shift to keep the stays and laces from chafing. How you flash yours (peeking out underneath a jacket, swaggering below a shrug or visible through a transparent blouse) is your business, but do be aware that male jaws are guaranteed to drop before this most enslaving of female intimate wear.

WHERE TO FLAUNT IT

The Ilfracombe Victorian Celebration (*www.victoriancelebration.org.uk*) is a week-long opportunity to bustle around in period clothing, and the Grand Corset Ball (*www.thecorsetball.com*) is a gala opportunity to flaunt the finest piece in your collection amid fellow tightlacers. More informally, wear your lacy pantaloons à la Bo Peep to a picnic on the grass (pack a pretty fan, a big straw hat and plenty of fresh lemonade), swing a croquet mallet through a billowing eyelet-edged skirt, or wear a high-collared muslin blouse on a date when you want to *look* fetchingly modest . . . how you *act* is up to you.

FOR VISUAL INSPIRATION: Snuggle up on the couch with these DVDs: *A Room with a View, Out of Africa, My Brilliant Career, Howards End, Finding Neverland* (J. Depp bonus appeal), *Titanic* . . .

SCENTS OF THE ERA: Guerlain's Jicky (1889), L'Heure Bleu (1912) and Mitsouko (1919); Floris's Edwardian Bouquet (1901) and Penhaligon's English Fern (1911). Like all the perfumes listed in this section, they are still available today.

— *Twixt, tween and 1920s*

By the teens and early twenties, the sands had slipped through the hourglass and a woman's waist was no longer moulded by the snug hug of laces and stays. For a brief spell in the early teens, French designer Paul Poiret, famed for his gorgeous jewel-toned gowns (check out *The Wings of the Dove* for the look), saw women take a step towards the Oriental with his hobble skirt, which so constricted movement that it soon fell out of favour. Other influences from the East – richly patterned fabrics and extensive use of velvets and satins – remained current through to the mid-1920s.

Over the course of that decade, the fashionable silhouette stretched long and lean. The focal point of the figure slipped downward, with bustlines flattening, waistlines dropping, revealing V-necklines front and back (to the horror of the old guard) and hemlines emphasised through overskirt tunics that added an extra flourish at knee level.

One of the most wearable vintage pieces of this era was also subject to the effects of gravity: the hat. Where it once sailed atop the wearer's head like a schooner masted with ostrich-feather plumes, the 1920s incarnation saw the brim disappear and the sides elongate as gracefully as the petals of a columbine – the cloche came into fashion. If you find a brilliant example in a shop, wear it like they did in the jazz age: pulled down tight, so that you tip your head back slightly to peer out from underneath. To counter-balance the helmet-like simplicity, kohl-rimmed lashes and red lips are a must, dangle earrings are sweetly tremulous, and starlight can flash from a wonderful marcasite brooch pinned at temple level.

Other eminently do-able 1920s accessories include a compact mirror (for checking the lippy), fur shrugs or stoles (or get the look with fake), ropes and ropes of big pearls (spilling over in charity shops) and bakelite bracelets (which, if authentic, ought to feel heavier than plastic versions).

Coco Chanel would approve. She emerged as a force in the early twenties with her relaxed approach to day dressing, including wide trousers for women and her signature boxy cardigan or jacket and tweed skirt, accessorised with the aforementioned (blatantly fake) pearls and a bag on a chain strap. Other important designers of the period include the brilliant Elsa Schiaparelli, Callot Soeurs and Madeleine Vionnet.

Jeanne Lanvin must also be singled out among these eminent names, for she brought the world the drop-waisted beaded dance dress so emblematic of the flapper era. These dresses, along with an Eton crop haircut, glistening exposed shoulders and slouchy grace, epitomise a time when girls just wanted to have fun – and did.

According to Annie at Annie's Vintage Costume and Textiles in Camden Passage, London, 'The best time to find vintage flapper dresses is between September and Christmas – when girls want something spectacular to wear over the holidays. The dresses suit a range of sizes and are quite light to wear, if decorated with sequins (which were made of gelatine in those days), or a bit heavier if embellished with glass beads. The perfect accessory is a little beaded evening bag.'

SEXY THEN . . . AND NOW

In olden days, a glimpse of stocking was something shocking but by the 1920s hosiery emerged from beneath layers of petticoats into the light of day, throwing off its drab black cast for a range of hues, from flesh to Easter-egg pastels, made all the more eye-catching with elaborate embroidered decoration. Silk was the high-end option, but rayon appeared as a lower-priced alternative – popular though it was, it did tend to bag and was extremely shiny (girls would powder their legs before going out!). The stockings stayed aloft thanks to fetching frilly garters or suspenders – and how much more enticing a look this is than your basic Boots tights bought on the fly during lunch hour. To flaunt silk stockings (and their support works), wear a deceptively long skirt with a tactically positioned slit.

WHERE TO FLAUNT IT

Come the warmer months, a floaty silk chiffon dress is perfect for an event such as Glyndebourne or Henley, where a drifting, dreamy nostalgia is so much an element of the day. Casinos and twenties garb are made for each other; throw down some chips, shrug the slidey strap back up on your shoulder and let the dice roll where they may. For an outdoorsy version, play the ponies at Newmarket wearing heavy binoculars, a hip flask and gloriously slouchy tweeds. Keep an eye out for the Floral Tea Dances sponsored at the Royal Opera House in London, where you can cha-cha in a floaty number. Come evening, how about a drink at the American Bar in London's Savoy Hotel, which earned its name in 1926 thanks to the introduction of American-style cocktails, foremost and deadliest being the Martini. Sip one and glimmer amid the sleek art deco fittings.

FOR VISUAL INSPIRATION: The costumes in these films and programmes are marvellous – *Brideshead Revisited*, *Bullets over Broadway*, *Enchanted April*, *The House of Eliott* (the BBC mini-series).

SCENTS OF THE ERA: For added twenties allure, consider spritzing the backs of your knees with a classic 1920s perfume, like Guerlain's Shalimar (1925), Molinard's Habanita (1926), Chanel No. 5 (1921), Lanvin's Arpège (1927).

—Something about the 1930s . . .

This decade ushered out the gamine in favour of an unapologetically feminine, seductive style. Silk and satin, hemlines dropped to the calf, flirty pleats, halter and cowl necklines, a waistline beautifully defined – at its natural point – with a belt bedecked with a jewelled buckle, possibly spun around to embellish the small of the back.

If you have a gorgeous back, or a well-defined bum, this is a decade that flatters you to the hilt. Designers such as Balenciaga, Mainbocher, Molyneux, Schiaparelli, Germaine Monteil and so many more took the plunge with backless evening dresses in lamé, silk chiffons and deliquescent satins, and framed the hips with snugly cut skirts. Fabrics clinging to, flowing over and cascading around the curves – in this decade, clothes revealed at the same time as they concealed, to devastating effect.

Body conscious in every way, the 1930s saw sportswear come to the fore. Pyjamas in cotton and linen (worn to the seaside!), bathing suits, shorts sets, stylish kit for bicycling, skating, tennis and more. All of these garments signified the wearer as healthy, outdoorsy, carefree and willing to have a go – just like you, no? In the 1930s these costumes were worn with one of the most flattering accessories going – a golden tan – which, thanks to San Tropez (the brand, not the beach), we can easily fake.

SEXY THEN . . . AND NOW

The bias-cut dress is a staple of the glamorous girl's closet – a frock that looks limp on the hanger blooms to life once filled with the female form. This is because the fabric – usually something luxuriously slippery like satin or crepe de chine – has been cut diagonally across the grain, creating the tendency to stretch and drape around curves rather than falling down straight atop them. (Due to the way these frocks sit on the body, it is important to seek a size or so larger than you would ordinarily wear, to ease entry and maximise slink.) Favoured by screen queens, bright young things at country weekends, Mata Hari extracting state secrets: this is where goddess dressing began.

WHERE TO FLAUNT IT

The art deco Burgh Island Hotel in south Devon offers an escape from the modern world into country house refinement, with guests encouraged to dress formally for dinner. The Café de Paris has been a Piccadilly institution since 1924, and where better to show off your thirties finery than in the ballroom that once hosted Lord Mountbatten and Cole Porter? Further north, Rogano bar and restaurant, a Glasgow institution, boasts an interior reminiscent of the *Queen Mary*, built down the way at the docks. For something completely different, how about wearing a vintage swimsuit to the Tooting Bec Lido in Wandsworth, London, Britain's oldest open-air pool and a classic of 1930s architecture (Brad Pitt filmed here for *Snatch*).

FOR VISUAL INSPIRATION: See how to wear these clothes in films set in the thirties: *Singing in the Rain, Cold Comfort Farm, The Thin Man* films, *I Capture the Castle, The Philadelphia Story, Gosford Park*.

SCENTS OF THE ERA: Dana's Tabu (1931), Worth's Je Reviens (1932), Jean Patou's Joy (1935), Elizabeth Arden's Blue Grass (1935) are all great accessories.

— Vintage on the Home Front

In June 1941, a new label appeared on British clothing – CC41, the two Cs, called 'the cheeses', looking like Pac-men on the munch. The tag designated garments produced under the wartime Civilian Clothing scheme, where austerity, practicality and durability displaced frivolous 1930s gowns that were good for a tango or two, then discarded. The standard-issue utility suit, purchased with ration coupons, had few embellishments (even pockets were a little-seen extravagance). The waist was nipped at natural height and the hemline rode just below the knee, fitted with a kick pleat or three. The shoulders were assertively broad, the lapels small and neat, the colours a sober black, navy or brown. The look was straightforward and remained largely unchanged from year to year – the government brooked no whimsical style innovations while the fighting continued.

'The stockings are dire. They have colossal seams . . . do they expect us to grow utility grooves?' As for the brassieres, 'they scratch like a vegetable grater . . . could hold a wild bull in leash . . .'
Time magazine, 1943

The war years inspired numerous accessories that complemented the 'make do and mend' pragmatism of the day: cork wedges, introduced by the original Salvatore Ferragamo, which lent inches of authority and were remarkably easy to wear (and still are if you can find them in your size!), turbans (useful for taming tumbling locks and/or disguising bad-hair days), and little brimmed hats home-embellished with feathers and other frippery.

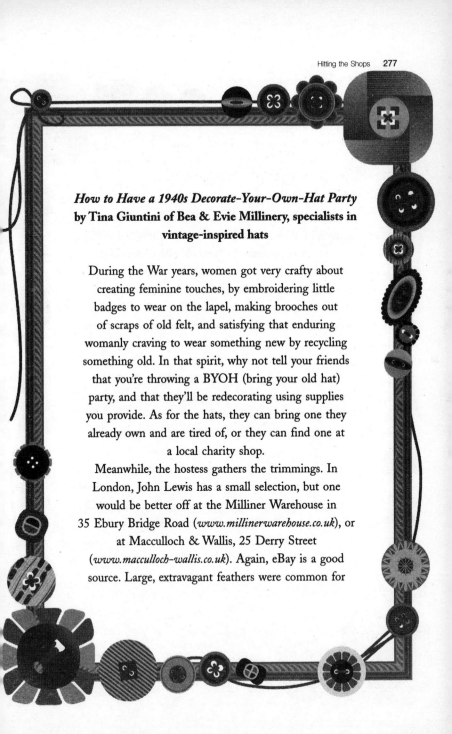

How to Have a 1940s Decorate-Your-Own-Hat Party
**by Tina Giuntini of Bea & Evie Millinery, specialists in
vintage-inspired hats**

During the War years, women got very crafty about
creating feminine touches, by embroidering little
badges to wear on the lapel, making brooches out
of scraps of old felt, and satisfying that enduring
womanly craving to wear something new by recycling
something old. In that spirit, why not tell your friends
that you're throwing a BYOH (bring your old hat)
party, and that they'll be redecorating using supplies
you provide. As for the hats, they can bring one they
already own and are tired of, or they can find one at
a local charity shop.

Meanwhile, the hostess gathers the trimmings. In
London, John Lewis has a small selection, but one
would be better off at the Milliner Warehouse in
35 Ebury Bridge Road (*www.millinerwarehouse.co.uk*), or
at Macculloch & Wallis, 25 Derry Street
(*www.macculloch-wallis.co.uk*). Again, eBay is a good
source. Large, extravagant feathers were common for

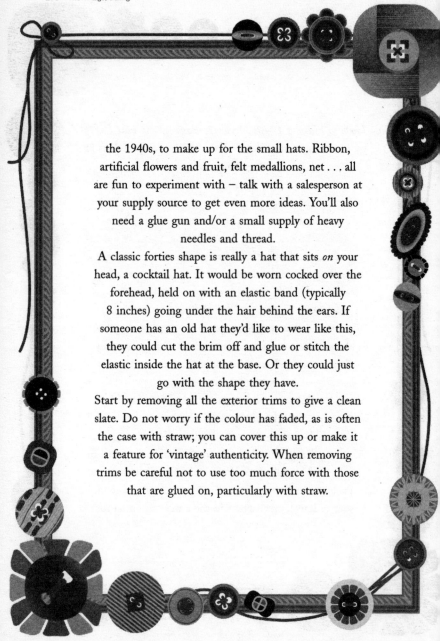

the 1940s, to make up for the small hats. Ribbon,
artificial flowers and fruit, felt medallions, net . . . all
are fun to experiment with – talk with a salesperson at
your supply source to get even more ideas. You'll also
need a glue gun and/or a small supply of heavy
needles and thread.

A classic forties shape is really a hat that sits *on* your
head, a cocktail hat. It would be worn cocked over the
forehead, held on with an elastic band (typically
8 inches) going under the hair behind the ears. If
someone has an old hat they'd like to wear like this,
they could cut the brim off and glue or stitch the
elastic inside the hat at the base. Or they could just
go with the shape they have.

Start by removing all the exterior trims to give a clean
slate. Do not worry if the colour has faded, as is often
the case with straw; you can cover this up or make it
a feature for 'vintage' authenticity. When removing
trims be careful not to use too much force with those
that are glued on, particularly with straw.

As for attaching the trimmings, it's fine to use a standard glue gun, but go carefully. It doesn't require much time to stick your decorations on – and if you don't like the hat you can remodel if you want to. With a glue gun, drying time is about two minutes. The best places to find inspiration are old movies, old magazines, costume dramas, museums (there is a hat museum in Luton) . . . or have a look at our website, *www.bea-evie.com.*

The longest I've worked on a bespoke hat (or a couture hat, as we say in millinery, which means everything was made by the milliner, the feathers dyed and trimmed, etc.) was thirteen hours in total – but for a fun gathering I would say two hours is as much time as you'll need.

Before your guests arrive, slip some Ella Fitzgerald, Peggy Lee or Bing Crosby on the stereo and mix up a batch of Singapore Slings or Mai Tais in honour of the Allied effort in the Pacific.

Not all was austerity in 1940s England – today's vintage shops spill over with deluxe crocodile bags in shades ranging from tawny to chestnut to glossy black, as well as fur wraps, stoles, collars and shrugs. If you prefer not to own animal-derived pieces, a Corde bag – an ultra-distinctive handbag constructed with glossy black, navy or deep brown cording worked into elegant geometrical patterns over the front, back, sides and base, closed with brass hardware – is an excellent alternative. These are timeless classics that add a casual glamour whether worn with a beautifully cut suit or jeans.

SEXY THEN . . . AND NOW

There's something about a lady in uniform – something dead sexy – especially if she can jump and jive to the brassy sounds of a swing band. Marc Jacobs, Jean Paul Gaultier and countless other mega-designers constantly reiterate the military theme, for who can resist the brass buttons, the braid and ribbon detail, the clean lines, the swagger . . . The trick to wearing authentic vintage military pieces fashionably is restraint, only one or two elements at a time, because nobody ought to look like a one-woman re-enactment of the Battle of Britain. Here are some examples of what you might find online or in shops dedicated to militaria (look on the internet for sources near you): thick corduroy Land Army trousers with leather lace-ups at the calves; a Wren officer's greatcoat; a WRAC service blouse accented with a neat black tie; a QUAIMNS military nurse tropical-weight top; and, of course, brilliant buttons, badges and other insignia for those occasions when the standard-issue bling just won't do.

Towards the end of the decade, in 1947, Christian Dior introduced his famous 'New Look'. Fashion became frivolous once again: wasp-waisted, full-skirted, soft-shouldered. Frocks, suits and ensembles were profligate with material; skirts had to go swish – and so they did on into the fifties.

WHERE TO FLAUNT IT

Have an urgent assignation at the Wolseley, London's elegantly styled all-day brasserie. Many historic railways have WWII-era weekends (see *www.HeritageRailways.com*). Come spring every year, the town of Haworth in West Yorkshire holds a 1940s weekend, complete with Spitfire fly-pasts and dancing in the streets. The Rhythm Lounge in London is the place for twenty-and-thirty-something swing lovers to enjoy a hip night out with a period buzz . . . serious jivers can sign up for a long weekend of instruction, workshops and crazy feet at one of the swing camps located around England (more at *www.jazzjiveswing.com*). Watch for u-boats off the pier at Brighton of an evening, wearing his Crombie coat.

FOR VISUAL INSPIRATION: Wear it like your forebears did – throw back your shoulders and show the world what you're made of. The nominees for best filmed 1940s costumes are: *The English Patient, Enigma, Hope & Glory, Pearl Harbor* (go on, see what the Yanks were up to, Kate Beckinsale looks splendid), and *End of the Affair*.

SCENTS OF THE ERA: Leave a waft of Piquet's Fracas (1948), Balenciaga's Le Dix (1947), Nina Ricci's L'Air du Temps (1948) or Dior's Miss Dior (1947) in your trail.

—*A fling with the fifties*

Whether your fashion passions incline towards big-screen goddess, gamine sylph, biker babe or rockabilly girl, the looks can be yours – and easily, too, since the clothes and accessories of this decade are easy to find in shops, on the internet and at exhibitions. Before you dive in, here is a more detailed field guide to the iconic fifties girls:

THE GODDESS
When she makes an entry, 'booma-chaka, booma-chaka' drums through the mind of every man in the room. As worn by Marilyn, Diana (Dors!), Ava and Grace, this look pledges allegiance to figure-hugging jumpers (prefer-ably angora or cashmere, embellished with tiny bugle beads or sequins for

evening), pointy nose-cone bras, knee-to-mid-calf pencil skirts and high spike heels. If a party's on, what eBay sellers love to call 'wiggle dresses' are the way to go. These down-and-kind-of-dirty descendants of Dior's New Look cinch the waist (made all the more hourglass with a 'waspie' corset). The dresses are frequently strapless, the better to show off bodacious shoulders and cleavage, which might be further framed with a fur wrap or stole. Skinny bangles, loads of them, polish off the presentation. An even more heightened incarnation of the fifties bombshell is the burlesque queen, a *stripteuse* as epitomised by the act of Dita von Teese. For amazing visual references to this special style (including lots of gorgeous period lingerie), see her two-books-in-one, *Burlesque and the Art of the Teese/Fetish and the Art of the Teese*. Local girl Immodesty Blaize has brought her act to the West End and can be tracked at *www.immodestyblaize.com*.

THE GAMINE

Here the icon is Audrey, and the feel is young actress or artist, simply but adorably clad in figure-skimming cropped capri pants (basic black preferred), ballet pumps or other flatties afoot, and a beautifully crisp white blouse, possibly with a Peter Pan collar, with tails knotted into a neat bow at the waist. The look can be geeked up with 1950s-style cat glasses. Beret and cropped hair also optional. This look is so classic, so enduring, it still passes for ultra-modern. Except maybe the cat glasses.

THE TEDDY GIRL

Be a bombsite Boudicca by first borrowing Audrey's cropped trousers and white shirt, then give the look a True Brit spin with a velvet-collared jacket, lace-up espadrilles, a coolie hat or straw boater and a cameo at the neck.

THE ROCKER GIRL

He's revved up the Harley and you're going for a ride: sweep your hair back in a red bandanna – wear a thick leather motorcycle jacket and vintage Levi's (the 'E' on the tag will be capitalised) turned up at the ankle. Spiky stilettos (white!) are the sexiest (if not exactly roadworthy) foot apparel. Heavy make-up, with pencilled brows and rouged lips, authenticates the look. (Note: unless you actually *are* going for a ride, the full-throttle version risks looking like you're auditioning for *Grease*: tone it down by substituting low-heeled black boots and scrub some of the slap off.)

THE ROCKABILLY

Inspired by the music of the skinny, youthful Elvis, this is a wonderfully girly look often expressed in tight-waisted floral or gingham frocks. Since rockabillies are dancers extraordinaire, skirts have exceptional swing – possibly with sunray pleats, or cut in a full felt circle and adorned with the classic poodle or other motifs. Pearls or a cheap 'n' cheerful plastic substitute hang from the neck, a charm bracelet dangles from the wrist and modest brooches may be pinned to the top (usually a cardie or twinset). If you're wearing a jacket, it's got a nipped waist, possibly a peplum, and three-quarter sleeves. A cute novelty handbag finishes off the look – possibly of raffia, or a boxy plastic number. Again, wearing the whole look – *especially* if it involves a poodle – is more fancy-dress than dressed to kill. Pick and choose your elements carefully. A playful felt skirt can be devastating if it's offset with a sophisticated lambswool or cashmere tank, and, if you really want to send some interesting messages, a leather dog-collar choker . . .

SEXY THEN . . . AND NOW

Where would a film noir heroine be without her stiletto heels, the better to clackety-clack down moody black and white alleys and grind the heart of her hired private eye into pulp? The shoes, possibly in snakeskin or alligator, had in their heel a real metal spike, which lent strength and durability but also wreaked havoc on fine wooden floors, leading to their banning in many older buildings. If you find a wonderful old pair of spike heels, make sure they fit comfortably, for at these heights any minor pinching will quickly become intolerable. Also think twice about wearing them on grass, for your mingling will be hampered if you keep getting stuck in 3-inch deep divots.

Walking gracefully in stilettos takes a bit of practice – think slow, swishy hips and away you go. Grand entrances are important; grand exits are, too.

WHERE TO FLAUNT IT

Rockabillies can meet like-minded swingers at parties sponsored by retro clothier Rokit (*www.rokit.co.uk*), and chicks who love to go vroom can ride on over to the Ace Café on the North Circular Road outside London (*www.ace-cafe-London.com*), where Marlon Brando and his gang of wild ones would have felt right at home amid the vintage Triumphs, leathers and classic rock 'n' roll. Would-be burlesque queens can look, learn and flaunt their finery at venues like London's Whoopee Club (*www.thewhoopeeclub.com*) and Lady Luck (*www.ladyluck.co.uk*).

FOR VISUAL INSPIRATION: *Rebel Without a Cause, Grease*, any Elvis movie, *Rear Window, The Aviator, Gilda*.

SCENTS OF THE ERA: Soften up the tough-girl vibe with a delectable period perfume, like Lancôme's Magie (1950), Estée Lauder's Youth Dew (1953), Dior's Eau Fraiche (1953), Dior's Diorissimo (1956) or Givenchy's Interdit (1957), Audrey's own favourite.

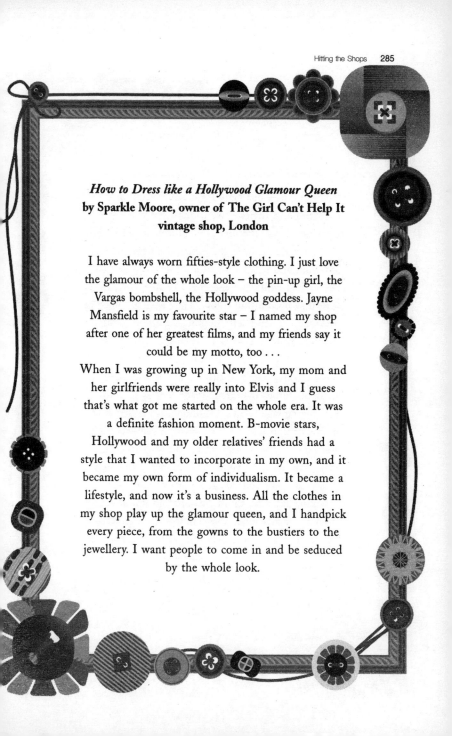

How to Dress like a Hollywood Glamour Queen by Sparkle Moore, owner of The Girl Can't Help It vintage shop, London

I have always worn fifties-style clothing. I just love the glamour of the whole look – the pin-up girl, the Vargas bombshell, the Hollywood goddess. Jayne Mansfield is my favourite star – I named my shop after one of her greatest films, and my friends say it could be my motto, too . . .

When I was growing up in New York, my mom and her girlfriends were really into Elvis and I guess that's what got me started on the whole era. It was a definite fashion moment. B-movie stars, Hollywood and my older relatives' friends had a style that I wanted to incorporate in my own, and it became my own form of individualism. It became a lifestyle, and now it's a business. All the clothes in my shop play up the glamour queen, and I handpick every piece, from the gowns to the bustiers to the jewellery. I want people to come in and be seduced by the whole look.

My shop is a distinctly American version of the forties and fifties – we didn't have the same restrictions and rationing as you did here, which you can see right away, in the prints, the flamboyance. The films and the photos from those days were shot in black and white, but the girls like Ava, Rita, Diana Dors, they lived in full colour. They were groomed by the studios, never left the house without looking immaculate – it was a head-to-toe stylishness. Getting the look is easy because even the drop-dead pieces I carry aren't all that expensive compared to modern clothes that aren't made half as well. Still, wearing vintage takes a bit of adjustment. At first, you might find that a fifties waistline feels too tight, too high. I've got a sign in my dressing room that says, 'Always hoist your boobs higher than you're used to – 40s and 50s glamour darts are placed pointing skyward, think outward and upward . . .'

These clothes make you stand differently, walk differently . . . it's definitely a more feminine way of carrying yourself.

Of course, no woman in the forties and fifties would leave the house without wearing a girdle, maybe a long-line bra – corrective underwear, I call it to be funny, but it's so sexy, too. Men go crazy for all the hooks and the snaps and the peekaboo – I've got one vintage bra, black lace, that's all support and no cup . . . you can just imagine. And then there's the seamed nylons.

The key to wearing clothes like this is not to overdo it, otherwise you'll come off unnatural, like you're in fancy dress. For a starter look, I'd suggest one of the cotton summer frocks. You can wear them with flat shoes, sandals, espadrilles, it can look completely modern, but with a little twist. Our evening gowns look very 'now' as well, like you just picked it up from Harrods. Really, looking like a goddess comes down to feeling like one – how you hold yourself, and being used to the clothes, being comfortable. Whether it's a big picture hat or a tight pencil skirt, you want to wear it like you were born to.

A Great Day Out

The Goodwood Revival, held annually in Sussex for three days in September, is a one-of-a-kind event: a historic race meeting featuring the kinds of cars and motorcycles that would have roared around the track during the heyday of the Goodwood Motor Circuit between 1948 and 1966. Not only are the cars authentic, all circuit staff and competitors wear period-appropriate clothing, and spectators are encouraged to do the same. The result? The times come to life in a swirl of pleats, seamed stockings, little veiled hats and ruby-red smiles. It's an unforgettable event, for the crowds, for the fish and chips wrapped in old newspaper, and for the thrilling sound of the gentlemen starting their engines . . . start yours, ladies, by having a closer look: *www.goodwood.co.uk/revival.*

— Swinging into the 1960s

If you've got a spiritual home in the go-go era, what an advantage you have over your cousins on the continent and in the US, for the greatest fashion talents of this decade were homegrown. Ossie Clark, Biba's Barbara Hulanicki, Gina Fratini, Bill Gibb, and the others whose wares filled the countless boutiques that lined the King's Road, and electrified the world with their outrageously new looks. Meanwhile, Courrèges, Pierre Cardin, Pucci, Rudi Gernreich, Yves Saint Laurent, Pierre Cardin and Hubert Givenchy did their best to keep up, and managed, now and again, to pull off something good.

The waist all but disappeared in the early sixties in favour of legs exposed to the very hilt – dressed girlie-cute in pale tights, cavalier in high boots or blatantly seductive in fishnet. If Mary Quant's Mod miniskirt is the brightest star in the chart of 1960s glam, of only slightly lesser brilliance are sheath dresses in outrageously colourful prints inspired by Op, Pop and Psychedelic art; the maxiskirts in deep-toned paisley velvet, snapping like mainsails on LSD; and unprecendented materials like citrus-hued patent leather, linked plastic discs, or even paper. Youth in all its incarnations was in the ascendant in this decade – which, at its most extreme, is Teletubby-playful in its fascination with geometric shape and eye-catching colour.

TROLLEY DOLLY

If you're looking for inspiration from the early sixties, peek at a page from the flight manual of the transatlantic trolley dollies, whose fetching looks made old-time air travel such a pleasure: a neat little A-line crimplene dress in a sunny, clear shade with big buttons and patch pockets, teamed with round-toed, chunky square-heeled courts and, as crowning glory, an immaculate pillbox hat.

FLOWER POWER

If you're into a mellower reading of the 1960s, you could jump ahead into the Age of Aquarius; channel your inner Flower Child with low-slung, skinny-thighed, big-belled jeans embroidered with peace signs and tiny flowers, topped with a skimpy tie-dyed T-shirt, a fabulous suede jacket and a stamped leather thong for your ironed-straight hair? Or an artsy-craftsy shepherdess dress down to the ankles, worn with floppy hat, patchouli and a blissfully spaced-out expression.

LUCY IN THE SKY

Love beads, baby, get you started on a more extreme version of this look – think Lenny Kravitz doing Jimi Hendrix and you've got it. Sergeant Pepper frock coats laden with epaulets, corded curlicues and brass buttons; ever-so-slightly flared striped trousers, winkle-picker boots (hanging on from the Teds a decade earlier) and a headband if you've got the nerve (and the flamboyant hair).

SEXY THEN . . . AND NOW

By the late sixties, crisp hemlines went the way of Vidal Sassoon geometric barnets: straight-edge was out, hanging loose was in, and fringe suddenly cascaded from every conceivable garment (even go-go boots), echoing the long, liberated tresses of the men and women who wore it. Fringe conceals, but only kind of, and it's irresistibly touchable, which is why it's so sexy at the midriff or the leg. On jackets, or on big leather bags, its animated flicks send a mustang-free message to the straights who are watching you go by. Girls who wear fringe know what they're about. Throw some on (in small doses, life isn't a rodeo), and flaunt your swinging style.

WHERE TO FLAUNT IT

What could be more sixties than the mud, sweat and tears ('The bloody *tent's* leaking!') of an outdoor concert? The original Isle of Wight festivals attracted musical luminaries like Jefferson Airplane and Bob Dylan.

Nowadays headliners run more to the line of Coldplay or Foo Fighters, but sixties stalwarts like Procol Harum and Lou Reed are on hand to lend tradition (and still-cracking talent) to the affair. Tickets sell out fast . . . If you're willing to travel, Eastertime for two decades running has brought European mods together for *The Italian Job* International Mod Rally (*www.modculture.co.uk*). Closer to home, The New Untouchables (*www.newuntouchables.com*) acts as a clearing-house for early 1960s culture fans, providing information on UK club dates, fashion shows and other rendezvous for like-minded souls. If you're into an evening of Rat Pack-style cool, check out the be-boppers at Ronnie Scott's, a London jazz institution.

FOR VISUAL INSPIRATION: Enjoy wonderful incarnations of this kaleido-scope of a decade with *Austin Powers* (way OTT, but there may be a mojo here for you), *Georgie Girl*, *The Graduate*, *Catch Me if You Can*, *Hairspray*, *The Stepford Wives*, *Alfie* (Michael Caine or Jude Law as special bonus material).

SCENTS OF THE ERA: Why not sample Rochas' Madame Rochas (1960), Hermès' Caleche (1961), Yves Saint Laurent's Y (1964), O de Lancôme (1968), Guerlain's Chamade (1969), and of course the all-natural oils so beloved of late-sixties chicks: full-on musk, ylang-ylang and jasmine.

Name to Know: Ossie Clark by Mark Butterfield, collector and proprietor of online shop C20 Vintage Fashion

I think Ossie Clark was the most talented and important British male designer of the twentieth century. He and his wife, Celia Birtwell, who was an equally gifted print designer, created some of the most breathtaking clothes of the late sixties and early seventies. As popular as he is among collectors, you can still find a good selection of his pieces in vintage shops, at auctions and on the internet. He first came into the public eye as a twenty-three-year-old fashion student, when David Bailey photographed his black and white, Op-art-inspired silk coat for *Vogue*. Not long afterwards he founded his shop Quorum, just off the King's Road, and it became a regular haunt of Brian Jones, Keith Richards (who wore Celia Birtwell print satin shirts), Marianne Faithfull, Anita Pallenberg and Pattie Boyd (George Harrison and later Eric Clapton's wife). Ossie designed stage clothes for Mick Jagger. The shop's driver, Dave Gilmour, gave up his job to play with Pink Floyd. We take it for granted today, but then the fusion of music and fashion was a completely new phenomenon.

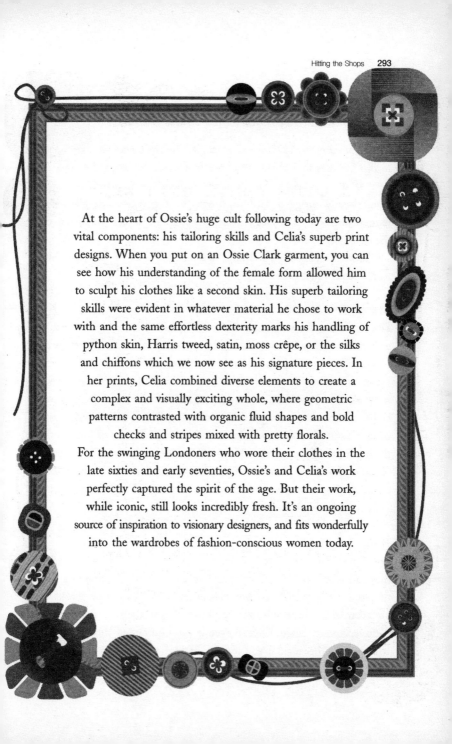

At the heart of Ossie's huge cult following today are two vital components: his tailoring skills and Celia's superb print designs. When you put on an Ossie Clark garment, you can see how his understanding of the female form allowed him to sculpt his clothes like a second skin. His superb tailoring skills were evident in whatever material he chose to work with and the same effortless dexterity marks his handling of python skin, Harris tweed, satin, moss crêpe, or the silks and chiffons which we now see as his signature pieces. In her prints, Celia combined diverse elements to create a complex and visually exciting whole, where geometric patterns contrasted with organic fluid shapes and bold checks and stripes mixed with pretty florals.

For the swinging Londoners who wore their clothes in the late sixties and early seventies, Ossie's and Celia's work perfectly captured the spirit of the age. But their work, while iconic, still looks incredibly fresh. It's an ongoing source of inspiration to visionary designers, and fits wonderfully into the wardrobes of fashion-conscious women today.

—And the beat goes on . . . the 1970s

The fashions of the 1970s are an ideal place for the novice vintage collector to dip her toes in – these pieces are fun, wearable, in good supply and, best of all, very affordable. And the options are tremendous, ranging from sweetly sprigged corduroy frocks to Ziggy Stardust glam – the hardest decision you'll face is which version of *That Seventies Show* calls the strongest.

Throw open the retro wardrobe and here are some of the classic head-to-toe looks you'll find:

ALL-ACTION ANGEL

Few could top the California cool of Angel Farah hanging out with the girls in Charlie's office, wearing a gorgeous white pantsuit in a stretchy poly blend with sharp wide lapels and crisp flares. Underneath she'd have on a dynamite slinky blouse in silk or other shiny fabric, open way low to show off skinny gold chains and a deep tan. Platform sandals lent authority to her kung-fu moves when the action got going. (Slinky blouses in silk or imitations are wall to wall in retro shops. If the collar of one you love is simply too flappy – that Huggy Bean look is *jive* on you, sister – consider the *Cheap Date* 'zine tip of having a tailor convert the collar to a button-down, which won't be too expensive and will freshen up the look considerably.)

BOHO BABE

For something completely different, cut to a wedding bash under a marquee in the middle of a Shropshire meadow, where the bridal party of Flora, Lady Whicker, wears classic Laura Ashley cotton frocks that are themselves mini-meadows of chintz. These dresses are starting to look very pretty again. Caveat: even if you find one in the right size, it will appear rather maiden auntie in its original state. So give it a makeover. Alter the waist to tight, and shorten the length to just below the knee.

Or try to achieve the same effect with a beautiful floaty chiffon scarf wrapped Obi-style around the waist. A cobweb-light ballerina cardie could be lovely knotted just under the bust. Lacy or fine fishnet tights – in pale pastels only – will add interest from the knees down. Top it with a graceful, wide-brimmed straw hat and you've got an essentially feminine look that's ever-so intriguingly faded, like a beautiful old summer photograph.

DANCE FLOOR DIVA

Meanwhile, back in town, Flora's black-sheep cousin Lady Marmalade is dazzling the not-easily-dazzled crowd at Annabel's with her second-skin silk jersey wrap dress and little else besides towering spike mules and an ankle bracelet. Seriously shiny from hair to heels, she knows four different ways to do the hustle. At the mirror-ball-and-strobe-light shoebox down the street, more budget-conscious dancing queens wear skimpy halters and bum-tight Calvins. (Wrap dresses are classic pieces that can go from modest to marauding give or take a couple of buttons. Diane von Furstenberg has done these up to the present day – if you find an older one or a decent substitute in silk or fine cotton jersey, it is well worth snapping up.)

PUNK PRINCESS

Snarling at the lot is the punk princess from the East End. Having spent her last pennies on *Never Mind the Bollocks*, she can't afford Vivienne Westwood's latest slash-and-chicken-bone T-shirts from SEX on the King's Road, and so has handcrafted her own version using her brother's hopelessly stained vest, a Jubilee tea towel, lashings of Ribena and a stapler stolen from the school office. Her skirt was her nan's, hacked short jaggedly at mid-thigh and safety-pinned to fit. Laddered tights and badly laced Docs complete the look. (Westwood's original punk gear is currently selling at auction for many hundreds of pounds. If you find an authentic piece, like a stencilled cheesecloth top or bondage trousers, consider wearing it like the iconic manifesto of an age it has since become, set against neutral elements. Or just throw it on over laddered tights. Anarchy knows no rules.)

SEXY THEN . . . AND NOW

Boob tubes. Misunderstood, misrepresented and, above all, misworn. Yet these skimpy holdalls of glitter-ridden elastic are cheeky, fun to wear and superbly flirty – if you know the simple dos and don'ts of carrying one off.

1) Make sure it fits. Since the tubes are so stretchy, some girls assume that one size fits all. If your flesh spilleth over (or under), you will look like a disaster – better to find a top that works better with your form.

2) Boob tubes magically magnify the presence (or absence) of what's underneath. If your endowment veers well off the norm, think twice about removing your cover-up (see 4, below). If it's droopy, a strapless bra could conceivably help, but a bra under a boob tube is pretty much missing the whole point.

3) Do you have spots on your shoulders or back? All the concealer in the world will not hide them, just make them look crusty. Go for a cover-up instead.

4) As is true with a corset, the *glancing presence* of a boob tube is usually a lot sexier than the full show. Wear a little cover: a shawl, a shrug, a teeny jacket. You can throw these off once you hit the dance floor – just be sure your boogying isn't so wild you drop the top as well.

WHERE TO FLAUNT IT

Throw on some (beautifully crafted) hot pants and find a great roller rink like Rollercity in Herts (*www.rollercity.co.uk*), or see the listings in your area's city guide for disco nights coming soon to a club near you. Wail along to 'Fernando' with an Abba tribute band. Take part in Danceline's star search for queen and king of the Freestyle Hustle at regional showdowns, culminating at a dance-off in Blackpool (*www.dance-lines.com*). Shuck off that seventies clobber and streak through a major public square.

FOR VISUAL INSPIRATION: Check out *Boogie Nights, Almost Famous, Klute, Saturday Night Fever* and *The Ice Storm*. Avoid Olivia Newton John in *Xanadu* – what a howler!

SCENTS OF THE ERA: Chanel No. 19 (1970), Eau de Rochas (1970), Yves Saint Laurent's Rive Gauche (1971), Revlon's Charlie (1973), Hermès' Amazone (1974), Cacharel's Anaïs Anaïs (1978).

—*It seems like just yesterday . . . the clothes of the 1980s*

Black leggings, a.k.a. leggins, looking as dodgy-dance-academy as ever, are back on our streets. Bubble skirts, too. Which can only mean one thing: it's time to dig the lace fingerless gloves out of the drawer, 'cause we're gonna get into the groove . . .

What goes around comes around, and this decade of glorious excess is currently undergoing an almighty ransack by the fashion establishment. White ruffles and frills à la Duran Duran have woken up and are a go-go on covers and editorial spreads; drainpipe jeans and Converse have experienced yet another incarnation thanks to the fashion stylings of indie front men. Have some fun the eighties way with these oh-so-now looking elements:

NEW ROMANTIC GEAR

A flouncy white blouse, a brocade waistcoat, some leggins (no stirrups, though – too naff even for hardcore re-enactors), elfin ruched ankle boots, a brooch at the collar, gold disc earrings as big as doubloons. Admit it: it's a cute look. And if you have the (skinny) legs for it, you can substitute a pair of jodhpur-cut corduroy or velvet paisley trousers.

TALKING HEADS GEAR

Did you catch David Byrne in the great concert film *Stop Making Sense*? In one scene he wore a jacket that was fifteen sizes too big. How we laughed, wearing our own dad's blazers with the sleeves rolled to the elbow, or a huge hairy mohair jumper that hung to mid-thigh. Big tops, tunics and jumpers of all manner were in. Even the cut of the sleeves was oversized: batwings, anyone?

DIANA GEAR

From unpromising beginnings shopping at the Sloane Street Laura Ashley for ruffle-collar shirts and theme jumpers, Diana went on to become one of the best-dressed women of the century, in Chanel-cut suits in gorgeous pastels, low court shoes, simple sheath dresses and fabulous custom-made gowns. The woman's dress sense was a harmonic convergence of style, suitability and *mettre en valeur*. We can but look at retrospectives, and learn.

ALEXIS CARRINGTON-COLBY-DEXTER-DEXTER-ROHAN-GEAR

On the other hand, there's this, but by God the woman could work a look. The power suits with shoulder pads as big as Cornish pasties. The jewel tones of the fabric – not to mention the actual jewels. The colour-coordinated shoes, even if the colour was tangerine. The incipient label-mania, expressed in Chanel quilted bags, Charles Jourdan shoes and Versace suits. Those of us stuck in rayon secretary dresses with a neckline bow, sensible pleats and skinny self-belts were meant to be terrified of Alexis as she chewed up a boardroom. Frankly, it worked.

Many eighties pieces may still be lurking somewhere in your wardrobe, but if they're not, car-boot sales, off-the-beaten-track charity shops, jumble sales and other venues that are fairly low in the fashion food chain are likely to offer 1980s cast-offs, as well as the usual retro outlets. Some items to avoid from the eighties (there are plenty): clapped-out, baggy-arse leggins (they were typically worn into the ground), shoddy merchandise (hoard your money for a gorgeous brocade bolero over a cheesy Flashdance one-shouldered sweatshirt), nostalgia-driven perms.

WHERE TO FLAUNT IT

Saturday nights at the Clapham Grand, London, or Fame, the Eighties Night, at Kennedy's in Dublin (check local guides for theme nights near you). Do some fashion research on the designer floor of Harvey Nicks, then splurge on a posh lunch at San Lorenzo. Elvis Costello, Bon Jovi and Queen Madge herself are still touring . . .

FOR VISUAL INSPIRATION: The perfect excuse to watch *Desperately Seeking Susan*, *Working Girl*, *Pretty in Pink* and *About Last Night* again.

SCENTS FROM THE ERA: There is only one, or at least that's what it seemed like back then: Giorgio of Beverly Hills.

A GREAT GIRLS' NIGHT IN

Get an omnibus *Dallas* or *Dynasty*, put a couple bottles of Bolly on ice, and have your girls over wearing whatever they can dig out that still fits. In between episodes, pogo dance to Depeche Mode and share your most heinous photos from the time when Cyndi Lauper was the epitome of cool.

How to Create a Vintage Face
by Jemma Kidd, make-up artist

I've loved make-up and the way it can transform a person's image for as long as I can remember. My professional interest took hold when I was modelling and watching my sister at shoots. It's the artistry that captivates me – maybe in another life I'd have been a painter. I also love teaching women how to enhance their features, because it can dramatically change not only how they look on the outside but how they feel on the inside. My school in Notting Hill trains people who share my passion for a career as a professional make-up artist, but women who want to learn how to do their faces in a fresh and flattering way can check out my website, *www.jemmakidd.com*, for detailed guides on creating all kinds of different looks.

Vintage fashion is so incredibly popular I don't really understand why vintage-y make-up isn't as well. I don't mean garish, stage-y looks – instead the sort of effect that subtly evokes the past, that makes you think 'that woman looks amazing, but how?' Here's how:

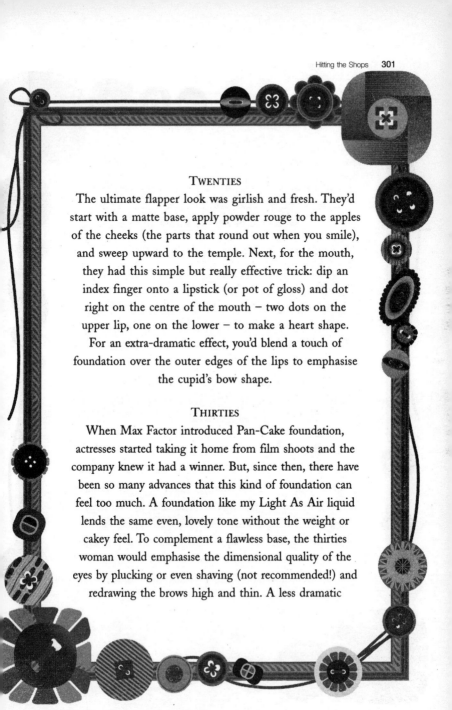

TWENTIES

The ultimate flapper look was girlish and fresh. They'd
start with a matte base, apply powder rouge to the apples
of the cheeks (the parts that round out when you smile),
and sweep upward to the temple. Next, for the mouth,
they had this simple but really effective trick: dip an
index finger onto a lipstick (or pot of gloss) and dot
right on the centre of the mouth – two dots on the
upper lip, one on the lower – to make a heart shape.
For an extra-dramatic effect, you'd blend a touch of
foundation over the outer edges of the lips to emphasise
the cupid's bow shape.

THIRTIES

When Max Factor introduced Pan-Cake foundation,
actresses started taking it home from film shoots and the
company knew it had a winner. But, since then, there have
been so many advances that this kind of foundation can
feel too much. A foundation like my Light As Air liquid
lends the same even, lovely tone without the weight or
cakey feel. To complement a flawless base, the thirties
woman would emphasise the dimensional quality of the
eyes by plucking or even shaving (not recommended!) and
redrawing the brows high and thin. A less dramatic

approach to getting the look is to apply a smokey grey or brown shadow in the crease of the upper eyelid and blend well with a brush.

FORTIES

The eyebrows grew back and became more emphatic in the forties – look at film stills of Lauren Bacall or Vivien Leigh and you see how browlines transformed from pencil-thin marks to proper arches. If your own brows don't have a lot of presence you can help them out with a like-toned pencil, lightly stroked over then blended. For a true-Brit forties mouth, wear a brownish-toned tint. Colours were more sombre during the War years, reflecting the overall mood of austerity.

FIFTIES

Women of the fifties knew how to make the most of their mouths. Joan Crawford, Marilyn Monroe, or my favourite, Ava Gardner, didn't just whack on some lippy and hope for the best. It was a *process*, starting with foundation to smoothly cover the lips and lend a base for the pigment to cling to. Next, using an extremely sharp lip pencil (for accuracy and a beautifully defined lipline), they'd

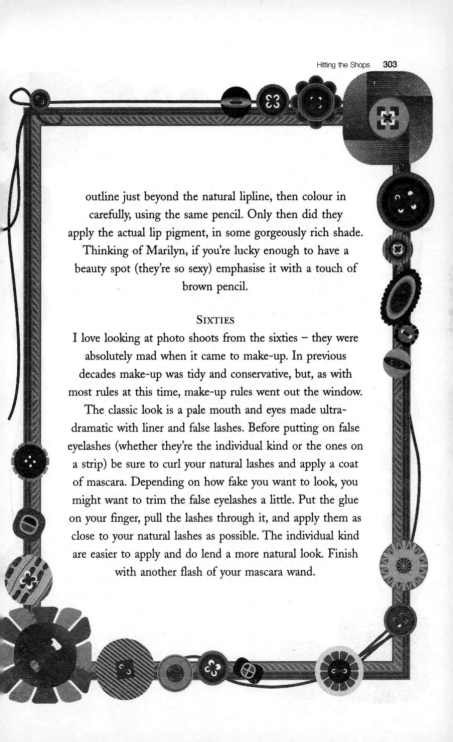

outline just beyond the natural lipline, then colour in
carefully, using the same pencil. Only then did they
apply the actual lip pigment, in some gorgeously rich shade.
Thinking of Marilyn, if you're lucky enough to have a
beauty spot (they're so sexy) emphasise it with a touch of
brown pencil.

SIXTIES

I love looking at photo shoots from the sixties – they were
absolutely mad when it came to make-up. In previous
decades make-up was tidy and conservative, but, as with
most rules at this time, make-up rules went out the window.
The classic look is a pale mouth and eyes made ultra-
dramatic with liner and false lashes. Before putting on false
eyelashes (whether they're the individual kind or the ones on
a strip) be sure to curl your natural lashes and apply a coat
of mascara. Depending on how fake you want to look, you
might want to trim the false eyelashes a little. Put the glue
on your finger, pull the lashes through it, and apply them as
close to your natural lashes as possible. The individual kind
are easier to apply and do lend a more natural look. Finish
with another flash of your mascara wand.

SEVENTIES

To me, the seventies are all about shimmer and glow. Put
three or even four complementary colours on the eye: the
middle-tone on the lid, something deeper in the crease, the
lightest on the browbone, and use the deepest colour as a
liner. Properly blended, the effect can be stunning – check
out photos of Jerry Hall on and off the catwalk. Mouths
were glossy and the shoulders shimmered (glittery cream or
dust-on powder is the way to go here) – if you're out for a
night dancing, it's a great opportunity to try out this look.

EIGHTIES

When I think of the eighties, one of the images that comes
to mind is Robert Palmer's video *Addicted to Love*. That
line-up of girls with their intensely red lips and eyes
dramatic with plum and burgundy tones was a classic look
of the time. It's easy to do a quick take on the eighties by
using an eyebrow brush to sweep your brows up to look
strong and dramatic, using a quick shot of hairspray on the
brush to help keep them in place. Back then, eyebrows
were like shoulderpads – the bolder the better.

Vintage Bride

Darling, you nailed him. Congratulations! Now on to more romantic parts of the equation, like what will you wear on this, the most unabashedly you-centric day of your life? The options are dizzying, as are the logistics, and your first impulse may be to go for a straightforward ceremony wearing a brand-new gown. *You will be beautiful* no matter what option you choose, but how much more memorable (and, cough, *less costly*, cough) is the vintage option. There's no denying it will take plenty of work, but if you've got the time and dedication to make it right, do it.

— *Making the decision*

Do you want a period wedding? Did you and your intended perhaps meet under circumstances (swing dance club?) that would make this kind of do most appropriate? Or are you taken with images of past bridal beauties (Grace, Diana, Her Majesty, Elizabeth Taylor) and long to recreate that look for yourself? Or are you simply devoted to the cuts and styles of a given period? Any of these makes you a great candidate for vintage bride.

PINNING DOWN YOUR LOOK

If you think you'd like to do a vintage wedding but aren't sure of which era to evoke, then save yourself tons of time and frustration by researching before you try on a single style. Your goal is to get a decade pinned down, for that will streamline your hunt considerably. Pore over old family photographs. Hunt the internet for inspiration (Gulden Brown, at *www.vintage-gown.com*, for example, has a spectacular vintage-wedding site). Spend a day in a library that has an excellent collection of old bridal magazines. Make photocopies, take extensive notes, and think very hard about whether a given era's style will actually suit you.

PLAN AROUND THE PITFALLS OF A VINTAGE GOWN

It may need to be cleaned, it will certainly need to be altered, and there may be damage that requires repair. So set a figure to spend – and then add a couple of hundred pounds for fixing-upping to make it perfect. Fragility is a huge issue with vintage gowns – especially if you plan to do any dancing. *Be absolutely sure* any dress you set your heart on will not come apart midway through the affair.

WHERE TO LOOK FOR VINTAGE GOWNS

If there is a shop anywhere within striking distance with a good selection of vintage gowns, by all means pay a visit. Otherwise, consider a vintage exhibition, which gives you the option of canvassing a number of dealers easily – let likely ones know what you're looking for and make sure they have your phone number. Internet vendors and eBay are also important sources, but, here, knowing your measurements is a must (allow some give, especially with 1930s bias-cut dresses), the vendor's trustworthiness must be demonstrated, you must get a thorough flaw report before putting any money on the table, and you must have the option of return if the garment is unsuitable. A lot of musts . . . but you're looking for the gown of your dreams, so expect a few hurdles. Off the vintage highway, dress agencies occasionally stock vintage gowns, or may have a non-bridal dress that may be suitable for the occasion. Charity shops sporadically get wedding dresses in, but this is nothing to count on. Do note, however, that Oxfam has speciality bridal outlets! Possibly in your area! Have a look at *www.oxfam.org.uk/shop/highstreet/bridal.htm* to see exact locations.

WHAT ABOUT MY BRIDESMAIDS?

It's a good idea to be flexible where your bridesmaids are concerned, because outfitting an entire party in near-identical vintage is a challenge that would tax even the most fire-breathing Bridezilla. Consider these alternatives: have your girls in matching colours, matching accessories or matching silhouettes only. According to Elizabeth Davies' wonderful website (*www.geocities.com/e2davies/brides.html*), one Nora Pennell of Lincs, who married in 1931, dressed her maids in pale blue, green and lemon, and they carried mixed sweet peas. The vicar called it a 'rainbow wedding' and said it was the prettiest he'd ever seen. As a final option, dress the bridesmaids in contemporary garb with a period accent.

I'D LOVE A VINTAGE RING . . .
This, by tradition, is up to the future husband, but you can gently steer him to Hatton Cross in London, or the Lanes in Brighton. Remember that stones can be removed and settings adjusted. If a family heirloom is destined for your finger, this might be an important consideration.

CHOOSE YOUR SETTING WITH YOUR ERA IN MIND
A church wedding may be your heart's desire, or you might opt for a setting with period resonance. Have a look on the internet for venues which have been approved for a civil ceremony – if you plan well ahead and it's within your budget, you could do a Victorian wedding at Wiltons Music Hall in London or a sixties-themed bash on the site of a James Bond film . . . among hundreds of other possibilities.

MAKING THE ANNOUNCEMENT
Set the tone of your party with some marvellous decade-appropriate invitations: a daguerrotype-style for a Victorian theme; a transatlantic steamship ticket for a 1920s wedding; a satin-backed card for a 1930s wedding; a crocheted snood-style wrapping for your 1940s do; an hourglass-shaped invite with a net border below for a rockabilly party; a Sputnik-styled 1960s stiffy; or a sequin-trimmed 1970s announcement. Let your imagination go wild and let your guests know that this isn't going to be one more nice (but a bit dull) affair.

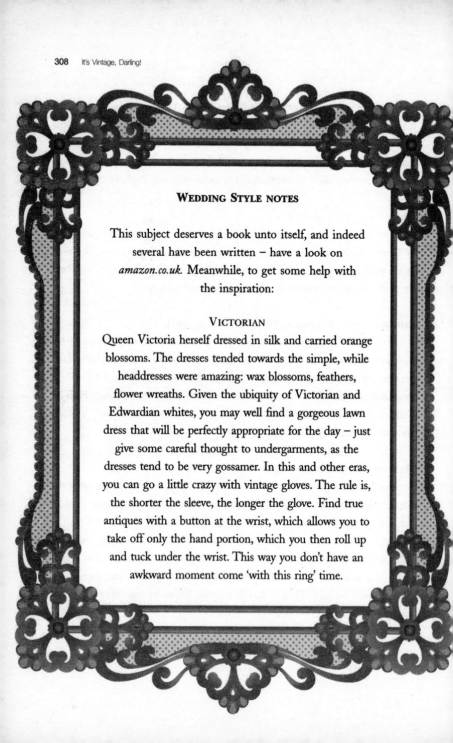

WEDDING STYLE NOTES

This subject deserves a book unto itself, and indeed several have been written – have a look on *amazon.co.uk*. Meanwhile, to get some help with the inspiration:

VICTORIAN

Queen Victoria herself dressed in silk and carried orange blossoms. The dresses tended towards the simple, while headdresses were amazing: wax blossoms, feathers, flower wreaths. Given the ubiquity of Victorian and Edwardian whites, you may well find a gorgeous lawn dress that will be perfectly appropriate for the day – just give some careful thought to undergarments, as the dresses tend to be very gossamer. In this and other eras, you can go a little crazy with vintage gloves. The rule is, the shorter the sleeve, the longer the glove. Find true antiques with a button at the wrist, which allows you to take off only the hand portion, which you then roll up and tuck under the wrist. This way you don't have an awkward moment come 'with this ring' time.

TWENTIES

Gowns, like other dresses, were unwaisted. A lace cloche or cap headdress could be a chic touch. Veils tended to be made of silk tulle, which hung straight down. If your dress comes to the knee, white stockings with flowered garters would work. If you find a beautiful beaded bag, why not use it as a holder for your bouquet?

THIRTIES

With natural waistlines settling back in, this is a decade to wear a fabulous waist corsage. Bias-cut silk dresses are a natural choice for this era, but don't stint on foundation garments because slithery isn't the most appropriate look at the altar. Big bouquets were *de rigeur* and white tulips might look spectacular with a columnar dress, like the blue Mainbocher number worn by Wallis Simpson (blue indicates a bride's faith in her husband's fidelity, in case you were wondering).

FORTIES

Wedding dresses were few and far between during the War years; most girls wore a borrowed dress or suit,

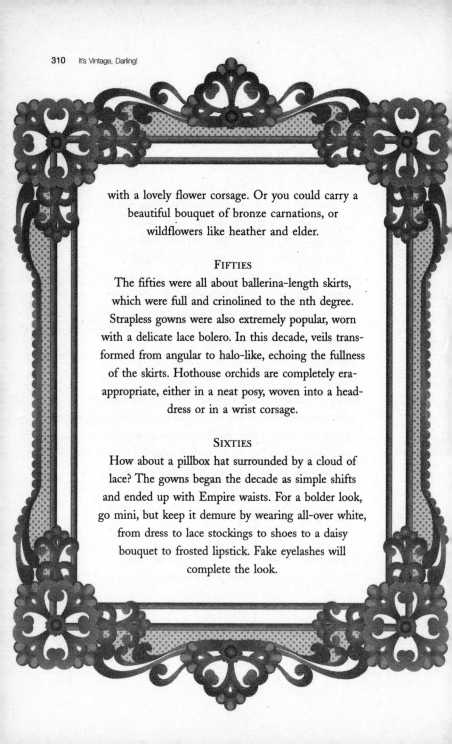

with a lovely flower corsage. Or you could carry a
beautiful bouquet of bronze carnations, or
wildflowers like heather and elder.

FIFTIES

The fifties were all about ballerina-length skirts,
which were full and crinolined to the nth degree.
Strapless gowns were also extremely popular, worn
with a delicate lace bolero. In this decade, veils transformed from angular to halo-like, echoing the fullness
of the skirts. Hothouse orchids are completely era-
appropriate, either in a neat posy, woven into a headdress or in a wrist corsage.

SIXTIES

How about a pillbox hat surrounded by a cloud of
lace? The gowns began the decade as simple shifts
and ended up with Empire waists. For a bolder look,
go mini, but keep it demure by wearing all-over white,
from dress to lace stockings to shoes to a daisy
bouquet to frosted lipstick. Fake eyelashes will
complete the look.

SEVENTIES

Sleeves were all over the map, from mutton-big above the elbow to Goth-ically flared down the wrist. Bib necklines were also big. If sophisticated seventies glam is more your style, look to Bianca Jagger and get married in a brilliantly cut white trouser suit. A white jumpsuit is also a possibility if you've got the figure and the nerve. Wear dangle globe earrings that glimmer and shimmer like little disco balls, but stop there – the only other sparkle should come from a diamond ring.

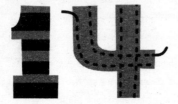

Sweet charity

For true believers, the charity-shop is less a shopping experience than a quasi-fanatical quest, complete with its own gurus, internet speciality pages and more. The late, lamented *Cheap Date* magazine was a trove of information on the charity-shop scene – another resource will surely rise to take its place.

While our motivations are as eclectic as the merchandise, most of us are irresistibly drawn to these places because they offer the best quality/price ratios in the known universe. Every second-hand shopper has heard the legend of how a friend of a friend found a Schiaparelli jacket (or whatever) priced in the single digits. While this could conceivably happen, it never does to anyone we actually know. The reason is simple: riches such as these are as rare as natural pearls, and finding them is extraordinarily hard work. Getting great quality at a charity shop is the sign of an Iron Woman connoisseur. If you've got the stuff, take your marks. But before we ready, set, go . . .

—A little background detail

To make the most out of the charity experience, it helps to understand the background and motivation of the shops. Broadly speaking, they are set up and run by major charities such as Oxfam, the British Red Cross and other not-for-profit organisations. Since people appreciate the good works of these charities, the shops may attract spectacular donations.

The atmosphere of a given charity shop can be dire or delightful, depending on who's managing the show. Typically, they're fluorescent-bright, no-frills rooms largely decorated by the merchandise. The clothing is usually railed up in an orderly way by male/female, adult/child, skirts/trousers/overcoats, etc. Better-organised shops indicate the size of the garments via little collars on the hangers or a note on the price tag; more often than not you have to determine the size yourself. Dressing rooms are small and often ill-lit. Hooks are not a given. The curtain that separates your naked haunches from the world and his uncle doesn't close all the way. It's all very endearing, really, as long as you remember that this isn't Selfridges.

> 'Thrift shops are, after all, where fads go to die . . .'
> **David Futrelle, *Salon***

—Always in stock

Like the swallows to Capistrano, certain garments always come home to roost in charity shops. They are, in no particular order:

- jeans that were stylish the year before last
- droopy jumpers
- sweatpants with missing drawstrings
- T-shirts bearing corporate logos
- see-through, ultra-stretchy, ultra-flammable-looking tops
- manky trench coats
- shoes looking like they crossed the Sahara and were spat on by camels

Then there's the merchandise *we're* after. Great finds like a pair of Marni linen trousers or a Kenzo ponyskin belt, mysteriously untouched while lesser items fly out of the shop.

As with dress agencies, the merchandise in a given charity shop tends to reflect the local dress code. This means glittery gowns brighten the rails in South Kensington, golf togs are a matter of course in St Andrews, cashmere is a likely find in Edinburgh. If a locale is chic, the area's charity shops reflect it. Residents do not travel far to unload the contents of their closets. Even organisations that distribute to a wide network of shops may channel their *pieces de resistance* to better areas.

By the same token, the least appealing goods are liable to appear in the most down-trodden neighbourhoods. Does this mean you should give such shops a wide berth? Not if you have the time to spare and enjoy taking a flutter. These shops make up for their mostly lacklustre merchandise with rare flashes of brilliance – pieces left untouched because the quasi-professional 'pickers' who haunt the better outlets don't bother coming. It's a long shot, but if you've got the time and the patience, it could be worth it.

—Rise of the thrift-store-as-boutique

In recent years, charity shops have adopted the boutique concept in a major way. At the shop or at a central distribution point, workers pull out

THE NEVER-ENDING TREASURE HUNT

'I believe that everything can end up in a thrift store, from originals of the Declaration of Independence tucked behind a bad watercolour, to brand-new 1930s men's shoes, to that one weird-sized screwdriver you've been looking for. Of course, it's pure chance where these items end up – whether it's at a thrift near you and on the day you choose to go – but thrifters are *ever* hopeful. It's like the lottery – somebody's got to win.'
Al Hoff, *Thrift Score*

big-name labels for display in 'designer' zones or dedicated stores. These goods are priced higher, reflecting their greater allure. Oxfam has a shop in exclusive Bond Street catering to that neighbourhood's ultra-posh tastes, while its Earlham Street shop appeals to the heart's desires of fashion students at the nearby Central Saint Martins Art College. The Salvation Army charity shop in Princes Street has a special line in cast-offs from the nearby West End theatres, while the Cancer Research UK shop in Marylebone High Street features designer cast-offs from the best addresses in Primrose Hill.

While an entire shop filled with decadent duds is a beautiful thing, more frequently we encounter individual rails or rounders with a handwritten 'boutique' tag posted hopefully above. These do give shoppers in a hurry a precise target, but be aware that the prices can be out of line (particularly for a designer's second/third-rung lines). Also, the winnowing system isn't perfect and fine pieces often languish on the regular rails.

—Priced to sell

Shops take one of two approaches to setting prices. Garments are either tagged individually according to quality and condition, or all items of a single type (coats, skirts) are ticketed at the same figure. The method shouldn't affect whether you shop at a given store – great bargains can be had either way. In terms of payment method, play it safe and assume they'll only accept cash or card-guaranteed cheques.

—Service

Anticipating marvellous service in a charity shop is like anticipating a marvellous meal at Pizza Hut – it's all about managing your expectations. Charity shops rely almost exclusively on volunteers – people doing hard work for little reward. They may be unaccustomed to sugar-coating their opinions. They may be way posher than you and adamant that you know it. They may be utterly lovely and helpful beyond all reason. Not knowing what you're going to get contributes to the inimitable charity-shop atmosphere.

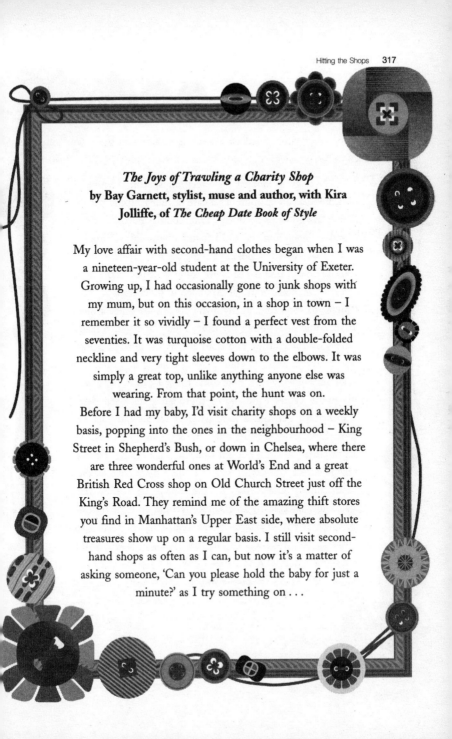

The Joys of Trawling a Charity Shop
by Bay Garnett, stylist, muse and author, with Kira Jolliffe, of *The Cheap Date Book of Style*

My love affair with second-hand clothes began when I was a nineteen-year-old student at the University of Exeter. Growing up, I had occasionally gone to junk shops with my mum, but on this occasion, in a shop in town – I remember it so vividly – I found a perfect vest from the seventies. It was turquoise cotton with a double-folded neckline and very tight sleeves down to the elbows. It was simply a great top, unlike anything anyone else was wearing. From that point, the hunt was on.

Before I had my baby, I'd visit charity shops on a weekly basis, popping into the ones in the neighbourhood – King Street in Shepherd's Bush, or down in Chelsea, where there are three wonderful ones at World's End and a great British Red Cross shop on Old Church Street just off the King's Road. They remind me of the amazing thrift stores you find in Manhattan's Upper East side, where absolute treasures show up on a regular basis. I still visit second-hand shops as often as I can, but now it's a matter of asking someone, 'Can you please hold the baby for just a minute?' as I try something on . . .

I like to go in looking for something specific – with a wardrobe as big as mine it's a case of filling precise needs. Doing so also helps me focus. Two months ago I was after a red cashmere jumper, and I found a beautiful one from N. Peal. Now I'm looking for the perfect leopard-print fake-fur coat. I find it helps give some structure to the hunt.

Of course you're always open to other finds.

I prefer to shop solo, at my own pace – sometimes a quick dash, sometimes taking my time. That way I get to really focus on the clothes, and don't feel as though I'm being rude by not wanting to chat. Having done it for years, I can scan very quickly – if there's one thing I can do very well it's give a second-hand shop a thorough going-over. Every so often I get into a state where I simply must have something, must acquire, but I think it's much more of an achievement to walk out with nothing, if nothing is there. This is such a wonderful way of finding distinctive clothes. Sometimes you see women – the showy-offy kind – who you know have spent an absolute fortune on their outfits, but haven't got an ounce of real style. They're dressing to impress, and it shows. To me, true style shines when you don't give a damn what others think, but you're dressing to please yourself.

— *Making the most of the charity-shop experience*

Whether you love or loathe charity shopping has less to do with a shop's qualities than with your approach to it. If you expect to strike gold in fifteen minutes or less, you are sitting up and begging for disappointment. Instead, slow down and clear your mind to a Zen state of calm, expecting nothing but the sensual pleasure inherent in clothing's texture, colour, line and detail. This state won't last, of course, but at least you'll get started in the right mood. Once you've been at it for a while and the going starts to get heavy, try to keep your sense of the absurd to the fore. When you stop seeing the lighter side of the goods and the characters shopping alongside you, it's time to go home. More advice:

GIVE YOURSELF ENOUGH TIME
Ah, the frenzy of playing beat the clock when you're only halfway through the acid-wash jeans. Charity-shop forays require double or even triple the time needed per square yard in other shops, thanks to merchandise volume, merchandise disarray, insufficient dressing rooms/mirrors, dismal lighting, the heavy flaw quotient and consequent need for careful checks. To keep a grip on sanity, give yourself as much time as you'll need.

SHOP FREQUENTLY
Your odds of finding excellent buys increase if you are a frequent visitor to the shop. Also, as you become familiar to and friendly with the employees, they may provide tips that would be withheld from unknowns.

APPLY YOUR QUALITY-DETECTION ABILITIES
Hand sensitivity is key on jammed charity-shop rails. Move deliberately, feel everything. Pull pieces that seem worthwhile, check out the size, hallmarks and condition, and then look at the price. Your goal is to move down a rack once and once only, so be thorough the first time around.

Try to avoid being dazzled by designer labels, or at least try to avoid letting them cloud your opinion – quality always comes first.

READ A CURRENT FASHION MAGAZINE BEFORE GOING IN
You'll arm yourself with information on fresh silhouettes, shapes and general trends, and be able to spot a doppelgänger on the shop rails. Like we've said, looking achingly fashionable is not the ultimate goal, but if a given shape or colour really suits you *and* it is on-trend, why not?

KNOW YOUR LABELS
Watch out for overpriced designer diffusion labels (often seen on boutique rails), keep a close eye out for potential counterfeits. If you let quality be your guide, brilliant pieces by a little-known name will occasionally leap out. I recently came across a lovely tweed suit piped with thin strips of real leather, and thought *Aha!* It was by Per Spook, one of the old-line Paris dressmakers, priced at £20 – couture-quality merchandise that went unrecognised and unsold.

MIND YOUR MANNERS
Treat the staff with respect, both to their faces and in how you handle and re-hang the merchandise. They're there because they're volunteering – in short, motivated by the best intentions. Suppress any urge to mock the goods – some might take your disdain personally. So, too, might shoppers whose financial situation is grim – they understandably resent the loud opinions of well-to-do brats. Finally, make a point of being open and generous rather than competitive. It makes for a happier environment, and you may get some great advice in return.

COMMON CHARITY SHOP PESTS

And then there's the less lovable quotient of charity-shop regulars. Again, Zen-like calm is the best line of defence, but if somebody's really pushing your buttons, a bit of decisive action is necessary.

THE RAIL HOG

You know the type. Forget moving for you, she wouldn't budge for a Brigadier General bearing down the aisle in a Sherman tank. There is only one effective way, short of a blunt instrument, to deal with her. Go around, saying very clearly, 'So sorry.' If she continues to guard a portion of the rack with her body, feel free to bump (careful if she's ancient), this time saying, 'Oh, I'm so sorry, I moved out of your way because I thought you were done with this section.' (P.S. Whenever someone is gracious enough to move for you, it's nice to acknowledge it.)

THE MIRROR HOG

One time I couldn't get a look in a mirror because a woman was hunched right up to it, engaged in some obscure business with her face. As it happens, she was plucking her eyebrows. With absurd situations like these, feel free to use the old 'so sorry' and loom very close, invading their personal space. But if someone at the mirror has a pile of clothes to consider (especially if the shop doesn't have a dressing room), the polite thing to do is to give her some breathing room and recommence searching, returning when the mirror is free.

THE FLINGER

If, out of laziness or the impulse to hide desired items, somebody drapes a piece of clothing over the rail on your path, say, 'Pardon me, did you want this?' and hand it right back. For your part, try to re-hang clothes as neatly as possible.

THE CRAZY

Be gentle. Give her a smile, then ignore her. Do not interact in any further way. She'll soon find a more responsive victim to pester.

DRESS APPROPRIATELY
This means two things:

1)   Dress down – non-descript clothing and minimal jewellery. You'll feel less stressed about tossing your own clothes onto the dressing-room floor. Also, people are more likely to be pleasant if you don't look like an It Girl who got lost on the way to Harvey Nick's.

2)   Ideally, your outfit should be form-fitting enough so that you can pull other garments on top of it, and still get a reasonable idea of fit. For me, this means slim-line bottoms and a form-fitting T-shirt, under an easy-off jacket or jumper.

STAY FOCUSED
Save visits to the record stack or knick-knack shelf until after you've finished up with clothes and accessories. It's amazing how distracting (and time-consuming) nostalgic junk can be.

DON'T FORGET PRICE ADD-ONS
You may need or want to dry-clean your second-hand shop buys prior to wearing. There's also mending and, possibly, alteration. Be sure to keep all of these figures in mind when tallying the true cost of an item.

BE REALISTIC IN YOUR GOALS
Face it – the really spectacular, high-quality items are more likely to be found at dress agencies or vintage shops, and you're going to have to shell out more than £5 to get them. Amazing treasures do crop up, but you're bound to be disappointed if you expect them. But if you're looking for a pair of jeans or something outlandish for a theme party I'd be amazed if you left empty-handed.

DRAG YOUR SISTER ALONG, GO WITH A FRIEND, OR MAKE ONE WHILE SHOPPING
Even the worst charity shop in the world (especially the worst charity shop in the world) can make for a splendid day out if you take the right approach, which is a lot easier to do with a like-minded accomplice.

Dreaming of Thrift Store Dresses
by Eithne Farry, author of Yeah, I Made it Myself

My best dream is the one where I head to a seaside
town for a day spent wandering around charity shops.
It's sunny and the air smells of salt and hot donuts,
and I've got that lovely buzzy feeling of the possible;
just thinking of all the cool stuff I'm about to find,
nestling on the rails of Help the Aged, makes me
happy. I open a door of a crammed little shop and
look over at the woman by the till. She's busy
unpacking a black bin liner full of recently donated
clothes. As I watch, she pulls out dress after dress –
and every single one of them is covetable – forties tea
gowns, fifties summer frocks covered in huge pink and
red roses or neat, crisp sixties tabards with scalloped
hems made up in jewel-bright colours. I find a plum
velvet opera cloak, a bubble-gum pink ruched halter
neck and a pair of gold dancing shoes. And, because
this is a dream, I get to buy it all for a ridiculously
small amount of money . . .

Even in the real world, charity shops and car-boot
sales and auctions in out-of-the way places can be a

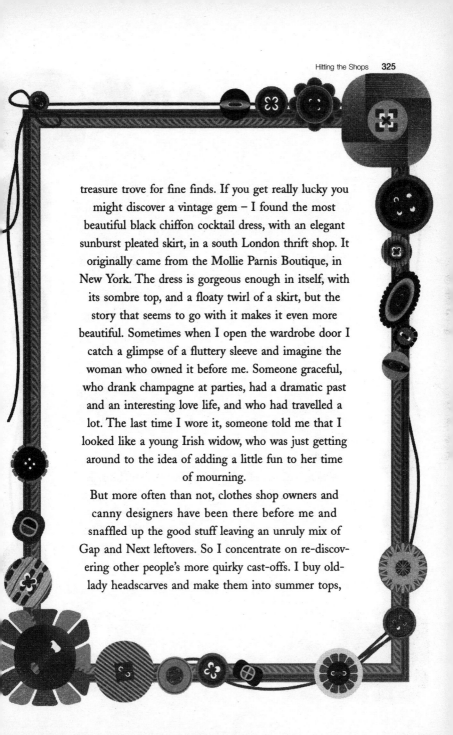

treasure trove for fine finds. If you get really lucky you might discover a vintage gem – I found the most beautiful black chiffon cocktail dress, with an elegant sunburst pleated skirt, in a south London thrift shop. It originally came from the Mollie Parnis Boutique, in New York. The dress is gorgeous enough in itself, with its sombre top, and a floaty twirl of a skirt, but the story that seems to go with it makes it even more beautiful. Sometimes when I open the wardrobe door I catch a glimpse of a fluttery sleeve and imagine the woman who owned it before me. Someone graceful, who drank champagne at parties, had a dramatic past and an interesting love life, and who had travelled a lot. The last time I wore it, someone told me that I looked like a young Irish widow, who was just getting around to the idea of adding a little fun to her time of mourning.

But more often than not, clothes shop owners and canny designers have been there before me and snaffled up the good stuff leaving an unruly mix of Gap and Next leftovers. So I concentrate on re-discovering other people's more quirky cast-offs. I buy old-lady headscarves and make them into summer tops, and add handles to cushion covers so that they become bags. I snip beautiful buttons from ugly old coats and sew them onto jackets, or boil-wash moth-eaten wool jumpers so that they get nice and felty. Then I cut the felted wool into flowers and add them to pockets or hems. And I L.O.V.E. old curtain fabric from the fifties, sixties and seventies – bold patterns, delicious colours, strange textures, they're just waiting to be turned into something wearable. My favourite dress is sewn from a curtain that I bought in a car boot sale. Before I transformed it, it had been hanging in a holiday caravan in Margate for years, brightening up the windows with its squares of gingerbread brown and egg yolk yellow. Now it brightens up my day every time I wear it.

And I've just bought a lemon-yellow linen tablecloth, which, with a little bit of snipping and stitching, is going be a very lovely A-line skirt. If I add a foraged shirt, with the sleeves cropped to the elbow and a corsage made from an embroidered handkerchief, I'll end up with a one-of-a-kind outfit. And that's a lovely feeling, knowing what you're wearing is totally original – no one else will have the match of it.

That's probably why I can't leave frocks, skirts or bags alone, I always have to tack something else on, even if it's only a scrabbly bit of knitting looped around a dress as a belt. When I was three I was sent a dress as a present from an aunt in America. It was pale pink and dotted with white spots; very lovely, but lacking a little something. So I took a dark blue biro and scribbled all over it. That was the very first thing that I customised; and, allowing for a few tidy teenage years, that's the approach I've taken towards clothing ever since. I either make something from scratch, adapt a shop-bought garment, or wear a thrift shop find.

So when the craving hits I'll head to the train station and find the nearest seaside town, and spend hours away from London, with a cheap-day return in my pocket and hope in my heart.

15

Dress agency confidential

OK, we shouldn't be dwelling on labels, but will you just take a look this line-up:

Dolce & Gabbana printed floral chiffon blouse: £45
Chanel Boutique pink and cream bouclé tweed shift: £275
L.K. Bennett red snakeskin boots: £35
Etro paisley silk skirt: £75

All immaculate, by the way, no visible wear whatsoever. This is but a sampling of the kinds of clothes currently on offer at my local dress agency. Granted, it's a killer dress agency, one of the best in London. The fact that it's not central means that countless women who are otherwise fashion obsessives will never visit. It's funny. We don't balk at going out of our way for a great pizza or a decent showerhead, but the thought of travelling to explore a new dress agency doesn't cross many minds, even those of die-hard second-handers. But isn't it worth the price of the tube, bus or train fare to profit from these kinds of opportunities? Especially if a given shop can outfit you for hundreds (or even thousands) less than you'd pay for equivalent pieces from department stores and retail boutiques? I say go for it, give it a try. (See the Directory for shop listings.) At worst you'll lose the train fare and a couple of hours' time; at best you'll gain a new pair of snakeskin boots to strut home in.

— *What to expect when shopping in a dress agency*

If, however, time is tight and you have fixed ideas about the styles and brands you're after, call an unfamiliar shop beforehand to make sure you're operating on a mutual wavelength. There's nothing worse than arriving at the shop with your heart set on a new frock for a wedding and learning there's nothing right in your size, or having a limited budget and discovering that the price tags are all in the high double and triple figures.

Certain clues can help you pre-evaluate the kinds of merchandise you'll find. Does the shop advertise in *Vogue*? *Big* clue, that one. Are the windows beautifully dressed with the kinds of things you'd like to wear? Where is it located? As mentioned earlier, a shop's offerings reflect the community dress code. Shops in well-heeled urban and suburban neighbourhoods are likely to feature current-season, flamboyant and expensive goods, as well as more international labels. A shop sharing a block with directional (read edgy) clothiers will get the stuff with the highest cool quotient.

It's unusual to come across a truly awful dress agency. The most frequent (minor) failings are inadequate lighting, overcrowded rails and, sometimes, a wee bit of attitude on the part of the personnel. I attribute this to the fact that a portion of their day is spent dealing with consignors from hell (sample dialogue: 'How can you *possibly* tell me that Prada suit hasn't sold?

Didn't you put it in the window like I told you!'). Never mind. You're there for the clothes.

—Keeping up appearances

Unlike charity shops, dress agencies are highly selective about the pieces they take on. The following guidelines intended for consignors are fairly universal starting points:

1) Very current items from the last 1–2 years.
2) New or gently used clothing:
     No stains or rips.
     No broken zips.
3) Items, including sweaters, must be cleaned, pressed and presented on hangers so they can view them quickly (clothing prepared properly sells best).
4) No mothball or smoke odours, or animal hair.

Keep in mind that it's the rare proprietor who won't accept a mint-condition Marni just because it's over two years old. The more chi-chi the name, the more flexibility there is in terms of age, especially if the piece is a classic. Do we care? Of course not. If the piece is beautifully made and enduringly stylish it will look great for years.

'It feels good to wear expensive clothes, especially when someone else paid for them the first time around.'
Caterine Milinaire and Carol Troy, *Cheap Chic*

— With a smile

Dress agencies prosper thanks to sincere and personalised service. If you become a regular customer at a given shop, here's the kind of treatment you can expect:

1) Top-quality assistance by sales help that truly knows the merchandise.
2) Offers of help with sizes and re-hanging unwanted items.
3) An honest opinion about the right styles for your figure.
4) Extra-mile efforts such as phone calls announcing that your preferred styles and sizes have come in.
5) A low-key education in the qualities of the best clothing.
6) The possibility of flexibility on shop hours (but only if you're an excellent customer).

Assistants often hope to own their own shop someday, and are consequently very keen indeed. How to tell the good from the bad? Great salespeople are honest. Poor ones, for some reason, feel they must fib. Watch out for narrowing of the eyes and fingers tapping chin while they work out what to say.

—Haggling dos and don'ts

This is a delicate area with dress-agency owners, and understandably so. It's not that they want to deny you a good deal – the problem is, most of the time, that the sale price or the profit has been fixed with the consignor, leaving no room for flexibility. This is why some owners get prickly if you ask for a discount. Others don't seem to mind. Certain experienced second-hand shoppers suggest always going for a discount, but my advice would be to do so only when:

1) The item has a flaw that may have escaped the owner's notice.

2) You're buying an unusually large or unusually expensive selection of clothes. If many of the pieces came from a single consignor (check the tickets for matching names or numbers), there may be more room for flexibility.

3) You have nerves of steel and don't mind a frosty reply.

— What to wear while shopping

If it's my first time in an upscale shop, I try to dress well. Over the years I've found that good rapport simply happens faster if I come in looking smart. Writer Tom Wolfe, in an interview with *The Times*, puts it much more elegantly: 'I realised early on that clothes are one of the few honest expressions people make about themselves. It's one of the ways people reveal how they think of themselves and how they want to be treated . . . People don't like to admit that these attributes reveal character, or that they are doorways into the soul, which I insist that they are.'

Still, practicality also enters the picture. It's good common sense to wear slip-on shoes and clothes with few buttons or other attachments. It's also better to wear hose instead of knee-highs, even underneath trousers. You'll get a more accurate sense of the proportions of frocks and skirts, and you'll have one less thing to dislike in the mirror (for the same reason, I try to remember to wear attractive underwear). When shopping for an evening dress that may involve support garments, either put them on or carry them along, so you can make the most realistic assessment.

—How to become a preferred customer

Contrary to popular belief, it doesn't mean spending bundles of cash (though this never hurts). You become a preferred customer by being a clever and considerate shopper, someone who appreciates and returns the shop's human touch. In brief:

1) Shop early and shop often. Let the owner get to know you, your tastes, your personality.
2) Spare thirty seconds for some friendly chit-chat with everyone on deck, no matter how rushed you feel. It will pay off the next time you go in.
3) Treat the clothes well. Remember to take your shoes off before stepping into skirts, shorts and dresses. Do not throw clothes on the floor. Wait until you're ready to leave the shop to freshen your lipgloss.
4) If you must criticise, do it like a diplomat.
5) Whenever possible, try to deal directly with the owner or manager. But don't monopolise her if the shop is busy.
6) Take advantage of the system. Most of the time, the tags hold the names or code numbers of specific consignors. If the same number crops up frequently in your picks, this is your kindred spirit on the other side of the consignment mirror. Tell the owner that you love this person's taste, and ask to be notified the next time she drops items off. This makes the owner a hero twice over.

—*How to profit from your purchases*

Spend enough time in dress agencies, and a little bell will go *ding* in your head. You have some fabulous clothing but, for one reason or another, some pieces are no longer right – you need more closet space, your figure has altered, your style direction has changed. Here's the great thing: just because the pieces are no longer objects of desire *for you* doesn't mean someone else won't love them. And this is where the dress agency comes in, from a completely different angle. It can be your partner in the happy retirement of pieces from your wardrobe.

WHERE THE TREASURES HIDE

1) The best merchandise in dress agencies often hangs within eyesight of the till, sometimes with security devices locking it to the rails. In shops with a good selection of top-ranked merchandise, designers may be sectioned off by name.

2) In the window. Smart shop owners put their most ravishing pieces on public view to attract passers-by. Sometimes they are willing to pull items out of display if there's a chance of making a sale.

3) At extremes of size. If you're an unusual fit, you may benefit where others fail.

4) On mannequins or up on the walls. Why decorate with posters when you've got Matthew Williamson originals instead?

5) In the back room. Often, premium merchandise is in a holding pattern, awaiting a steam or tag. If you're a good customer on excellent terms with the owner or staff, you can ask if anything wonderful is out back, getting the jump on others.

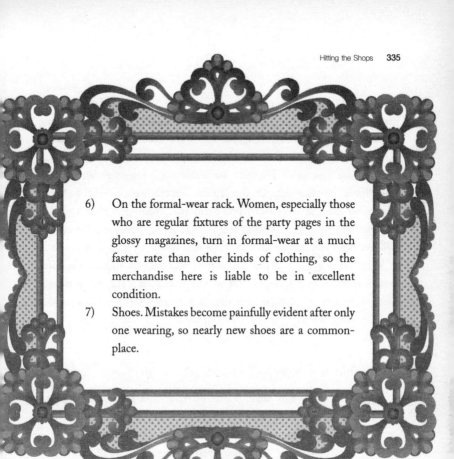

6) On the formal-wear rack. Women, especially those who are regular fixtures of the party pages in the glossy magazines, turn in formal-wear at a much faster rate than other kinds of clothing, so the merchandise here is liable to be in excellent condition.

7) Shoes. Mistakes become painfully evident after only one wearing, so nearly new shoes are a commonplace.

There are all kinds of reasons to feel good about channelling clothes back into the second-hand flow. For starters, it's environmentally and socially sound. Fashion can and should be fun, fabulous, frivolous – but there are realities at work, too. It always astounds me that people can throw away perfectly wearable clothing without a second thought, when the slightest additional effort would help lessen the world's solid waste, benefit the have-lesses and lighten the environmental impact/utility ratio of the garments' manufacture. These are reasons enough to keep good clothes in circulation, but then there's that other one . . .

Your bank account benefits as well as your soul. The trick lies in playing the game sensibly. If you buy second-hand clothing at a great price, in new or almost-new condition, and care for it meticulously, it's theoretically possible to break even or *even make money* reselling it.

These are a lot of ifs. It's more likely that you'll simply recoup some of your initial investment. If the goods are showing slight signs of wear, most dress agencies won't take them on. Donating to charity may be the best way to go. If the item is a vintage piece, the considerations are different, and you may be able to sell it to a dealer for cash on the spot.

What follows are some rules on how to play the game. Once this information is under your belt, you will be able to negotiate the entire second-hand cycle – from purchase to active duty to retirement – knowing that you're making the most out of your clothes.

—How not to resell clothing – a personal tale

A number of years ago, when I was working in a low-paying job and desperate for cash, I came up with what seemed like a cunning plan to earn it: sell off some recently cleaned garments to one of the best dress agencies in my area. Approaching the shop, I was very nervous, as though I were doing something wrong (boy, was I ever). I meekly approached one of the saleswomen, who led me into the back room and took a few seconds to look over my garments. A few seconds! She looked up and, in the kindest possible way, said there was no way they could sell them. She was very gracious (to the shop's eternal credit), but all the same I left feeling crushed. Back then, I didn't understand even the simplest principles of how to resell. Today, after a decade's experience dealing with all kinds of owners, it's a different story. Here's what I've learned:

THE THREE GOLDEN RULES
1)   *The label (or the quality) must fit the shop's image.* My High Street items – while desirable in other places – were no match for this particular

shop's Escada, Donna Karan and Valentino. The label or the quality has to be up to standard or else it will look like a poor relation.

2) *The finer the shop, the less tolerant they'll be of wear and flaws.* Despite the recent cleaning, my jumper was bobbly, and the seam above the slit was starting to gap on one of the skirts. While barely noticeable in the course of day-to-day wear, these were definite demerits when it came to making a sale.

3) *In better shops, the clothing's age really counts.* All of my pieces, while classic in style, still looked a few years out of date. In fact, compared with the shop's offerings, they looked frumpy. Why hadn't I noticed that before?

The answer is simple – on my previous visits, I had been looking at the merchandise as a buyer rather than as a seller. Now I know better. When reselling clothes, you work as a team with the shop owner, and you need to craft an approach that meshes with their own.

—*Putting on a selling hat*

The skills required to sell at dress agencies are similar to, but distinct from, the buying skills outlined in the previous chapters. In short, you must:

1) Accurately analyse the type of merchandise sold in the target shop.
2) Present yourself as a valuable present and future supply source.
3) Know the shop's particular policies.
4) Provide a clear idea of the piece's retail value.
5) Sell your garment's merits convincingly.
6) Negotiate intelligently.
7) Avoid walking away with regrets.

Now let's take a closer look at the underpinnings of these skills:

ANALYSE THE TYPE OF MERCHANDISE THE SHOP SELLS

◉ Look carefully around the shop first – never consign any garment 'cold'. You want to be sure it fits with the rest of the merchandise – that is, the quality is on a par, neither much better nor much worse than what's currently on the rails.

◉ A shop won't take a winter coat in April because they won't want to store it until the autumn. Bring in seasonal clothes just before the season begins.

◉ Don't set your sights too high with once-trendy pieces. Both owners and customers dislike garments that look blatantly last year.

◉ Likewise, unusual garments can be a hard sell. I once tried to consign a beautifully made, brand-new pair of designer formal shorts, only to have three shops turn me down flat. Why? Because every garment has a season unto heaven, and that particular season was hell for formal shorts. The same goes for things like catsuits, micro-minis, unusually coloured suede and leather items, extremely long sweaters, fur, silk suits and a host of other offbeat styles that appeal only to a limited audience. With pieces like these, you might have much more luck with a vintage or retro shop.

> **Connoisseur's Tip:**
> If you are consigning high-calibre scarves and jewellery, your chances of making a sale are greatly increased if you can bring in the original boxes as well. Why? Because people craftily buy such items as gifts, and it's far more convincing to present them as new if they come in the original packaging.

PRESENT YOURSELF AS A VALUABLE PRESENT AND
FUTURE SUPPLY SOURCE

◎   Many owners say it doesn't matter, but I *always* dress well when consigning – great outfit, accessories, smudge-free mascara. A well-groomed appearance simply lends more lustre to your goods.

◎   It's smart to imply you have a closetful of similar stuff at home (which is true, right?). Do this by bringing a casual air to the proceedings, letting the owner see your fine labels (rather than pointing them out), and being neither a snob nor a quivering wreck – simply a woman with great taste in clothes.

◎   Consigning clothes that show a bit of wear is often easier when the owner doesn't know you. Here's why – if you're a regular shopper in somebody's shop, she may conclude that any pieces you present are also second-hand, meaning she has to sell *third-hand* goods. Ironic as it may be, many owners find the idea loathsome. If your garments are in fantastic shape this shouldn't be an issue but, again, if they're not, you may gain a slight advantage by taking them to less familiar surroundings.

KNOW THE SHOP'S POLICIES

◎   *Always* call ahead to enquire about the shop's clothes-viewing policy (some only consider consignments on specific days). Find out if there's a minimum number of pieces (some shops don't like to take single items). Also, if there's any doubt, ask about the timetable for seasonal goods. If the shop has a written consignment policy, ask them to send it to you. Then go ahead and set up an appointment. Even if they say 'come in whenever', try to pin down a time during a calmer part of the day – you're less likely to wait should the owner or manager get tied up.

◎   Always assume the merchandise must be freshly dry-cleaned. If you can bring it in the plastic, all the better.

◎   Before negotiations begin, ask to see the consignment contract (if the shop has one in writing), and question any points you don't understand. If they don't have a contract, be sure you:

1) Understand the mark-down system. You will make less money if your garment hasn't sold within a set period of time and the price is lowered. Better to know this sooner rather than later.

2) Are aware of any hidden costs for paperwork or other administration.

3) Are clear on how you get paid. By cheque at the end of the month? Or some other method?

4) Know whether it is your responsibility to check on the status of consigned items (it usually is). Beware that if you don't, you might lose the piece altogether (more on this below).

PROVIDE A CLEAR IDEA OF THE PIECE'S RETAIL VALUE

◎   Whenever you *buy* a second-hand piece, try to obtain its original retail price from a knowledgeable person at the shop. If it's unknown, perhaps some retail research will shed light. Once you get the figure, jot it down, preferably in your second-hand notebook. Besides reinforcing your shopping smarts, it will be invaluable when it's time to resell.

◎   Most shops won't ask how old a garment is unless the wear is obvious (in which case they're looking for excuses to say no). Replying 'I've had it for a year' is acceptable, outright lying is not. If you're going to be shot down, do it with your integrity intact.

SELL YOUR GARMENT'S MERITS CONVINCINGLY

◎   If the shop owner doesn't appear to see the value of your item (perhaps it's a foreign or otherwise unfamiliar make), gently point out the quality details. When she starts nodding, you've convinced her not only of the piece, but of your own expertise.

Negotiate intelligently

◎ Check out the prices of garments similar to yours on the shop's racks. Reckon on making about half that amount (as the shop usually takes 50%).

◎ As paradoxical as it may sound, point out any flaw before the subject of money comes up. Why? So that the shop takes it into account on the ticket price, and can't cave in to a customer's demands that the price be lowered – a rude surprise for you later on.

◎ Try to get the owner to name a price first. If she seems interested in your garment, ask 'How much do you think you could sell it for?' If her response sounds good, next ask 'And would I get half?' If either answer surprises you, be sure to ask (nicely) why it's so.

◎ If you're asked for your selling price, you have two options. Either name a quarter of the original retail price, or half of the ticket price of a comparable garment in the shop, whichever is higher. Either way, you'll be able to defend your position. Remember that the age and the condition of your piece are critical factors. The better these are, the higher you can reasonably go.

Avoid walking away with regrets

◎ There will be occasions when you don't see eye to eye with a shop on price. Make every effort to find out why they feel as they do (this will arm you for future encounters), decline graciously and leave on a pleasant note. Remember – it's business, not personal, and you don't want to burn any bridges. Then, try your luck with another shop.

Once you've made an agreement

◎ Keep track of your consigned garments. Most shops stock items for a given period only. I once had the very bracing experience of eavesdropping on a shop owner and manager as they decided how to clear out their unsold stock. It soon became clear that the highly valued and/or famous consignors would get a courtesy phone call before their clothes were shipped off to charity; the 'nobodies' got no warning at all. The lesson? Most shops don't have the time, inclination or manpower to keep consignors posted on what's up with their clothes. It's up to *you* to check periodically on your garments' progress, and up to *you* to collect pieces that don't sell. If you don't, you risk losing your items. If the shop does not have a written statement about their particular policy, be sure you know exactly what's expected.

16

International second-hand

Holiday on the Med – been there, done that, have the sun damage to prove it. Culture-vulture tour of a European capital – one cathedral is breathtaking, but ten? Snowboarding in the French Alps – fantastic, except for that cumbersome take-home ankle cast.

Why not try a different kind of getaway, one with a whole new spin? Put all the money you've saved by shopping second-hand into an amazing trip to a fabulous destination, where you can do *loads more shopping* second-hand?

Stay with me on this one, because the possibilities are incredible. You could do a long weekend in New York City, following Carrie Bradshaw's Manolo-prints at great vintage and retro shops like *Marmalade* and *Star Struck* downtown. Or hit Barcelona, where at *La Gauche Devine* you can have a glass of *tinto* and admire an art exhibition as a break from browsing the vintage couture. Or duck out of the sun on Bondi Beach with a dive into *Puff 'n' Stuff*, whose collection of retro trainers fits right into the sporty Aussie vibe. Or go stark raving banshee in Tokyo, where *Hanjiro Harajuko* has enough trash and treasure to merit a couple of days' digging.

It's really the only thing to do, once you've conquered the second-hand horizons in your area. Go west, young woman, and east, and north, and south. Experiencing second-hand shopping in another country is just as rewarding as discovering a new cuisine or seeing a world-famous postcard come to life, because you're working the racks right alongside the natives. What better way to immerse yourself in a culture? And, strange as it may seem, visiting a shop overseas could be the *least* foreign aspect of being in a new land. For second-hand shopping, like love, is a universal language. Smart girls all over the world adore a brilliant find – be it vintage or (almost) brand new. No matter how exotic the location, the shopping protocol is pretty much the same. You're in there. You know what to do.

The United States has a second-hand sensibility so firmly entrenched that thrifting is a culture unto its own, with books, 'zines and megastores celebrating mining for diamonds in the rough, while in other countries flea markets act as the clearing-houses of slamming cheap. In sophisticated urban centres, no matter where the locale, you'll find dress agencies profiting from the usual designer suspects (Prada and Gucci are beloved from Abu Dhabi to Zermatt), but with the added interest of locally loved labels. And most foreign countries have a place for vintage clothing, either in dedicated boutiques or at markets or, increasingly, in shops-within-shops, as fashion-forward department stores realise that a vintage section is extremely good for the bottom line.

—Shouldn't I be getting real culture instead?

All right, all right, forsaking great museums, cathedrals, plazas and cafés for extended binges in the local charity shops is not the highest and best use of holiday time. But really, there's only so much museum-going and café-sitting a body can take. If your significant other objects, fire back with these plausible rationales:

1) It gets you off the tourist track and into the soul of a foreign city. Second-hand shops tend to cluster in neighbourhoods ignored by the package-tour crowd, and so offer a fascinating way of seeing how the bohemian locals really act, dress and have fun.

2) Finding these places develops your ability to read maps and use local transportation (blokes will *love* this one). Get somewhere successfully and you have that wonderful feeling of being a *traveller*, someone who can go anywhere and find anything you choose.

3) You'll be visiting a place where English is probably not a given, and you'll see that it doesn't matter. Enthusiasm (and cash) speak volumes for you.

4) You'll be exposed to labels and styles that are deeply unfamiliar, and therefore an excellent challenge for your new skills.

— *A word on sizes*

In other countries, the size designations will be foreign, too. The British and continental European versions translate (more or less) as follows (other size conversions are readily available on the internet by searching with keywords 'size conversion', 'clothes' and your destination country):

United Kingdom

8	10	12	14	16	18	20	22	24

European

38	40	42	44	46	48	50	52	54

American and Canadian

4	6	8	10	12	14	16	18	20

As for shoe size, add '33' to your current size to get the continental European equivalent. For the US equivalent, add 2 to your size (but, for goodness sake, *always try everything on*!)

For a taster of what you can expect, come along on a quicky world tour . . .

— New York City

Where to begin? With the drop-dead dress agencies on upper Madison Avenue, like *Michael's* and *Encore*, which have been unclothing the best-dressed women in the world for decades (and clothing them too, not that they'd tell). Or thrift stores ranging from the football pitch-sized *Salvation Army* depot on far West 56th street, or the bijou *Out of the Closet* on East 81st, or the fabulous cluster of glittering thrifts (*Spence-Chapin, Memorial Sloan-Kettering, Irving Institute*) on upper Third Avenue. Great vintage finds can be snagged at the many shops that litter the downtown area, or, in a more condensed, easy-shop version, at the *Manhattan Vintage Clothing* show and the *New York Vintage Fashion and Textiles Show* (check the internet for dates and times).

— Paris

As few as ten years ago, it was hard to find inexpensive second-hand clothing (*fripes*) in Paris, apart from Sunday forays at the *Marche aux Puces* and *Marche Clignancourt* flea markets, or at the still-going-strong *Mouton à Cinq Pattes* in the boulevard St-Germain and rue St-Placide. But the French are nothing if not fashion-conscious, and they have jumped on the retro bandwagon. *Come on Eileen* in the rue des Taillandiers in the trendy 11th arrondissement is a wonderful emporium of vintage finds, as is *Wochdom* in the rue de Condorcet in the 9th. For vintage of more distinguished lineage, there is *Gabrielle Geppert Vintage* in the Palais Royale, or, just down the arcade, the grande dame of them all, *Didier Ludot*, where the most exquisite creations from the foremost ateliers are put on display. Meanwhile, dress agencies (*depot-ventes*) make amends for the high prices with a bounty of riches, from last season's Chanel suits to the hottest looks from APC. *Réciproque* on the rue du Pompe in the doughty 18th arrondissement is one of the biggest (and best) in the world, and *Chercheminippes*, not far from the Printemps department store on the rive gauche, runs a close second. *Les 3 Marchés de Catherine B*, a jewel box of a shop in the St-Germain de Prés neighbourhood, stocks only Hermès and Chanel. All are easily accessible by metro from the heart of town and are a worthy destination for a few hours' break from the Louvre and *patisseries*.

— *Milan*

Come bella you'll look, *chiara*, after a successful expedition to *Cavalli e Nastri* on the via Brera, where you'll find everything vintage, from wedding gowns to accessories. Designer labels from all decades reside at the *Cento Borse* in the via Giangiacomo Mora, and *Franco Jacassi* in the via Sacchi could easily outfit latter-day Ginas and Sophias in ultra-sophisticated vintage style.

— *Los Angeles*

Beverly Hills, baby, is home to the spectacular haute-couture (and only slightly less *haute* bog-standard couture) specialist *Lily et Cie*, the go-to boutique for all of young Hollywood on the hunt for a gown to wear to their latest premiere. The prices are as stunning as the customers. *Decades* and *Decades Two* on Melrose Avenue specialises in 1960s and 1970s top-end glad rags (*D1*), as well as more contemporary pieces (*D2*). An entirely different experience can be had at *Wasteland*, also on Melrose, which has rack upon rack of browseables going back to the 1940s. If you hate the thought of missing out on the fabled LA sunshine, why not visit *Jet Rag* on North La Brea, which holds Sunday parking-lot sales, competing with the flea market extravaganzas at the *Rose Bowl* (opens at 5 a.m. on the second Sunday of the month) or at *Pasadena City College* (a more easy-going 8 a.m. start on the first Sunday of the month).

—*Amsterdam*

Running neck and neck with Barcelona as the most romantic city in the world after Paris, Amsterdam is further enhanced by a number of fine dress agencies, like *Lucky Lina*, which features contemporary women's and children's wear at gentle prices, and *Second Best*, offering exclusive names in a lovely shop. Restore yourself with a cosy beer or hot chocolate in one of the hundreds of cafés that dot the canals, then head off to *Lady Day* in the city centre, well in the running for the best vintage shop in town.

—*Copenhagen*

Young, vibrant, with a delightful café culture, Copenhagen's charms are considerable. Some noteworthy stop-ins on the local second-hand scene: *KK Vintage*, on Skt. Peders straede, holds a nice selection of vintage finds, and *Kitsch Bitch* in Laederstraede boasts a friendly owner and a fine selection of 1950s–60s era clothing and goods. Other shops cluster in Larsbjornstraede and Studiestraede.

—*Making your own discoveries in foreign lands*

When visiting a new city, the last thing you want to do is to waste time trying to find second-hand outlets that may not exist in the first place. That's why it's important to do as much initial research as you can before you go. Regrettably, no single guidebook lists the second-hand shops in the world's major cities (a publishing opportunity if ever there was one). However, the **individual city guides** – especially those from Time Out, Lonely Planet and Rough Guide – offer a wealth of *bonnes addresses* of second-hand shops. Another source is **shopping guides** to countries and individual cities, for example Suzy Gershman's *Born to Shop* titles. An hour or so spent in a good library or bookshop should get you started on possibilities. While you're at it, find a dictionary of your destination country's language and write down their words for 'second-hand', 'clothing', 'vintage', and anything else of special interest (note that the term 'second-hand' won't translate easily).

Another at-home option is combing the **internet** for information. Try typing the name of your city along with the usual keywords (keeping an eye out for antique and flea markets, which usually host at least a few sellers of vintage clothes). As with all internet research, results will vary widely depending on the general availability of the information you desire, the time you can devote and how you go about tracking it down. Another thing: stores come and go, but web pages can be up there forever – be sure that the information you're viewing is current.

Once you're at your destination, have a word with the hotel's concierge (they are paid to hunt down this sort of information, and the unusual nature of the request may set their detective instincts blazing). If there's no concierge, or if he or she seems unhelpful, try asking a friendly young woman on the hotel staff. You may get a blank look, but there's an equal chance that she has some personal favourites to share. Whomever you speak with, avoid misunderstandings by:

1) Being as clear as possible about the kind of clothing you seek. In some countries, second-hand equals nasty old cast-offs, and you don't want to waste your time. Explain that you want high quality, good names, and you are willing to pay a good price.

2) Bear in mind that how you look could determine where you are sent. If you're wearing a trackie and trainers, the shops suggested are likely to be filled with similar goods. If you are dressed smartly, you will likely be sent to the better addresses.

3)   Use terminology that people can understand. 'Dress agency' doesn't translate in most countries, likewise 'charity shop' may draw a blank. 'Vintage' should be understood, but if you really get stuck you could try something like 'antique clothing' (which may result in a trip to an armour store, but chainmail is an interesting look . . .).

4)   Make sure you obtain the shops' hours. Many smaller ones won't open until the afternoon, or will close for siesta, or close at 5 p.m., or won't be open at all on, say, Monday, or in August. Better to find out in the comfort of your hotel than on the street in front of a locked door.

5)   Ask your helper to jot down the names and addresses, and, better yet, circle the locations on a local map.

And then there are some firm **don'ts** you should also keep in mind:

◎   **Don't** go anywhere without a good map. At best you'll get frustrated, at worst you'll get lost, and who needs that kind of hassle on vacation?

◎   **Don't** go into any neighbourhood unadvised by hotel staff. If you feel uncomfortable in a particular place, heed your instincts and turn back.

◎   **Don't** go too far out of your way. Even if there's a great dress agency out in the suburbs somewhere, the travel time and aggravation are probably not worth it.

◎   **Don't** go anywhere without checking the hours first. Again, this is not the occasion to waste time on closed shops.

◎   **Don't** assume that you can pay with a card. Cash is always the safest bet. Count your change carefully, especially at markets.

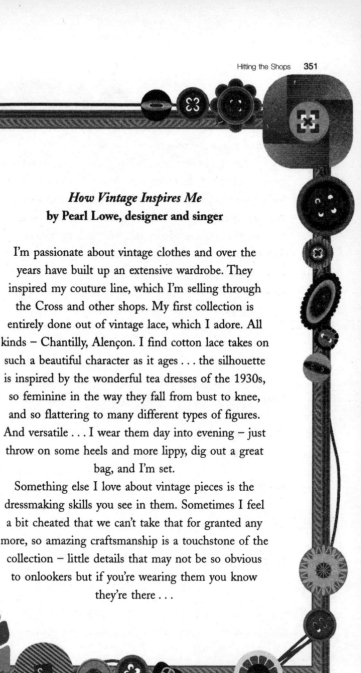

How Vintage Inspires Me
by Pearl Lowe, designer and singer

I'm passionate about vintage clothes and over the years have built up an extensive wardrobe. They inspired my couture line, which I'm selling through the Cross and other shops. My first collection is entirely done out of vintage lace, which I adore. All kinds – Chantilly, Alençon. I find cotton lace takes on such a beautiful character as it ages . . . the silhouette is inspired by the wonderful tea dresses of the 1930s, so feminine in the way they fall from bust to knee, and so flattering to many different types of figures. And versatile . . . I wear them day into evening – just throw on some heels and more lippy, dig out a great bag, and I'm set.

Something else I love about vintage pieces is the dressmaking skills you see in them. Sometimes I feel a bit cheated that we can't take that for granted any more, so amazing craftsmanship is a touchstone of the collection – little details that may not be so obvious to onlookers but if you're wearing them you know they're there . . .

My parents were in fashion – my mother had a shop in Covent Garden – and as a kid I was always so into shopping. At seven or eight I'd think nothing of marching into a store and asking, 'Oh can't you *please* get that one in my size?' My mum was a designer fan and had this gorgeous Missoni mint-green scarf that still looks great, absolutely timeless.

I put so much thought into what I wear – what a disappointment to spend a fortune for a special occasion only to see someone else wearing exactly the same thing! This happened to me once at a party – and it was a £4,000 Alexander McQueen frock! This is where vintage and one-of-a-kind pieces are such an advantage. You *know* your look is unique.

The 1920s and 1930s are a special time – it almost feels like I have a spiritual home there. When I sing, mood is sultry, smoky, atmospheric – I did a gig at Ronnie Scott's Jazz Club, surrounded by photos of Billie Holiday and other greats, and it felt so right. My grandmother actually performed in this era – she was a saxophonist in England's first all-girl

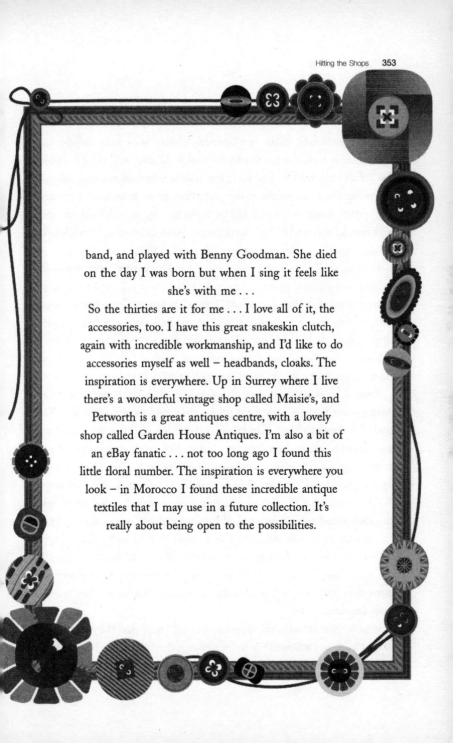

band, and played with Benny Goodman. She died
on the day I was born but when I sing it feels like
she's with me . . .
So the thirties are it for me . . . I love all of it, the
accessories, too. I have this great snakeskin clutch,
again with incredible workmanship, and I'd like to do
accessories myself as well – headbands, cloaks. The
inspiration is everywhere. Up in Surrey where I live
there's a wonderful vintage shop called Maisie's, and
Petworth is a great antiques centre, with a lovely
shop called Garden House Antiques. I'm also a bit of
an eBay fanatic . . . not too long ago I found this
little floral number. The inspiration is everywhere you
look – in Morocco I found these incredible antique
textiles that I may use in a future collection. It's
really about being open to the possibilities.

—A few final words

There's a word used in the employment industry to describe abilities that transfer easily from one job to another – such skills are said to be 'portable'. You'll find that that's exactly what your clothing connoisseurship will turn out to be. Once you've got quality detection, fit assessment and personal style points down pat, you'll feel at home in any second-hand situation anywhere in the world. And, on a deeper level, developing your clothing connoisseurship touches upon other life areas as well.

For one, you'll find yourself increasingly willing to **trust your own skills**. Relying on your own senses to detect the best frees you from the marketing barrage so many others succumb to. Instead of jumping on a hot trend just because some fashion copywriter says so, you will actively weigh it against other options – ultimately choosing the smartest all-round buy. Sure, you'll still go for the occasional famous name or fashion fad, but because you *know*, rather than *hope*, it makes you look good.

Related to this, being a savvy second-hand shopper means routinely checking out the retail arena for prices, styles and quality indicators. This kind of **research ability** – turning available information to your own advantage, doesn't have to stop short at clothes. When it's time to buy a new stereo, a car, a flat, you will know how to survey the market. Decisions that are informed by facts rather than by feelings *always* result in better deals.

Another area that clothing connoisseurship actively develops is **self-knowledge and self-acceptance**. While some might argue that knowing your hip measurement and figure flaws has little to do with being a happy, well-centred person, I disagree. Knowing them and, more importantly, managing them through well-chosen garments, means you can stop worrying about how you look and refocus on more important stuff – yes, there is more important stuff.

Finally, women who are expert in second-hand chic know this above all: just because you weren't born into money, don't have a high-paying job, or weren't blessed with trophy good looks, **doesn't mean you have to settle**

for second-best. Your wardrobe can be as exquisite, as up-to-date, as eye-catching as you choose. And if this gives you the confidence to take on the world in other ways, your accomplishments will go well beyond buying great clothes.

Directory

Now you know what to look for, here's where to look!

All information is correct at the time of going to press.

— Museums and Organisations

Bexhill Museum of Costume & Social History
The Manor Gardens
Upper Sea Road
Bexhill-on-Sea
East Sussex
TN40 1RL
01424 210 045
www.bexhillcostumemuseum.co.uk

The Bowes Museum
Barnard Castle
County Durham
DL12 8NP
01833 690 606
www.durham.gov.uk

Cavalcade of Costume Museum
The Plocks
Blandford Forum
Dorset
DT11 7AA
01258 453 006
www.cavalcadeofcostume.com

Chertsey Museum
33 Windsor Street
Chertsey
Surrey
KT16 8AT
01932 565 764
www.chertseymuseum.org.uk

Devonshire Collection of Period Costume: Totnes Costume Museum
Bogan House
43 High Street
Totnes
Devon
TQ9 5NP
01803 862 075

Gallery of Costume, Platt Hall
Rusholm
Manchester
M14 5LL
0161 224 5217
www.manchestergalleries.org/html/costume/goc-home.jsp

Kensington Palace, Royal Ceremonial Dress Collection
London
W8 4PX
020 7937 9561
www.hrp.org.uk

Museum of Costume and Textiles
51 Castle Gate
Nottingham
NG1 6AF
0115 915 3500
www.nottinghamcity.gov.uk

Museum of Costume
The Assembly Rooms
Bennett Street
Bath
BA1 2QH
01225 477 752 / 01225 477 789
www.museumofcostume.co.uk

National Museum of Scotland
Chamber Street
Edinburgh
EH1 1JF
0131 225 7534
www.nms.ac.uk

Northampton Museum – Boot and Shoe Collection
Guildhall Road
Northampton
NN1 1DP
01604 838 111
www.northampton.gov.uk/museums

Shambellie House Museum of Costume
New Abbey nr. Dumfries
DG2 8HQ
01387 850 375
www.nms.ac.uk/costume

Victoria & Albert Museum, Department of Textiles & Dress
Cromwell Road
South Kensington
London
SW7 2RL
020 7942 2000
www.vam.ac.uk

— Internet Reference Sources

The Antique Corset Gallery (www.antiquecorsetgallery.com)
A guided tour through the last 250 years of corsetry.

The Costumer's Manifesto (www.costumes.org)
The go-to site for professional costumers – incredibly detailed info here.

The Costume Society (www.costumesociety.org.uk)
Special interest group formed of collectors, curators, designers and vintage lovers. Offers special events, lectures, a journal.

Fashion Era (www.fashion-era.com)
Spendid site featuring extensive information on twentieth-century fashion history.

Go! Vintage (www.angelfire.com/la3/govintage)
Excellent UK-based site offering guidance, directories and links about vintage clothes.

Just-Pleats (www.just-pleats.co.uk)
Hire agency for pleated clothing from the 1950s, 1960s and 1970s.

The Vintage Fashion Guild (www.vintagefashionguild.org)
International collective of vintage lovers with great resources and chat groups.

— Internet Vintage-Clothing Sources

www.babylonmall.com (collective of vintage sellers, fun links)

www.bartonandbarton.com (French and UK vintage clothing and home-ware)

www.c20vintagefashion.co.uk (extensive collection, many British 1960s greats)

www.ebay.co.uk (many vendors have online shops)

www.odditiesantiques.com (specialists in antique and vintage textiles)

www.sleeknchic.com (largest online resource for vintage lingerie)

www.truffleshuffle.co.uk (1980s retro specialists, especially strong in T-shirts)

www.vintagevixen.com (superb US site with extensive reference material and links)

www.vivalafrock.co.uk (daywear, eveningwear, bridalwear and home collection)

— *Vintage Expositions*

Ann Zierold Textile & Vintage Fashion Fairs
Cheshire & University of Manchester
enquiries@annzieroldfairs.co.uk

Battersea Vintage Fashion, Accessories & Textiles Fair
Battersea Arts Centre
London
SW11 5TN
020 7223 6557
www.vintagefashionfairs.com

Battersea Vintage Fashion Fairs
16 Garden Road
Bromley
Kent
BR1 3LX
020 8325 5789

Blind Lemon Vintage Fairs
07790 578 605
www.blindlemonvintage.co.uk

Frock Me!
Chelsea Town Hall
London
SW3 5EE
020 7254 4054
www.frockmevintagefashion.com

London Vintage Fashion & Accessories Fair
Hammersmith Town Hall
London
W6 9JV
020 8748 3020
info@pa-antiques.co.uk

Vintage Fashion Fair
Earl's Court
London
SW5 0LX
www.uniqueeventsoflondon.com/fashion-fair.htm

— *Markets*

LONDON
Alfies Antique Market
13–25 Church Street, NW8 8DT
Tue–Sat 10.00–6.00

Brick Lane and Cheshire Street
Between Bethnal Green Road and Whitechapel Road, E1 6PU
Sun 6.00–1.00

Camden Market – The Stables Market
West of Chalk Farm Road, NW1 8AH
Sat–Sun 9.00–5.00

Camden Passage
Upper Street and Essex Road, N1 8EG
Wed 7.00–4.00; Sat 7.00–5.00

Grays Antique Market
1–7 Davies Mews, W1 5LP
Mon–Fri 10.00–6.00

Greenwich Market
Greenwich High Road, SE10 9HZ
Sat–Sun 9.30–5.00

Portobello Market
Portobello Road, W10 5ET
Mon–Wed 8.00–5.00; Thu 8.00–1.00; Fri–Sat 8.00–6.00

Roman Road
E3 5LU
Tue, Thur and Sat 8.30–5.00

Spitalfields Market
Commercial Street, E1 6BG
Thur 9.00–4.00; Sun 11.00–4.00

Swiss Cottage Market
Eton Avenue, NW3 3NR
Fri–Sun 9.30–4.30

OUTSIDE LONDON
Affleck's Palace
52 Church Street
Manchester
M4 1PW
0161 834 2039
www.afflecks-palace.co.uk

Iveagh Market Hall
Francis Street
Dublin 8
Tue–Sat 9.00–5.00

Snape Antique & Collectors Centre
Snape Maltings
Saxmundham
Suffolk
IP17 1SR
01728 688 038

—Vintage Shops

LONDON
Annies
12 Camden Passage
N1 8EG
020 7359 0796

The Antique Clothing Shops
282 Portobello Road
W10 5TE
020 8964 4830

Appleby
95 Westbourne Park Villas
W2 5ED
020 7229 7772
www.appleby.com

Biba Lives Vintage Clothing
13–25 Church Street
NW8
020 7258 7999
www.bibalives.com

Blackout II
51 Endell Street
WC2H 9AJ
020 7240 5006

Butler & Wilson
189 Fulham Road
SW3 6JN
020 7352 3045
www.butlerandwilson.co.uk

Cenci
4 Nettlefold Place
SE27 0JW
020 8766 8564
www.cenci.co.uk

Circa Vintage Clothes
8 Fulham High Street
SW6 3LQ
020 7736 5038
www.circavintage.com

Cloud Cuckoo Land
6 Charlton Place
N1 8AJ
020 7354 3141

Cornucopia
12 Upper Tachbrook Street
SW1V 1SH
020 7828 5752

Crazy Clothes Connection
134 Lancaster Road
W11 1QU
020 7221 3989

Dolly Diamond Vintage Clothing
51 Pembridge Road
W11 3HG
020 7792 2479
www.dollydiamond.com

Emporium
330–332 Creek Road
SE10 9SW
020 8305 1670
www.emporiumoriginals.com

Flashback
50 Essex Road
N1 8LR
020 7354 9356
www.flashback.co.uk

Gallery of Antique Costume & Textiles
2 Church Street
NW8 8ED
020 7723 9981
www.gact.co.uk

The Girl Can't Help It
Alfies Antique Market
Unit G100
13–25 Church Street
NW8 8ED
020 7724 8984
www.thegirlcanthelpit.com

Marshmallow Mountain
G5, Kingly Court
49 Carnaby Street
W1B 5PW
020 7434 9498
www.marshmallowmountain.com

Modern Age Vintage Clothing
65 Chalk Farm Road
NW1 8AN
020 7482 3787
www.modern-age.co.uk

The Observatory
20 Greenwich Church Street
SE10 9BJ
020 8305 1998
www.theobservatory.co.uk

One of a Kind
253 & 259 Portobello Road
W11 1LR
020 7792 5284/5853

Palette London
21 Canonbury Lane
N1 2AS
020 7288 7428
www.palette-london.com

Peekaboo at Topshop
Topshop (Vintage)
Oxford Circus
W1D 1LA
020 7636 5733
www.topshop.com

Pop Boutique
6 Monmouth Street
WC2H 9HB
020 7497 5262
www.pop-boutique.com

Rellik
8 Golborne Road
W10 5NW
020 8962 0089
www.relliklondon.co.uk

Retro
(men's)
34 Pembridge Road
W11 3HL

(women's)
20 Pembridge Road
W11 3HL

(home furnishing)
30 Pembridge Road
W11 3HL
020 7792 1715
www.musicandvideoexchange.co.uk

Ribbons & Taylor
157 Stoke Newington Church Street
N16 0UH
020 7254 4735

Rokit
101 & 107 Brick Lane
E1 6SE
020 7375 3864

225 Camden High Street
NW1 7BU
020 7267 3046

42 Shelton Street
Covent Garden
WC2H 9H2
020 7836 6547
www.rokit.co.uk

Sheila Cook
42 Ledbury Road
W11 2QA
020 7792 8001

Steinberg & Tolkien
193 King's Road
SW3 5ED
020 7376 3660

Virginia
98 Portland Road
Holland Park
W11 4LQ
020 7727 9908

What the Butler Wore
131 Lower Marsh
SE1 7AE
020 7261 1353
www.whatthebutlerwore.co.uk

— Vintage Shops Outside London

With special thanks to Carolyn Garlick at Go! Vintage (www.angelfire.com/la3/govintage) for her research into shopping outside the capital.

NORTH WEST
Bulletproof
41 Hardman Street
Liverpool
L1 9AS
0151 708 5808

Decades
20 Lord Street West
Blackburn
Lancashire
BB2 1JX
01254 693 320
www.decadesemporium.co.uk

Live Again
77 Newport Street
Bolton
BL1 1PF
01204 527 803

My Goodness
10–12 Hilton Street
Northern Quarter
Manchester
M1
07731 917 738

Phaedra
104 Shakespeare Street
Southport
PR8 5AJ
07713 785 687

Pop Boutique
34 Oldham Street
Manchester
M1 1JN
0161 236 5797
www.pop-boutique.com

Rags to Bitches
60 Tib Street
Manchester
M4 1LG
0161 835 9265
www.rags-to-bitches.co.uk

Somewhere in Time
Quiggins Centre
12–16 School Lane
Liverpool
L1 3BT
0151 706 0796

Vintage Clothing Company
Afflecks Palace
52 Church Street
Manchester
M4 1PW
0161 832 0548
www.affleckspalace.co.uk

Vintage Clothing Company
Ground Floor
Quiggins Centre
12–16 School Lane
Liverpool
L1 3BT
0151 707 0051
www.pop-boutique.com

Vintage to Fetish
Afflecks Palace
52 Church Street
Manchester
M4 1PW
0161 835 4078

SOUTH WEST
Bees & Graves
3 Clifton Arcade
Boyces Avenue
Bristol
BS8 4AA
0117 973 0500

Clifton Hill Antique Costume & Textiles
4 Lower Clifton Hill
Bristol
BS8 1BT
0117 929 0644

Glad Ragz
50 Churchgate
Wiltshire
LE1 4AJ
07796 347 344
www.gladragz.com

Happy Days
Cutcrew Sawmill
Tideford
Cornwall
PO12 5JZ
01752 851 402

Katze
55 Gloucester Road
Bristol
BS7 8AD
0117 942 5625

Kitts Couture
Kitts Corner
51 Chapel Street
Penzance
Cornwall
TR18 4AF
01736 364 507
www.kittscouture.co.uk

RePsycho
85 Gloucester Road
Bristol
BS7 8AS
0117 983 0007

Sobeys
34 Park Street
Bristol
BS1 5JG
0117 929 8923
www.pop-boutique.com

The Yellow Shop
74 Wolcott Street
Bath
BA1 5BD
01225 404 001

Vintage Clobber
920 Christchurch Road
Boscombe
Bournemouth
BH7 6DJ
01202 433 330
www.vintageclobber.com

Vintage to Vogue
28 Milsom Street
Bath
BA1 1DG
01225 337 323

SOUTH
Bead Games
40 Cowley Road
Oxford
OX4 1HZ
01865 251 620

Uncle Sam's
25 Little Clarendon Street
Oxford
OX1 2HU
01865 510 759

MIDLANDS
Back in Fashion
38 High Street
Tutbury, Burton on Trent
DE13 9LS
01283 814 964

Celia's Vintage Clothing
66–68 Derby Road
Nottingham
NG1 5FD
0115 947 3036
www.celias-nottom.co.uk

Corsets and Crinolines
29 Lansdowne Grove
Wigston
Leicestershire
LE18 4LU
0116 224 5361
www.corsetsandcrinolines.com

Gas Works
24 Salter Street
Stafford
Staffordshire
ST16 2JU
01785 226 868
www.gasworksoline.co.uk

Mondo
8/9 Saddler Gate
Derby
DE1 3NF
01332 295 233
www.mondoclothing.co.uk

Retro Styling
St Wilfred's Hall
63 High Street
Kibworth
Leicester
LE8 0HS
0116 279 6229
www.retrostyling.co.uk

Tea Gowns and Textiles
28 & 30 Broad Street
Leominster
Herefordshire
HR6 8BS
01568 612 999
www.vintage-fabrics.co.uk

The Wardrobe
6 Royal Arcade
Silver Street
Leicester
LE1 5YW
01162 538 983

Urban Village
The Custard Factory
Digbeth High Street
Digbeth
Birmingham
B9 4AA
0121 244 5160
www.urban-village.co.uk

Wild Clothing
4–6 Broad Street
Nottingham
NG1 3AL
0115 941 3928

Yo-Yo
7 Ethel Street
Birmingham
B2 4BG
0121 633 3073

YORKSHIRE & LINCOLNSHIRE
Blue Rinse
9 & 11 Call Lane
City Centre
Leeds
LS1 7DH
0113 245 1735

Echoes
650a Halifax Road
Eastwood
Todmorden
OL14 6DW
01706 817 505

Ego
2 The Strait
Lincoln
LN2 1JD
01522 514 264

Era
Carlton Antiques, Salts Mill
Victoria Road
Saltaire, near Leeds
BD18 3AA
01274 592 310
www.cissieandbertha.com

Freshmans Vintage Clothing
6–8 Carver Street
Sheffield
S1 4FS
0114 272 8333
www.freshmans.co.uk

Groovy Boutique
46 Savile Street
Hull
HU1 3EA
01482 327 543

Priestley's Vintage Clothing
1 Norman Court
Grape Lane
York
YO1 7HU
01904 631 565

Sugar Shack
14 Headingley Lane
Leeds
LS6 2AS
0113 226 1020
www.sugar-shack.co.uk

NORTH EAST
Attica
2 Old George Yard
Off Highbridge
Newcastle-upon-Tyne
NE1 1EZ
0191 261 4062

Dr Funkenstein
23 Derwent Street
Park Lane Shopping Village
Sunderland
SR1 3NV
0191 567 1971
www.drfunkenstein.net

Retro Modern
29 Highbridge
Newcastle
NE1 1EW
0191 232 5514

Royal Vintage
4a Worswick Street
Newcastle-upon-Tyne
NE1 6UN
0191 230 3040

SOUTH EAST
Bohemia
104 High Street
Hythe
CT21 5LE
01303 267 020

Juju
24 Gloucester Road
North Lane
Brighton
BN1 4AQ
01273 673 161

Harlequin Vintage
31 Sydney Street
Brighton
BN1 4EP
01273 675 222
www.harlequin-vintage.co.uk

Rockaround
Unit 8
Bristol & West Arcade
Friar Street
Reading
RG1 1JL
0118 956 0588

Starfish Retro Clothing
25 Gardner Street
Brighton
BN1 1UP
01273 680 868

To Be Worn Again
51 Providence Place
Brighton
BN1 4GE
01273 624 500

24a Sydney Street
Brighton
BN1 4EN
01273 680 296

Wardrobe
51 Upper North Street
Brighton
BN1 3FH
01273 202 201
www.decoratif.co.uk

EAST
Moons
24 The Thoroughfare
Ipswich
IP1 1BY
01473 254 299

Past Caring
6 Chapel Yard
Albert Street
Holt
NR25 6HG
01263 713 771

SCOTLAND
Armstrongs
64–66 Clerk Street
Edinburgh
EH8 9JB
0131 667 3056
www.armstrongsvintage.co.uk

Armstrongs Vintage Clothing
83 Grassmarket
Edinburgh
EH1 2HJ
0131 220 5557
www.armstrongsvintage.co.uk

Circa
34 Halley Drive
New Albion Estate
Glasgow
G13 4DL
0141 952 4411

Flip
59–61 South Bridge
Edinburgh
EH1 1LF
0131 556 4966
www.flipstores.com

15 Bath Street
Glasgow
G2 1HY
0141 353 1634
www.flipstores.com

Godiva
9 West Port
Grassmarket
Edinburgh
EH1 2JA
0131 221 9212
www.godivaboutique.co.uk

Herman Brown
151 West Port
Edinburgh
EH3 9DP
0131 228 2589

Mr Ben Vintage Clothing
Unit 6
King's Court
King's Street
Glasgow
G1 5RB
0141 553 1936

Retro
8 Otago Street
Kelvin Bridge
Glasgow
G12 8JH
0141 576 0165
www.retro/clothes.com

Retro Rebels
355–359 George Street
Aberdeen
AB25 1HD
01224 622 344

Rusty Zip
14 Teviot Place
Edinburgh
EH1 2QZ
0131 226 4634

Saratoga Trunk
Unit 10
61 Hydepark Street
Glasgow
G3 8BW
0141 221 4433
www.saratogatrunk.co.uk

Starry Starry Night
19 Dowanside Lane
Glasgow
G12 9BZ
0141 337 1837

Victorian Village
93 West Regent Street
Glasgow
G2 2BA
01413 320 808

IRELAND
Jenny Vander
50 Drury Street
Dublin 2
00353 (0)1677 0406

Redstar
28 Waterloo Street
Derby City
BT48 6HT
02871 288 895

WALES
Drop Dead Budgie
10–12 Royal Arcade
The Hayes
Cardiff
CF10 2AE
02920 398 891

Gusto
7 Terrace Road
Aberystwyth
SY23 1NY
01970 612 555

Hobos
214 Oxford Street
Swansea
SA1 3BE
02920 341 188

Tails & The Unexpected
10 Victoria Road
Penarth
Vale of Glamorgan
CF64 3EF
02920 704 499 / 07974 344 639
www.tailsandtheunexpected.com

—Australia

Blue Spinach
348 Liverpool Street
Darlinghurst
+61 (0) 2 9331 3904
www.bluespinach.com.au

Bondi Markets
Bondi Beach Public School
Warners Avenue
Bondi
Sydney
Sun 10.00–5.00
+61 (0) 2 9315 8988

Broadway Betty
259 Broadway
Sydney
+61 (0) 2 9571 9422

C's Flashback
Shop 32
277 Crown Street
Surry Hills
Sydney

Diva's Closet
(By appointment)
+61 (0) 2 9361 6659

Puff 'n' Stuff
Shop 3
96 Glenayr Avenue
Bondi
Sydney
+61 (0) 2 9130 8471

Retrostar Vintage Clothing
Level One
Cathedral Arcade
37 Swanston Street
Melbourne
+61 (0) 3 9663 1223

Shag
Brunswick Street
Centre Way Arcade
Melbourne
259 Collins Street
Melbourne
+61 (0) 3 9663 8166

130 Chapel Street
Windsor
Melbourne

The Corner Shop
43 William Street
Paddington
+61 (0) 2 9380 9828

The Rokit Gallery
80–85 George Street
The Rocks
Sydney
+61 (0) 2 9247 1332

The Vintage Clothing Shop
Shop 5
147 Castlereagh Street
Sydney
+61 (0) 2 9267 7155

Zoo Emporium
332 Crown Street
Surry Hills
Sydney
+61 (0) 2 9380 5990

— Dress Agencies

LONDON
The Anerley Frock Exchange
122 Anerley Road
SE20 8DL
020 8778 2030

Bang Bang
21 Goodge Street
W1F 0PJ
020 7631 4191

Butterfly Dress Agency
3 Lower Richmond Road
Putney Bridge
SW15 1EJ
020 8788 8304

Catwalk
52 Blandford Street
W1U 7HT
020 7935 1052

Change of Heart
The Old School
59c Park Road
N8 8DP
020 8341 1575

Designer Bargains
29 Kensington Church Street
W8 4LL
020 7795 6777

Designs on Her
60 Rosslyn Hill
NW3 1ND
020 7435 0100

Deuxieme
299 New King's Road
SW6 4RE
020 7736 3696 / 07976 293970

The Dress Box
8 Cheval Place
SW7 1ES
020 7589 2240

Dress for Less
391 St John Street
EC1V 4LD
020 7713 5591
www.dressforless.uk.com

The Dresser
10 Porchester Place
Connaught Village
W2 2BS
020 7724 7212
www.dresseronline.co-uk

Frock Market
50 Lower Richmond Road
Putney Bridge
SW15 1JT
020 8788 7748

Jasmine
65 Abbeville Road
SW4 9JW
020 8675 9475

Lady's
10 High Street
E11 2AJ
020 8989 7530

La Scala
39 Elystan Street
SW3 3NT
020 7589 2784

The Loft
35 Monmouth Street
Covent Garden
WC2H 9DD
020 7240 3807
www.the-loft.co.uk

Resurrection Recycle Boutique
3a Archway Close
N19 3TD
020 7263 2600

Revive
3 High Street
Wanstead
E11 2AA
020 8989 8030

Salou
6 Cheval Place
SW7 1ES
020 7581 2380

The Second Look
236 Upper Richmond Road West
SW14 8AG
020 8878 7233

Seconda Mano
114 Upper Street
N1 1QN
020 7359 5284

Sign of the Times
17 Elystan Street
SW3 3NT
020 7589 4774

Stelios
10 Cheval Place
SW7 1ES
020 7584 4424

Tresor
13 Cale Street
Chelsea
SW3 3QS
020 7349 8829

Twice as Nice
228 Battersea Park Road
SW11 4ND
020 7720 2234
www.twiceasnicedressagency.com

Wellingtons
1 Wellington Place
NW8 7PE
020 7483 0688

— Dress Agencies Outside London

Too numerous to list . . . to find shops in your area visit fashionfizz at
www.biz.fashionfizz.co.uk and use keywords 'Dress Agencies in
[your region]'.

— Charity Shops UK

To find local store listings, visit the Association of Charity Shops
(*www.charityshops.org.uk*), whose website has a shop locator, or consult
listings at these charities' websites:

Age Concern
www.ace.org.uk/AgeConcern/shop.asp

All Aboard
www.allaboardshops.com/where-we-are.htm

Barnardo's
www.barnardos.org.uk/shop

British Red Cross
www.redcross.org.uk/whereintheuk.asp?id=42119

Cancer Research UK
www.cancerresearch.uk.org/shopping

Marie Curie
www.mariecurie.org.uk/shop

Notting Hill Housing Trust
www.nottinghillhousing.org.uk/content.aspx?id-content=112

Oxfam
www.oxfam.org.uk

Salvation Army
www.salvationarmy.org.uk

Scope
www.scope.org.uk/shop/scopeshops.shtml

Sue Ryder
www.suerydercare.org/getinvolved/shopsdirectory.asp

Traid
www.traid.org.uk/shops.html

— Charity Shops Australia

St Vincent de Paul Society
www.vinnies.org.au/advertising/2004-wiggles.cfm

The Salvation Army
www.salvos.org.au/contact/stores/index.php